THE ONE

In Defense of God

THE ONE

IN DEFENSE OF GOD

J. DAN GILL

Editor in Chief
21st Century Reformation

21st
CRP

21st Century Reformation Publishing

Nashville, Tennessee

THE ONE: *In Defense of God*

Published by 21st Century Reformation Publishing— Nashville, Tennessee
www.21stcr.org

Book Design by Sharon E. Gill

Published in the United States of America

Dewey Decimal Classification: 253
Subject Heading: BIBLE \ THEOLOGY \ CHRISTIAN DOCTRINE

Library of Congress Cataloging-in-Publication Data

Gill, J. Dan (James Daniel)
The One: *In Defense of God* / J. Dan Gill — 1st ed.
p. cm.
Includes bibliographical references and indexes.
ISBN 978-0692682401
1. Christianity. I. Title.

Personal Pronouns: Pronouns which reference God are not capitalized in this book. That is also the case with the majority of English Bible translations (KJV, NIV, ESV, NLT, NRSV, etc.) and conforms to the Chicago Manual of Style which is widely considered a leading authority on grammar and usage. Lack of capitalization here is not to infer any disrespect for the Deity.

Dedication

To everyone who has desired to know God,
but religion kept getting in the way.
This book is for you.

CONTENTS

Thanks

My heartfelt appreciation goes to every person who has written or spoken in defense of the one true God. I am indebted to all of you. I give particular thanks to Anthony Buzzard, Joel Hemphill, Joe Martin, Dale Tuggy and others whom I am honored to call colleagues and friends. Likewise, thanks to those who were kind enough to read the manuscript and provide useful recommendations.

Special thanks to my wonderful family including Sharon, our two daughters, two extraordinary sons-in-law and amazing grandchildren. It is an exceptional blessing to share with you our mutual faith in the one true God of heaven and earth!

Thanks to 21st Century Reformation which believed in this project and in me. Also I give particular thanks to Sharon who with considerable genius designed this book and to my dear and gifted friend Sarah Jimenez whose final proofing and suggestions were most helpful.

Introduction

Seeking God

You will seek me and find me if you seek me with all of your heart.

— God (Jeremiah 29:13)

If we begin at the beginning, then we begin with God. He is first in terms of time and priority. I could cease to exist, yet our planet and life on it would go on. Without him, however, there would be neither life nor the planet. No one in the universe is as important as he is. And, if he is the most important being that exists, then the cardinal thing would be for us as human beings to accurately know about him: better yet, to actually know him for ourselves.

In the quest to know God, who is at the end of the quest? If we say that we believe in God, in whom do we believe? How shall we ever really know him if we are uncertain about who he is? Human history is an odyssey of speculation about God. From early times, people have created gods who were then believed to be responsible for the conditions of our world.

Some seek to find God as nature or humanity; others propose to find "God" in the form of an impersonal cosmic force. How shall we find him if we do not know who it is we seek?

God hardly needs defending. Yet, because of misunderstandings and misrepresentations, the truth about God does require clarification and defense. It is not possible that humanity at large has apprehended the truth about him when we are at ever opposing views about him. We have found ourselves with gods of our own making. Such gods can be no better than we who have made them.

Who then is worthy of our faith? Faith goes to the heart of who and what we are as human beings. For something so valuable to be misdirected is tragic. People who do not consider the object of their faith carefully value their faith too little. We should know with confidence that our trust is vested in that which is true.

The God of the Bible is faith-worthy. He is beyond nature and humanity. He is our Creator. We are in his image. He is *the* cosmic power. Yet, he is our Father. All others fall short of him. If it is truly God that we would know, then it is the God of the Bible we must seek. And *he* will show us the way. God alone is able to satisfy our desire to know him. He who is infinite will bring us to himself. Hence, this is not a quest reserved to the intellectual giants among us. It is the desire of God that "ordinary people" would know him.

But will not our imperfections prevent us from approaching one who is perfect? No! It is his promise that says, "You will seek me and find me." However, let all of humanity know with certainty, he will not be known by those who seek him by their own cleverness. Rather, God himself says that he will be known by those who seek him "with all of their hearts" (Jer. 29:13).

But this is not a journey for people of weak constitution, the faint of heart. Those who would really know the true God have always been and continue to be men and women of courage. They are people who are willing to move out of their comfort zones: those willing to look beyond the moment — beyond their friends — to see what others are so often missing. People who, in their desire to know God, are willing to question everything they know — or think that they know — about him. For those people, God will be found. And the rewards are wonderful. It is as the poet said in "The Road Not Taken":

I shall be telling this with a sigh
Somewhere ages and ages hence:
Two roads diverged in a wood, and I,
I took the one less traveled by,
And that has made all the difference.

— ROBERT FROST

So let us seek. We will learn of the God of the Bible, from the Bible. Let us take a fresh look at what it tells us about our Creator. The Bible is his story: his message to all who desire to know him. In this present book, we will make our quest primarily through the Old Testament Scriptures — the Hebrew Bible. It is his record by his prophets and people of old. They saw him wonderfully. Let us ascend the mountain with them and see him as they did. As we go, we will also give attention to the words of Jesus and his earliest followers. In a future book, we will take up matters of Jesus and God. There our focus will be more directly on the New Testament Scriptures.

Who can write a book about God? The definitive book about him has already been written. It is the Bible. It was written by his prophets and his people of old. It was written by the early followers of Jesus. In the Bible we have a matchless record of God's words to all humanity. They are words that reach even us today.

Why is it important? First, it is important to God. As surely as he exists, it is his desire that we would know him, and know him as he really is. Secondly, it is of paramount consequence to us: Only by knowing our Creator can we understand who *we* are and his purposes for us. And, how shall we say that we love creation, ourselves and our fellow human beings, if we do not know and love the one who created us? And can we really love him, if we are uncertain about who he is and what he is like?

In seeking for knowledge, fortune and fame, people have explored our planet and outer space. They have scaled mountains; descended into oceans. They have sometimes given their lives in pursuit of the knowledge of our world and the universe. Yet, for all of this, there is no quest so wonderful — so meaningful — as the search to know our Creator.

The most profound of all human thought is not the expanse of the universe, but rather contemplation of its Creator. The air we breathe — our very lives — are literally from him. When we have exhausted all superlatives we will say he is "THE ONE!"

The truth is always before our eyes,
It is our hearts that do not see.

— J. DAN GILL

Chapter One

The One Who Is

The fool has said in his heart, "There is no God."

— Psalm 14:1

With a sense of anticipation I made my way to the War Memorial Building in Nashville, Tennessee. Renowned atheist Madalyn Murray O'Hair was going to be speaking. Ms. O'Hair — best known for her successful lawsuit to exclude official Bible readings from public schools — was founder of the organization known as American Atheists.[1]

As a young man in college I determined that I should be open-minded. I took paper and pen to make notes. I listened to Ms. O'Hair speak and answer questions from the audience. At the conclusion of her presentation, I looked at my notepad and saw that it was empty. I came to the realization that Ms. O'Hair, the best known atheist of her time, had made no points in her speech that were helpful to an open-minded inquiry. What I had heard was an anti-religious diatribe in which she hurled insults and curses at the Christian world. I realized that

I was not hearing from one of the great minds of the century. Rather, I was listening to an angry, troubled person.[2]

Following my trek to hear Ms. O'Hair, I decided to research the writings of other skeptics and atheists. To my surprise, the more I read the more I was convinced that "God is." In fact, reading their works helped remove any doubt. In a contest between noted atheists and the God of the Bible, God won both my mind and heart. I found that his wisdom and love surpass the opposition of his detractors.

To the people of the Bible the existence of God is never in doubt. There are no chapters of the Bible devoted to explaining that he is. It is he who has extended to us the privilege of life. His existence can be no less real than our own. To them, our adage: "I think, therefore I am" might well be rephrased as: "I *can* think, therefore God is." Philosophies that would doubt the existence of God are not new. Such notions were known in Bible times. To God's people, however, those ideas were foolishness, and trusting in God was the only thing that made sense. For them, faith was the intelligent choice, the reasonable choice.[3]

We Need Not Doubt

Denying the existence of God (atheism) or denying that we can be confident of his existence (agnosticism) are now sometimes considered thoughtful, intelligent positions. To the people of the Bible, however, such ideas were illogical. His people of old were never in doubt about God's existence.

God — The Master Scientist

> By his wisdom the LORD founded the earth, by understanding he established the heavens (Prov. 3:19).

Galileo – Newton – Faraday! These three men are clearly among the great minds in the history of science. And all three believed in a Creator. To them, they were studying God's world.[4] To those can be added a host of other scientists who both now and in the past have believed in God. Recently we can particularly note Francis Collins who led the National Human Genome Institute and was instrumental in founding the National Center for Advancing Translational Sciences (NCATS).[5]

Scientific advances are wonderful. However, some have thought that the more we learn of our world, the less we find a need for God. To the people of the Bible, the precise opposite is true. It is by wisdom and understanding that God has created all things. It is *his* world and the more we learn of it, the more we learn of him. He is in fact the "master scientist" of the universe.

For me, there is no choosing between science and God. To choose true science is to choose him. And science has never competed well as a substitute for God. Scientists know in part, but he knows all things. Science may improve our lives, but he gave us life.

The primacy of God's wisdom is spoken of throughout the Scriptures. People may not understand how he accomplishes the things he does. However, it is a consistent theme of the Bible that he does all things by his extraordinary understanding and wisdom.[6] He is the God of reason; the God of intelligence. His creation declares him:

> The heavens are telling the glory of God; the skies are proclaiming his handiwork (Ps. 19:1).

And might we not say that one who is intelligent and powerful enough to have created our world might have done so *either* in a few days *or* over great expanses of time? The earth can be as recent or as old as people may think it to be. In either case, he was there. The God of the Bible is from everlasting to everlasting. This God not only exists; he always has and always will:

> Before the mountains were born; before you brought forth the earth and the world — from everlasting to everlasting you are God (Ps. 90:2).

Again, he is the ultimate source of wisdom:

> For the LORD gives wisdom. Knowledge and understanding come from his mouth (Prov. 2:6).

Humanity learns by sharing in God's wisdom. How ironic that we, because of our knowledge and understanding, would then imagine to doubt him. What a tragedy that we who seek knowledge would miss the ultimate source of knowledge. And, as his creation we will never outgrow the need for our Creator.

Skeptics and the Bible

> For the word of the LORD is right; he is faithful in all that he does (Ps. 33:4).

Many who are skeptical of the Bible are victims of bad theology — their own! It is notable that atheists and agnostics make poor theologians. Skeptics have often not bothered to educate themselves meaningfully in the Scriptures. When approaching the Bible, they frequently do so with preconceived ideas and a lack of objectivity. They then proceed to "prove" their preconceptions by their own biblical misinterpretations. The resulting assaults on the Bible tend to be unsound or at times even inept. If one is going to attempt to use the Bible to make a point against the Bible, it would seem incumbent upon him or her to get it right.

Skeptics are also frequently victims of the bad theology of people in the religious world. Views may be colored by popular interpretations of some who teach from the Bible but unfortunately do not understand it. Skeptics and non-skeptics alike are often drawn into simplistic notions of God. He is sometimes pictured as a one-dimensional being who bears little resemblance to the God of power and wisdom who made our world.

In a similar vein is the failed logic of the revisionists. Thinking to depreciate the Scriptures from a historical standpoint, they sometimes insist that kings like Saul, David and Solomon were products of the imaginations of later generations. It is proposed that the biblical records about such leaders were developed "after the fact" in order to create a "positive" history for the nation of Israel. However, revisionists then fail to resolve: What then was "the fact"? Where did the monarchy come from? How did there come to be a lineage of kings who are of the House of David? They do not satisfactorily resolve such crucial questions. Inevitably the proposals of revisionists for resolving them are less credible than the Bible records themselves.[7]

Again, in the rush to unfounded ideas, revisionists have often unwittingly shown their own theories to be false. They fail at this critical juncture: The biblical records regarding the kings in question are brutally honest. They bring us leaders who are often weak, faithless and at times even contemptible. By the reasoning of the revisionists themselves, these are the very kind of records that would never have been "created" by later people seeking a "positive" history for their nation. Interestingly, the revisionists by their own logic have given credibility to the scriptural records they thought to diminish.

There is nothing compelling in the arguments of the skeptics. To the people of the Bible, it is *God* who is true. It is those who would doubt him who are themselves to be doubted. We should always have a healthy skepticism toward the skeptics.

Humanity Was Not Created Evil

> And God looked at everything he had made and saw that it was very good. And it was evening and then morning, the sixth day (Gen. 1:31).

God is by definition perfect. He did not create evil in humanity (Eccl. 7:29). When he made human beings he recognized them, together with the balance of creation, to be good. Some have conjectured that evil in mankind is evidence that God does not exist. In the matter of evil, what is at stake is not so much the existence of God as his nature. How can human beings be evil when the God who made them is good?

But evil is not a commodity. Moral evil relates to the state of our hearts and minds as people. As God's creation, we are allowed to think and to choose between good and evil. Happily, we as human beings have often chosen to do good. Unfortunately, we have also chosen to do much evil.

It is not reasonable that we as humanity would choose evil and then blame God for *our* decision. Both choice and responsibility rest with us. God did not create evil; neither does he take pleasure in it. The better question might be, Why did God create us: beings with the ability to choose to do evil? Clearly God created human beings as capable of choosing to love him — or not; to do good — or not. He chose to create us rather than beings who would robotically do only as he programmed them to do. And seeing that our Creator made us with the intent that we would do good, it is important that we choose good and refuse evil:

> And to man he said, "The fear of the Lord, that is wisdom! To depart from evil is understanding!" (Job 28:28).

Isn't our ability to choose an essential aspect of what makes us human? To be absent of that, it would not have been human beings God created, but something else. Would we wish away our own existence as the human race because of our tendency to do evil? Or do we consider our existence wonderful, even though we do wrong and often suffer at the hands of one another? If we answer "yes" to that question, then perhaps we are drawing near to the heart of God in this matter. He too saw value in a humanity which could choose.

God created human beings out of love. He bears with us in the hope that we will depart from evil. The continuing existence of evil is evidence of the goodness of God. If it were not for his kindness, people in whom evil dwells would all be destroyed without mercy. Evil in humanity is allowed to exist because God is kind and because he loves us as his creation. The existence of the atheist or doubter is in itself an indication that God exists and that he is a God of kindness and patience.

Hardship, Pain and Suffering

We experience wonderful things. However, we also encounter great hardships. If God is good, why do we experience pain and suffering? But notice that here again what is at stake is not so much the existence of God as his nature.

As we have seen, humanity has collectively chosen to do evil. That brings with it collective consequences. Hardship, pain and suffering are some of those consequences. As human beings we benefit from the good that is done by our fellow man. However, we bear consequences for the evil acts they do as well. We are all in this boat together. We should not blame God because of our choice to do evil to one another. Like it or not, our welfare as individuals is tied to the actions of our husbands, wives, children, parents, strangers and human governments. We as individuals are also victims of our own bad choices.

Yet, in all of this there is a paradox: Even suffering and pain are not without benefit to the human enterprise. These things are important teachers. Our propensity to do evil is often moderated by pain and suffering. They help us to learn that God's way is right; that we should choose to do good and not do evil; that we should love our neighbors as ourselves. The fact that pain and suffering are not without benefit is also seen in some very noble things. When misfortune befalls a neighbor, it often causes people to sacrifice by providing help and care. Here, we find even heroic deeds: what is best in us is brought to the fore.

Perhaps most wonderfully, we see people rise through their own hardships to show us beauty and strength in humanity. They help us to see the value of life. A person of particular inspiration has been Fanny J. Crosby. Millions of people have been lifted — even transformed — through the words of her poetry and songs. Yet, most may not know that the woman who penned the words to "Blessed Assurance," "Pass Me Not, O Gentle Savior," "To God Be the Glory," and "Near the Cross" was blind almost from the time of her birth.[8] At the age of eight, she wrote her first poem:

Oh, what a happy soul I am
Although I cannot see;
I am resolved that in this world
Contented I will be.

How many blessings I enjoy,
That other people don't;
To weep and sigh because I'm blind,
I cannot, and I won't!

Why doesn't God do away with evil, pain and suffering? The Bible assures us that he will do exactly that — in his time and in his ways. The Scriptures confidently point us to a day in which evil will be eliminated from the earth:

> But the meek shall inherit the land and delight themselves in abundant peace. God will swallow up death forever; and the Lord GOD will wipe away tears from all faces, and he will take away the reproach of his people from all the earth. The LORD has spoken (Ps. 37:11; Isa. 25:8, ESV).

That is the hope that our Creator extends to us as his creation. He himself will swallow up death forever; he will wipe away our tears. In that day, both moral evil and natural calamity will no longer be a problem. Humanity will no longer live in the shadow of pain and suffering. Until that time comes, let us all learn to trust God and abstain from evil. Let us never suffer because of our own wrongdoing. And, if we suffer, let it be with grace; let it draw us nearer to God; let it somehow benefit our fellows.

> I thank God for my handicaps, for through them, I have found myself, my work, and my God.
>
> — HELEN KELLER

Bad Religion — An Argument Against God?

A review of the writings of notable skeptics from Bertrand Russell till now reveals a common factor: a barely veiled contempt for all that is religious. Hatred for religion proves to be a psychological root for the crusading efforts of many atheists. Shrouding themselves in the notion of higher plateaus of thinking, many skeptics are actually motivated by the unfortunate irrationality and inhumanity of some religious people. I am persuaded that without "bad religion" to fuel the fire, much of the steam would go out of atheistic crusading. In fact, if it were not for the abuses of some religious people, there would be far fewer agnostics and atheists.

Human religions have often been terrible. As our saying could go, "With friends like these, God has no need for enemies." In the minds of some, "bad religion" is reason not to believe in God.

However, the matter of evil in religion fails in opposition to the God of the Bible. He is not the friend of bad religion. On this point, it is interesting that there is a bit of common ground between God and the skeptic: God is also distressed by the religions of man. He too is grieved by the ignorance and arrogance of many who are religious.

In contrast to bad religion, it must be noted that some of the greatest atrocities ever committed against human beings were carried out by atheists. Terrible evils were perpetrated under the banner of forced atheism by Communist regimes in the twentieth century. People suffered and died in as great numbers under the influence of such atheistic visionaries as Lenin, Trotsky, and Stalin, as under any other form of thought in human history. If the evil deeds of men are reason for not believing in an ideology, then it is certain that no one should ever believe in atheism.[9]

Yet, in all regards, the God of the Bible does not compromise. There is a consistent recognition in the Scriptures that human beings can be evil in either religious or non-religious garb. In either event, God is not moved:

> You are not a God who takes pleasure in wickedness; evil cannot dwell with you (Ps. 5:4).

What God desires today are people who will "light a candle rather than curse the darkness"; people who will learn his wisdom and depart from evil; people who will share in his virtues.

> The existence of the atheist or doubter is in itself an indication that God exists and that he is a God of kindness and patience.

Faith Versus Reason?

> Wisdom and strength belong to God; counsel and understanding are his (Job 12:13).

It is a popular misconception that faith and reason are of necessity at odds with each other. In reality, right reason is never in contradiction to true faith. Unbelief is reasonable only if there is no God. If God exists, the only thing that is at all reasonable is to trust in him. Faith is not a substitute for knowing. True faith is about knowing: Knowing God!

And does not reason lead one to faith? Does not the existence of a marvelous universe lend itself to the *reasoning* that our world has a Creator? God cannot be found in a test tube. But does not the existence of both the test tube and the scientist lend itself to the *reasoning* that there is a God?[10] The decision to believe in the God of the Bible is itself an exercise in reason.

At the same time, we often fail to recognize the limitations of science. We may ask, "What *did* go bang? And what did it bang into?" If nothing is beyond space and matter as created by the big bang, where did that nothing come from? Such are the questions that we ask our scientists. Such are the questions that they ask themselves. Yet it would seem that science runs aground at such a point.

For example, the popular theoretical physicist Stephen Hawking has suggested that the universe may have come about by "spontaneous generation." Effectively proposing that perhaps "stuff happens," he asks the public to believe that everything came from nothing.[11] In a similar vein, biologist/atheist Richard Dawkins observes: "The fact that life evolved out of nearly nothing, some 10 billion years after the universe evolved out of literally nothing, is a fact so staggering that I would be mad to attempt words to do it justice."[12]

It is difficult for the rational-minded person to see why such ideas as "things came from nothing" would be thought reasonable, but that it is unreasonable to believe that all things came from God. It would seem that for atheists with an anti-religious bias, any argument will do so long as it doesn't involve God! As for science, in spite of all of its advantages, it can never lead humanity well in regard to the most fundamental issues of creation, so long as the best it can offer is that "stuff just happens."

Likewise, science sometimes errs by failing to celebrate the extraordinary differences between human beings and the balance of creation. Science has done well in exploring the similarities between humanity and other forms of life on our planet. Such relationships are recognized in the Bible itself. All living beings have the same Creator and share much in common with one another. But will we as human beings overlook the obvious? Will we fail to recognize rightly our own exceptional place in the world?

Presently, the Bible does a better job than science of bringing into focus the astounding differences between humanity and the balance of creation. It is the Bible that tells us that human beings are uniquely made in the image of their Creator (Gen. 1:27) and that it is humankind that is capable of knowing and emulating him. It is the Bible that tells us we are created not only with the potential, but also the responsibility of being good managers of our world (Gen. 1:28).

When will science take us from meaninglessness to meaning? When will it provide our children with a view of themselves that moves beyond base evolution to ultimate responsibility? Will we always tell our children that humanity is simply the accidental development of crude chemical interactions and then be surprised that they have little regard for themselves, other human beings and the balance of creation?

Our human enterprise cries out for meaning. So long as science fails to provide that, human beings will rightly continue to seek elsewhere for the answers to our greatest questions. The God of the Bible gives us those answers in unparalleled fashion.

In a similar vein, neither can science lead humanity in terms of ethics and essential questions of human morality. A science which is itself tethered to a supposedly random, mindless development of humankind is not on a good footing to raise us above that same random mindlessness regarding what human character and morality should be. We see why it is widely agreed that ethics is not in the purview of science but rather of philosophy and religion.

Scientists have brought us many benefits. However, it is also scientists, from Leonardo da Vinci till now, who have tended to give themselves — their considerable knowledge and skills — to finding and developing ways of making war and human destruction more horrific. It is the saddest of commentaries on scientists that they have too often failed to rise above the human drive to injure and destroy their fellows. Jesus did rise above those things. Thoughtful scientists who may be humbled by their failures in these regards might also realize how much that they still need to learn from him.

What Can Science Prove?

We enjoy seeing descriptions in the news telling us about the latest scientific advances. However, one headline we have never seen and can expect <u>not</u> to see is, "Scientists Disprove the Existence of God!" Science cannot prove empirically that God does not exist. This leaves the person who professes an affinity toward science — while claiming the need for "absolute" proof — in an embarrassing position. Atheists have often argued that the existence of God cannot be proven on empirical (experimental) grounds. Whether that is true or not, all must accept that it is certain science cannot prove that God does *not* exist.

When asked to empirically disprove the existence of God, atheists often cry "foul," saying we cannot expect them to do that.[13] They indicate that asking them to do so is not in keeping with scientific possibilities. But is it unfair to ask them to prove that God doesn't exist — simply because they can't? It is an inherent weakness of science that it cannot empirically prove this negative. It is not the scientist's fault — but it certainly isn't the believer's fault either.[14]

It is not possible for credible scientists to point us to the unfathomable expanse of our universe and then assure us that God is not there — or beyond it. It requires an atheist to make that assertion. In the light of science, atheism is an unproven theory.[15]

Atheism in Retreat

Atheism is not science. Atheists are people who do not believe in God — often for very *non-scientific* reasons. They are attempting to use science to bolster their position. It should always be kept in mind that there is nothing in true science that compels a person to be an atheist.

The person for whom belief in God makes the most sense out of his or her own existence, needs not fear the arguments of the atheist. Atheism supports a negative that it cannot definitively prove. Atheists have suffered from their own lack of empirical evidence in this matter, a matter in which atheists themselves have often insisted on empirical "proof" from believers.

Unable to establish the non-existence of God on an empirical basis, atheists have tended to be left with non-empirical reasoning in a broader sense. Here, it is argued that a "reasonable" person would not believe in God. In this is sometimes found an unfortunate superior, even condescending attitude on the part of some atheists: People are deemed "unreasonable" unless they agree with the atheist!

Believers welcome the atheist to a discussion on the grounds of either empirical or non-empirical evidence. However, we see that for atheists themselves, the resolution of the matter of the existence of God actually comes down not to any definitive proof, but rather to their own non-empirical reasoning. They reason that because evil exists, or because there is pain and suffering, or because of the hypocrisy of many religionists, then God does not exist. However, as we have seen, such questions do *not* prove that God does not exist. Neither do these matters necessarily impugn his character. Science in the 21st century has not provided us with any compelling reasons why we should abandon faith. Neither can we expect it to do so in the future. Atheists attempting to use science will continue to assert more than they can prove. But in the end they have failed.

The existence of the agnostic is often a particular discomfort to the atheist. Some agnostics believe that science and religion are at a stalemate regarding the question of the existence of God. The possibility of such a stalemate is an idea that the atheist desperately wants to disallow. Hence, we see the atheist's unhappiness with the agnostic in such cases. At the same time, agnostics are sometimes caught up in the unproven assumption that the existence or non-existence of God must ultimately be determined on narrow scientific grounds. Indeed, the Creator of the universe is not to be found in a test tube. But why would we suppose that he would be knowable to his creation in only such limited fashion? God invites the atheist and the agnostic to come to know him through faith and reason.

I love science. I also love faith. I find these loves to be mutually consistent. People have at times been drawn into believing that science is more definitive in this matter than it actually is. Likewise, people have often failed to appreciate that there is an integral relationship between faith and reason.

How valid is any reasoning that would lead people to deny their own Creator? The questions posed by atheists are simply not enough to justify abandoning God. Choosing to doubt him or to trust in him is not just an academic exercise. The stakes are high for us in this matter. If indeed God exists, then for human beings to deny him is to deny their own Father.

30 Minutes as an Atheist

A friend told me, "I was once an atheist for about 30 minutes." That was a way of describing a brief episode in his earlier years. Rebounding from a painful encounter with bad religion, he had questioned God. Similar experiences are found too often. That is particularly the case among younger students who may be impressionable and lack a sound education in issues of faith. Most such episodes are short-lived and typically give way to surer, healthier faith in people's lives. Such was the case with my friend who had regained his equilibrium and moved forward, stronger in his faith. He went on to become a professor of New Testament studies at a Christian college — sharing his love for God with ministers in training as well as many other young people over a long and successful career.

The atheist who never questions his or her atheism is shortsighted. What is brought to us by bad religion is unfortunate. But what is being handed humanity by atheistic crusaders is just as unfortunate. I would rather always be in quest of the true God than to settle for either of those alternatives.

> In the light of science,
> atheism is an unproven theory.

Why Faith?

> And Abram believed in the Lord, and the Lord counted it to him as righteousness (Gen. 15:6).

The God of the Bible can be described as the one who loves faith. Abram believes him and that is of great value to God. The Bible at its center is not an ancient book about the exploits of great men and women. Rather, it is the story of the one who is God and the people who trust in him.

To believe, to have faith, is more than to assent that God is. It is the decision to trust in, adhere to and rely on him. Faith is sensible. It is at the heart of God's plan for dealing with human beings. Rather than wealth, wisdom, power or even human virtue, there is something that he counts of more value. It is faith. God is drawn to those who will trust in him. God's choice to receive our faith is born out of his love and mercy.

It is because of his wisdom that he favors faith. Faith is for people of all eras. It is amazing that the God of the Bible made himself known to people in ancient times. To know God did not require waiting on scientific advances. Trusting in him was possible for Abram who lived centuries before Christ. It is just as possible now for a person living centuries after. The enterprise of faith is not foolishness. It is brilliant and wonderful.

Today, it may be said that some are "faith-phobic." Fear of faith is sometimes rooted in aversion to the thought that to embrace it would result in being responsible to God for the way in which we conduct our lives. However, failure to believe in God does not at all change the fact that he exists. True faith is based on the conclusion that as our Creator, he uniquely knows what is right and best for us. Faith rejoices in the confidence that God is inclined to be merciful and patient toward us even in our shortcomings. Faith comes from the resolve of a person that to trust God is better than to trust in others. The decision to have faith issues forth in a life of trust.

Faith is *not* something that just happens to one. To have faith is a choice that a person makes. Real faith is truth on God's terms. It is the placing of our confidence in eternal fundamentals of our existence. God knows that there is a distance between him and humanity. It is his choice that faith would be the bridge between us and him. To the people of the Bible faith is never "magical." It is how our faith affects the heart of God that makes it effectual. He loves faith because it comes from honesty and humility on our part. It comes from the recognition of a timeless truth. That truth is: We need him.

And the benefits of such faith are great. After all, it is our Father with whom we are connecting.

I Choose God

> "For my thoughts are not your thoughts, neither are your ways my ways," says the Lord. "For as the heavens are higher than the earth, so my ways are higher than your ways and my thoughts higher than yours" (Isa. 55:8, 9).

I might have been an atheist had it not been for God. I have found that he is greater than doubt. For me, his wisdom and kindness are irresistible. His ways truly are higher than our ways. The more that I come to understand his ways, the more I am in awe of him. To disregard him is to miss our own purpose in life. If indeed he created us, then it is certain that he did so for a reason. We can only answer the question, "Why are we here?" by approaching the one who put us here. It is when we find him that we truly find ourselves.

We are not alone. It would be a tragedy to live our lives as though we were. It is God who calls us to something greater than ourselves. We are his creation and are living because of his goodness. We should honor him in our lives. The message of the God of the Bible is to "get connected." It has been his choice to receive our faith. It is our choice whether or not to have it. I have looked at faith — I have looked at doubt. Faith is better. I choose God.

Chapter One

Notes

1. Ms. O'Hair, famously described by *Life* magazine as the "most hated woman in America," founded American Atheists as the Society of Separationists in 1963. She was the president until succeeded by her son Jon Murray in 1986. He and his mother continued to run American Atheists until their kidnapping and murder in 1995 by a former employee of the organization.

2. Ms. O'Hair raised her children as atheists, and the famous case to exclude Bible readings and recitation of the Lord's Prayer from public schools was brought in the name of her oldest son Bill Murray. (*Murray v. Curlett,* Combined by the U. S. Supreme Court with *Abington School District v. Schempp,* 374 U.S. 203 83 S. Ct. 1560, 10. L. Ed. 2d 844, 1963). Bill Murray later converted to Christianity and championed the cause of Christ. He wrote a book chronicling his growing up as the son of Madelyn Murray O'Hair. William J. Murray, *My Life Without God* (Nashville: Thomas Nelson Publishers, 1982).

3. There are many works available which consider the full range of a *priori* and *a posteriori* theistic proofs. It is not the author's intent to review those here. Rather, the chapter at hand takes a fresh look at the hearts and minds of the people of the Bible with regard to their confidence in the existence of God.

4. It is a misconception to assume that scientists are necessarily atheists or agnostics. The atheistic cause has tended to be led *not* by scientists but rather by some in the fields of philosophy and political activism. There are people in the scientific community who not only believe in a Creator, but who also profess Christ.

5. For more on Collins see *Wikipedia,* "Francis Collins," last modified January 26, 2015, http://en.wikipedia.org/wiki/Francis_Collins. Also note Collins' book, *The Language of God: A Scientist Presents Evidence for Belief* (New York: Free Press, 2006).

6. The Scriptures tell us that God "spoke" and creation took place (Gen. 1:3, etc.). However, the Scriptures also say that beyond his

speaking, God accomplishes all things by his unfathomable understanding and wisdom (Ps. 104:24; 136:5; Jer. 10:12; 51:15).

7. Revisionists (also known as biblical minimalists) have found interest for their ideas in recent years. A Public Broadcasting System presentation (*The Bible's Buried Secrets,* Nova, Nov. 18, 2008) gives a somewhat biased view in favor of the perspectives of the revisionists. For a more balanced consideration of the revisionist controversy note two books by William G. Dever: *What Did the Biblical Writers Know and When Did They Know It?* (Grand Rapids: Wm. B. Eerdmans Publishing, 2001) and *Who Were the Early Israelites and Where Did They Come From?* (Grand Rapids: Wm. B. Eerdmans Publishing, 2003).

8. For a recounting of Fanny Crosby's amazing life read Edith L. Blumhofer, *Her Heart Can See: The Life and Hymns of Fanny J. Crosby* (Grand Rapids: Wm. B. Eerdmans Publishing, 2005).

9. The terrible deeds of atheists of course in no way justify or diminish the great evils committed by various religionists over time.

10. For an introduction to the considerable work which has been done on arguments from design see Kenneth Himma, "Design Arguments for the Existence of God," *Internet Encyclopedia of Philosophy,* http://www.iep.utm.edu/design.

11. Stephen W. Hawking and Leonard Mlodinow, *The Grand Design* (New York: Bantam Books, 2012).

12. Richard Dawkins, "From tail to tale on the path of pilgrims in life," *The Scotsman,* April 9, 2005.

13. A popular response by skeptics is that "neither can science disprove the existence of unicorns or fairies." That only establishes, however, that there are yet other things that science cannot disprove. And what scientist is there who has ever had such a question posed to her who did not wish — even for a moment — that she could empirically disprove the existence of unicorns? If she could, it might mean there was a dimension to science that is not presently known. From a practical standpoint, few people are concerned about the existence of unicorns. Great numbers of people, however, are keenly concerned about the existence of a Creator. And, the reasons for believing in God seem far more compelling to them than anything to do with unicorns.

14. Attempts by some atheists to argue that a negative can be proven inevitably involve a subtle shifting from the question of empirical evidence to *reason* in a larger — less scientific— sense. In any event, the existence or non-existence of God is hardly comparable to

mundane matters in which one may feel confident that something does or does not exist in a particular — limited — environment.

15. That does of course leave the philosophical arguments to consider. For an excellent overview of those see Dan Howard-Snyder's contribution to *Reason for the Hope Within*, ed. Michael J. Murray (Grand Rapids: William B. Eerdmans Publishing, 1999), chapter 4.

Chapter Two

The Pretenders — Gods of Our Making

My soul thirsts for God, the living God. When can I come and appear before him?

—Psalm 42:2

Quaint and beautiful, Kyoto had been the capital of old Japan. As a young Christian, I was visiting missionaries there. The city was filled with wonderful historic sites including the Imperial Palace which had been the emperor's residence for over a thousand years. While I was taken with their history, I found myself even more fascinated with the pleasantness and traditions of the Japanese people.

Traveling on in Japan, I inquired about their religions. I talked with people about their beliefs, and toured two of Japan's noted Buddhist monasteries. I discovered that the nation was largely a melting pot of eastern philosophies: Shinto and Buddhism influenced by Confucian principles.

Yet, for all of my inquiries, it was difficult to understand exactly what the faith of the Japanese people was really about. I began to realize that they too often struggled with that matter.

As the time was drawing near for me to leave Japan, I visited a Christian church in Yokohama. I struck up a conversation with a Japanese man of college age. I told him that I was a Christian traveling in his country and had been trying to understand better the religions of the land. His response was immediate: "I too am a Christian!" He went on to talk about his conversion to Christianity. Then he said these words: "Knowing God! The difference is about knowing God!"

In those few words, he had contrasted the religions of the land with his new Christian faith. He had lived on both sides of a great religious divide. The beliefs into which he was born had brought him to a great "cosmic unknown." However, they had only left him with a sense of incompleteness. He had thirsted to know God. In his Christian faith, he found what he had been missing in the religions of his youth. I left Japan with memories of a fascinating culture and beautiful land. However, it was the words of the young man in Yokohama that rested most on my mind:

"Knowing God!" he said.
"The difference is about knowing God!"

Human history is replete with a myriad of religions. People have worshipped gods of their own invention: some made with their hands; others fashioned only in the imaginations of their minds. But the one who really is God made us. We should serve the God who made us, not the gods which we have made. He is the only one worthy of the name "Sovereign of the Universe." Clearly this God excels all. Surely, he alone is God.

Idols— Gods Made by Human Imagination

> Their land is full of idols; they bow to the work of their hands, to what their fingers have made (Isa. 2:8).

The people of the Bible had a simple but clear understanding: A true God cannot be fashioned by human beings. It is not just that gods of our making are inferior to the God who made us; it is that they are not real at all. To make and worship such gods is an injurious falsehood. It takes honor from the one who really is God, and harms people by diverting their attention away from their Creator. In Jeremiah we find an exposition about the futility of making and serving idols:

> A tree from the forest is cut down and worked with an axe by the hands of a craftsman. They decorate it with silver and gold; they fasten it with hammer and nails so that it cannot move. Their idols are like scarecrows in a cucumber field, and they cannot speak; they have to be carried, for they cannot walk. Do not be afraid of them, for they cannot do evil, neither is it in them to do good (Jer. 10:3–5, ESV).

We should serve the God who made us,
not the gods which we have made.

It has always made sense that God would be someone greater than his creation. It fails the test of reason that we can make gods who are then our superiors (Ps. 115:1–8). The prophet Isaiah also speaks with irony about the man who makes a god with his own hands.[1] He says that such a man cuts down a tree and then:

> Half of it he burns in the fire. Over the half he eats meat; he roasts it and is satisfied. Also he warms himself and says, "Aha, I am warm, I have seen the fire!" And the rest of it he makes into a god, his idol, and falls down to it and worships it. He prays to it and says, "Deliver me, for you are my god!" (Isa. 44:16, 17, ESV).

Polytheism is the belief that there is more than one god. In polytheism, we sometimes find entire pantheons of gods. People often picture a plethora of deities acting in concert — or in competition with one another. Known to us in mythology, they are gods made in the image of humanity at its worst. They embody all of our evil doings. They represent nothing better than us.[2] While the nations held to idol gods, even pantheons of gods, the people of the Bible saw only one who is God. By his own power, he alone made all things. He is our Father and he shares his place as God with no one.[3]

Deism — A Missing Creator?

> "Be still, and know that I am God; I will be exalted among the nations, I will be exalted in the earth." The people said, "The LORD of hosts is with us; the God of Jacob is our fortress" (Ps. 46:10, 11).

God speaks: "Be still and know that I am God." His people respond: "The LORD of hosts is with us." The God of the Bible is involved with his creation. It makes no sense that one with such great wisdom and love would create the world and then care so little for it as effectively to abandon it. Yet, that has been the view of some people over time. This idea of an uninvolved Creator is referred to as deism.[4]

Such a notion is not worthy of the God of the Bible. This God loved creating and loves what he created. In humanity is found an aspect of his creation that is capable of having relationship with him, sharing in his creativity and loving the things that he loves. It is not logical that the one who created us with those potentials would then stand entirely aloof from us. As Creator, the earth is actually his *ongoing* possession. The psalmist speaks to him saying, "The heavens and the earth are yours; you founded the earth and all that is in it" (Ps. 89:11).

To propose that he would be an uninvolved Creator challenges reason. The very excellence of his creation is a testimony to the kind of God he is. He is not one who would set the world in motion and then walk away from it. Let us all come to say with his people of old, "The Lord of hosts is with us."

Pantheism — Is Nature God?

> It is good to give thanks to the Lord, to sing praises to your name, O Most High; to proclaim your steadfast love in the morning, and your faithfulness at night. For you, O Lord, have made me glad by your work; I sing for joy at the works of your hands (Ps. 92:1, 2, 4).

Great mountains reach heavenward. The expanse of seas and oceans seems boundless. The heavens are filled with spectacular views. In amazement we look at creation. It is beautiful, majestic and awesome. We feel our spirits lifted when we realize that we are in the midst of such grandeur. To the people of the Bible, all of this gives reason to worship our Creator. The more they saw the wonder of creation, the more they proclaimed the awesomeness of God.

It has been rightly said, however, that there is little that humanity cannot "mess up." That includes our understanding of God and his creation. An idea referred to as pantheism confuses God with nature. It proposes that in nature we are literally seeing God. In pantheism, creation and God are one and the same. This unfortunate reasoning underlies various unsound philosophies including nature worship and much that is found in eastern religions.[5]

To confuse nature with God is a painful misunderstanding. In doing so, people are in awe of creation but then fail to give honor to its Creator. Our world is God's landscape. It is his painting. God's creation inspires us to know him. We can learn much about a creator by observing his creation. It is beyond reason, however, that we would view a painting itself as literally being the artist.

It would be bewildering to the people of the Bible that one would venerate creation while failing to glorify the true God as its Creator. Their understanding of God and of our world far exceeded nature worship and any sort of pantheism. The 104th Psalm is a beautiful song which extols the wonder of nature. In it, the writer at the same time magnifies its Creator:

> **You** make springs gush forth in the valleys; they flow between the hills; they give drink to every beast of the field; the wild donkeys quench their thirst. Beside them the birds of the heavens dwell; they sing among the branches. From **your** lofty abode **you** water the mountains; the earth is satisfied with the fruit of **your** work. **You** cause the grass to grow for the livestock and plants for man to cultivate, that he may bring forth food from the earth and wine to gladden the heart of man, oil to make his face shine and bread to strengthen man's heart. The trees of **the LORD** are watered abundantly, the cedars of Lebanon that **he** planted (Ps. 104:10–16, ESV).

The words above envision the wonders of nature. Yet, seven times they make reference to the God who created it. The psalmist then further observes:

> May the glory of the Lord endure forever; may the Lord rejoice in his works. I will sing to the Lord as long as I live; I will sing praise to my God while I have my being (Ps. 104: 31, 33, ESV).

Creation is cause for God to rejoice in his works. And it gives reason for the psalmist to sing praises and glorify him. His people in the Bible will climb to the highest mountain, view the expanse of nature, and cry out with praises to the God of heaven and earth. It is he who has brought such wonderful things into being.

God Is Not "Us"

> For I am God and not a human being (Hosea 11:9).[6]

Humanity is marvelous: chief of God's creation in this world. Human beings uniquely have the ability to understand and appreciate his creativity. Yet, we are not God:

> So God created man in his own image. In the image of God he created him; male and female he created them (Gen. 1:27).

Human beings are made in the image of God. Yet, by definition, the image of something is not the thing itself.[7] It is an extension of pantheism that blurs the distinction between God and humanity. However, while we are not God, recognizing that we have been created in his image is critically important. It is essential to understanding our role in the world. That role is to govern our lives and God's world in accordance with his wisdom — his will (Gen. 1:28). It is to aspire to be like him. It is to forever honor him as our Creator and as the only true God:

> For you are great and do wonderful deeds. You alone are God (Ps. 86:10).

He alone is God. No other being in the universe, including us, shares that place with him. If we genuinely seek for God, it is "him" that we will find: him alone.

God Is Not an "It"

> Do not be afraid, for I am with you. Do not be dismayed, for I am your God. I will strengthen you and help you; I will sustain you with my righteous right hand (Isa. 41:10).

The God of the Bible has individuality and character. This God speaks and when he does he says, "I" am with you. In contrast to that, another idea frequently found in some philosophies and particularly in eastern religions brings us to a god sometimes described as the "life-force" or "cosmic unknown." This concept also has roots in pantheism. Indistinguishable from the cosmos, this god is essentially an *it*. The God of the Bible, however, is both knowable and known. He is known through his prophets and people of old. He is known through his creation:

> The heavens are telling the glory of God; the skies are proclaiming his handiwork (Ps. 19:1).

The God who gave us individuality and character has individuality and character. The gods of the "cosmic unknown" are less than us. We are knowable. They are *not* knowable — for they do not exist.

New Age?

Peculiarly termed "New Age," the movement by that name is actually an amalgamation of rudimentary philosophies from ages gone by. As variations on the theme of pantheism, New Age includes everything from "nature worship" and "humanity as god," to "god as a cosmic unknown."[8] Popularized by some in the entertainment industry, the movement has found interest in recent years. Some may have seen the miniseries "Out on a Limb"[9] in which actress Shirley MacLaine stands at the ocean side proclaiming; "I am God." I for one am greatly disappointed if Shirley MacLaine is God.

New Age religion is a confluence of ideas that simply do not match the realities of our world. In a pantheistic "all is one" philosophy, Shirley MacLaine together with the balance of humanity is believed to be god. Oddly, however, most of us just don't know that we are. But what kind of god is it that doesn't know that he or she is god?

Again for many people in New Age, God is not an individual. To them there is no essential distinction between God, a human being, and a tree. However, reality would indicate a good deal of difference between a human being and a tree and, I should think, an even greater difference between us and our Creator.[10]

New Age sometimes brings to us the idea that there are many realities. Here, each human being is said to create his or her own reality. New Age philosophers do not resolve what happens when the supposed "realities" are in conflict with one another. In such a world, we are left to suppose that no one is ever really wrong and none are ever delusional. It might be said, however, that such a thought is itself delusional.

In such a world, even good and evil are sometimes not seen as distinct from one another. The dark realm of Wicca, the occult, magic and astrology are all at home in New Age. Even Scientology and Satan worship find a place there. It would seem that anything is welcome in New Age except for the God who made us and objective truth that comes from him.

All in all, New Age fails. Its ideas failed the test of reason while they were still "Old Age." It is certain that putting them together under a new umbrella still leaves only failure. New Age and its various philosophies are not at all wise. With their notion that "everything is God" it turns out that effectively "nothing is God."

The New Age movement has been fostered by a number of self-help gurus and eastern mystics. These often even purport to embrace Christ. However, to embrace Christ one must embrace his words: his teachings. With regard to that, New Age proponents are entirely selective. When it suits their purpose, they construe his teachings to be in harmony with their own philosophies. At the same time, they ignore or disregard as spurious the great body of teachings by Christ which are clearly in opposition to them.[11]

For example, Christ was never ambiguous about the distinctions between good and evil (Matt. 12:34, 35). He never taught such things as Wicca, the occult, magic or astrology. He rejected Satan worship and served only the one true God (Matt. 4:8–10). He never saw the world in pantheistic terms. He clearly saw a distinction between all of creation and the God who created it (Matt. 19:4). He never embraced reincarnation. Rather, he taught that we are created beings with the hope of unending life only by resurrection (John 6:40). Neither did he espouse a humanism that places humanity at the center of its own universe, distorting our importance, while at the same time diminishing the one who made us.

Jesus taught that God has individuality. He presented to us his God — his Father. He taught us that his God is also our Father (Matt. 6:9–13, John 20:17). He declared that his Father is in fact the "only true God" (John 17:3).

Pluralism — Do All Roads Lead to God?

It is sometimes said that the religions of the world are actually worshiping the same God from different perspectives. However, that is not an idea found in the Bible. It is clear that none of the varied philosophies we have reviewed in this chapter lead to the God of the Bible.

The common problem with the various theories we have considered in this chapter is that they ultimately lead people away from God. If we follow after anyone or anything else, we will miss him. If, as in deism, we think he has abandoned us, we will not seek him. If we imagine that nature or human beings are God, or that God is a cosmic unknown, we will not look to him — nor will we find him. We are hindered from knowing him because of doubt, self-reliance, arrogance, and humanity's determination to do evil. We are led away from him by the roads of pluralism: roads which, while promising to lead us to truth and spiritual enlightenment, in reality only take us into a philosophical fog.

The many roads of pluralism do not lead to the God of the Bible. They meander away from him. Will we trade the God who gave us character and individuality for a "life-force"? Will we trade away our own Father for a "cosmic unknown"? If we do, everyone loses. God loses the love and honor that he should receive from us as his creation. We as people lose because we fail to know and honor our own Creator.[12]

Knowing God

> But if from there you will seek the LORD your God, you will find him if you search for him with all your heart and soul (Deut. 4:29).

I would rather forever be in the state of seeking the true God than to live in a fog of philosophies that only obscure the truth about him. For me, to know him is worth everything. It is the pleasure of God that we would know him. As we look at the cosmos, we might think that in the larger scheme of things we as human beings are entirely unimportant. Yet, to God we *are* important. We are important enough for him to have created us. And he is mindful of us. It is his desire for us to know him. Otherwise, why would he have made us with the ability to do so? There is no other being in all of this world's creation that has the ability to really know our Creator.

I could have grown up as did the young man I met in Yokohama. My life too might have been filled with thoughts of an "impersonal cosmic force." However, had such been the case, I hope that I would have been like him in this regard: that my heart would have cried out to know the living God. Today, I do not even recall that man's name. However, I find myself in awe of him. I dedicate this chapter to him, and to every other person who has peered through the veil and hungered to know God.

Chapter Two

Notes

1. Idolaters typically believe that their god inhabits the idol when it has been properly consecrated. They would insist that the wood or stone is not in itself their god. In any event, idol worship is abject foolishness in that it treats an inanimate object as though it were living. Any form of idol worship is unacceptable to the God of the Bible (Ex. 20:4, 5).

2. Of course the Greek pantheon is well known to us in mythology. Roman mythology was particularly syncretistic, borrowing heavily from the Greeks. There have been and still are a number of pantheons of gods found in human religions.

3. There is a consideration of the word "God" (*el, elohim, theos*) in its honorific sense for human beings in chapter 9 of this book.

4. Deism as a movement was a phenomenon of the 1600s and early 1700s. The development of American deism was an extension of the movement in Europe. Some notable Americans were deists. Those include Thomas Paine and Ethan Allen. While modern adherents frequently allege that certain other important historical figures were deists, they often claim more than they can prove. For example, assertions that George Washington was a deist are not well founded. He was noted for his personal prayers and saw God as guiding the creation of the nation. For an easy but reliable overview regarding the faiths of Washington, Adams, Jefferson and others, see Alf J. Mapp, Jr., *The Faiths of Our Fathers* (New York: Fall River Press, 2006).

5. Pantheism from the Greek *pan* (all) and *theos* (god): thus, the notion that everything is god. It is the belief that "God is not a personality ... that God and the universe are one and the same." *Webster's New World College Dictionary*, 4th Edition (Cleveland, OH: Wiley Publishing Company, 2007).

6. For other references indicating that the God of Israel is not a human being, note Numbers 23:19 and 1 Samuel 15:28, 29.

7. That human beings are in the image of God is prima facie evidence that they are not God. Image is defined as "A reproduction or

imitation of the form of a person or thing; esp. an imitation in solid form: STATUE." Merriam-Webster's Collegiate Dictionary, 11th Edition (Springfield, MA: Merriam-Webster, Inc., 2014).

8. While New Age adherents are not entirely uniform in their views, the idea is fairly universal among them that there is really only "one thing" and the apparent "many things" are appearances or mis-perceptions of it. Hence, pantheistic perspectives tend to underlie most New Age philosophies. A fairly comprehensive evangelical response to the New Age movement was written by Russell Chandler, religion writer for the *Los Angeles Times*: Russell Chandler, *Understanding the New Age* (Nashville: Word Publishing, 1988).

9. The miniseries "Out on a Limb," producers: Stan Margulies and Colin Higgins, ABC Television, 1987, was a for television adaptation of MacLaine's book by the same title: Shirley MacLaine, *Out on a Limb* (New York: Bantam Books, 1983).

10. Dr. Dale Tuggy explains that for some New Agers, Hindus, etc., "'God' is the one thing there is, the one real individual entity if not a person. They would then say that the world of many things is illusory or else that it is 'less real' than the ultimate." Dale Tuggy, personal correspondence, December 5th, 2014.

11. It is only those who are poorly informed regarding the life and teachings of Jesus who are taken with the works of opportunists who have used his name while essentially denying his teachings. Some persons who have been notable for doing that include Wayne Dyer, Deepak Chopra and Fritjof Capra.

12. For a review of the subject of pluralism, I suggest: Harold Netland, *Encountering Religious Pluralism: The Challenge to Christian Faith and Mission* (Downers Grove, IL: InterVarsity Press, 2001).

Chapter Three

God of the Universe— Shepherd of Men

The Lord *is my shepherd, I shall not want. He makes me lie down in green pastures, he leads me beside still waters, he restores me. He leads me in paths of righteousness for the sake of his name.*

— Psalm 23:1–3

What is God *Really* Like?

The one who is seated on the throne of the heavens leads David on the hills of Judea. The God of the Bible is sovereign over the universe. Yet, his eyes are upon his people. He cares for them. The true God is a God of relationships. The 23rd Psalm contains some of the most poignant words ever found in human language. Throughout our world they are better known than the constitutions of great nations. We are moved by the words of this psalm because we are drawn to David's God. We too desire such a shepherd.

There are none among human beings or their gods who can compare to him. An imagined "cosmic unknown" really is unknown and cannot help us. God is referred to in the above lines from the 23rd Psalm four times as "he." The true God is an individual, not an "it" or a "they." He has character and is knowable.

They Knew Him by Name

The Lord is YHWH

When David wrote about "the LORD" being his shepherd, he was actually calling him by name. Linguists, Bible scholars and the best of our Bible translations tell us that the word "LORD" when found in all capital letters in our Bibles is actually a stand-in for יהוה the name of God (YHWH or YHVH). The English Standard Version states, "As is common among English translations today, the ESV usually renders the personal name of God (YHWH) with the word LORD (printed in small capitals)."[1] This device has been used by major translations over time, including the Authorized Version (King James).

Thought to have been pronounced "Yahweh" by many or "Yahwah" by some, that name occurs some 6,823 times in the Hebrew Bible.[2] It is the single most frequently occurring word in the Old Testament.[3] According to the New American Standard Bible, the name ceased to be spoken by Jews of old, "because of reverence for the great sacredness of the divine name."[4] When reading the Scriptures aloud they would often speak a Hebrew word for Lord (*adonai*) rather than pronounce the name. When the Hebrew Bible was translated into Greek, Aramaic and Syriac, words with the meaning of "lord" in those languages were employed rather than writing the name. Due to lack of use, over time people became uncertain about the pronunciation.[5] All of this led to the substitution of the English word "LORD" (all capital letters) in most English translations.[6] In this present book, the author uses "LORD" and "YHWH" interchangeably.

What was intended out of reverence, however, had unanticipated consequences. Using the word "LORD" rather than God's name leaves us with a somewhat nondescript reference that sounds more like a title or office than a personal name. David had a closeness to God reflected in the fact that he called him "YHWH." By ceasing to use his name, we lost some of that sense of intimacy. Nevertheless, familiarity with the name and even accuracy regarding its pronunciation are of little value if we do not know who God is and do not have connection with him for ourselves.

When I see the word "LORD" in my Bible, I find it inspiring to remember that it is actually God's name that is intended. When I think of that, I feel a kinship with David and all of God's people of old who did speak his name. Reflecting on that name also reminds me that the true God is an individual with a personal name and is not an impersonal force or power. And it reminds me that YHWH is a single individual. The name YHWH in its thousands of occurences is consistently accompanied by singular verbs and pronouns. It is YHWH who is the God of the universe. And *he* is the shepherd of men.[7]

He Is Their Father

> I saw the Lord sitting on a throne, high and exalted, and the train of his robe filled the temple (Isa. 6:1).

Isaiah sees a vision of YHWH. Seated on the throne of supreme majesty, he is the most extraordinary being in the universe. The prophet is overwhelmed by his splendor and glory. However, he is also struck by his purity.[8] God's perfection causes Isaiah to suddenly be aware of his own imperfections. The God of the universe seems unapproachable:

> Then I said, "Woe is me! I am doomed! It is because I am a man of unclean lips ... and I have seen the King, the LORD of hosts" (Isa. 6:5).

Later in Isaiah we find another prophecy about God. In contrast to the earlier vision, the prophet exclaims:

> For surely you are our Father, though Abraham does not know us and Israel does not acknowledge us. You, O LORD, are our Father; Our Redeemer from of old is your name (Isa. 63:16).

It is the same God in both cases. However, we now see that the God of the universe is the Father of his people. He is indeed approachable. He is capable of "compassion" (v. 15). And this one who is their Father is the only one who is God:

> From days of old, no one has heard, no ear perceived, nor has any eye seen a God besides you, who works on behalf of those who wait for him. But now, O LORD, you are our Father. We are the clay, you are the potter; all of us are the work of your hand (Isa. 64:4, 8).

If we were to see God, we would likely react as Isaiah did. We too would be overwhelmed by his glory and majesty. Standing before him, we might find ourselves suddenly aware of our failings and weaknesses. But we would also see that he is a God of "tenderness" and "compassion." He is not distant and uncaring. He is approachable; the Father of his people.

And in the presence of such greatness, we would know with absolute certainty that he alone is God. It is impossible that there would be another like him:

> With all that I am I will exclaim, "Who is like you, Lord? You deliver the weak from those too strong for them, the poor and needy from those who rob them" (Ps. 35:10).

He sits in the heavens but has concern for the troubles of human beings. In him we find not only someone greater than ourselves, but someone better than ourselves. He is the only one worthy to be called the God of the universe. His goodness is complete. God by his nature defines goodness.[9] This God is not only supreme in power but also in virtue. He is incomparable in qualities and character and he desires that people would be like him. He is our Father. But to truly be his people, we must love the things that he loves. We must love our fellow human beings.[10]

This God won the hearts of his people. The people of the nations sometimes serve their gods from stark fear and vulgar desires. In the Bible, we find people who serve their God because of his qualities. They admire him. They esteem him. His goodness is beyond measure. Who is like YHWH? No One!

They Sing of Him

His impassable excellence is acclaimed in the songs his people sing. The Book of Psalms is a collection of 150 of their songs. Again and again they celebrate the virtues of their God.

They Sing of His Love

> Praise the Lord! O give thanks to the Lord, for he is good; his love endures forever (Ps. 106:1).

"His love endures forever" were familiar words to those who sang the songs of the Bible. Those words are found in the Book of Psalms some 34 times. They are in the opening words of four Psalms. They are a captivating refrain in each of the 26 verses of the 136th Psalm.

He is worthy of their love. They love him for his virtues and because he cares for them. To truly be his people they must emulate his love. Some of the most powerful words ever directed to human beings are found in his instruction that one should love his neighbor even as himself:

> Do not take vengeance or bear a grudge against any of your people, but love your neighbor as yourself: I am the LORD (Lev. 19:18).

He takes the same thought yet further when he instructs his people to love even the foreigner — the stranger (Lev. 19:34).

They Sing of His Faithfulness

> I will praise you with the harp because of your faithfulness, O my God; I will sing praises to you with the lyre, O Holy One of Israel (Ps. 71:22).

His people can depend on him. He changes not (Mal. 3:6). Two key ways in which he never changes are found in the above phrase, "O Holy One of Israel." First, he does not change in that he is "The One." Their Father has always been, and always will be, the only one who is God.

> Therefore you are great, O LORD God! There is no one like you, and there is no God besides you, according to all that we have heard with our ears (2 Sam. 7:22).

Second, he never changes in that he is holy. By his great love and mercy he may deal with people at various times in different ways. He sometimes works with them according to their ability to comprehend. With extraordinary patience, he leads people from where they are to where they need to be. He himself, however, never changes. His character remains the same. Well-doing always pleases him; evil never does. In opposing evil, he sometimes brings sharp judgment, calamity and even destruction to bear. In his time, he will put an end to all cruelty and inequity on our planet. Yet, today and always, he is the shepherd of his people and the helper of those who will flee evil and seek him. Notice these words from the 23rd Psalm:

> Even though I walk through the valley of the shadow of death, I will fear no evil, for you are with me; your rod and your staff comfort me. You prepare a table before me in the presence of my enemies; you anoint my head with oil; my cup overflows (Ps. 23:4, 5).

His faithfulness is a source of comfort; he is a God of constancy and fidelity. He is neither uncertain nor fickle. Wholly dedicated to his people, he is ever their protector and help (Ps. 18:2). His loyalty to them is certain, never in doubt. And again, they are to be like him. Their dedication should also be certain; their faithfulness unswerving.

They Sing of His Righteousness—He Is a God of Justice

> Righteousness and justice are the foundation of your throne; constant love and faithfulness go before you (Ps. 89:14).

Throughout history people have tended to reduce God to caricatures of his true self. He is the most powerful being in the universe. Yet, he is not as an angry puppeteer dangling human beings according to whims. He is fair and just in all that he does. He is the judge of all the earth and his judgments are right. Righteousness and justice are essential aspects of his nature (Ps. 33:5). He rightly hates evil. It is not possible to truly love that which is good without opposing the evil that wars against it. He is the ultimate judge of all of the earth (Ps. 96:13). All who do evil have reason to greatly fear him. But to those who will be his people, he is the source of their comfort.

Again, to be like him, his people must seek to be righteous. It is by righteousness that human beings shall approach this God (Ps. 15:1, 2). We must not allow the distinctions between good and evil to be blurred (Isa. 5:20; Amos 5:15). Without exercising equity in our judgments, we are not being like him. How can we really be his children without dispositions of hearts and minds which favor true righteousness?

> Doing righteousness and justice is more acceptable to the LORD than sacrifice (Prov. 21:3).

If we do not know justice that is higher than ourselves, then we really know neither justice nor God. In the presence of the true God we rise above ourselves: above war, strife, self-absorption and inequity against our fellow human beings. And it is he himself who will lead his people in the ways of righteousness. Recall again, in the 23rd Psalm he leads "in the paths of righteousness for the sake of his name" (v. 3).

They Sing of His Mercy and Compassion

> He has made his wonderful works to be remembered; the LORD is merciful and compassionate (Ps. 111:4).

The God of justice is also the God of mercy. His is a throne of mercy where judgment is tempered by goodness. The disposition of God toward humanity is one of kindness. He made us. He is for us and wants us to succeed. Though we incline ourselves to evil, he allows us to live; to enjoy this world and perhaps to seek after him.[11] He loves those who are righteous but is merciful even to the unrighteous:

> The Lord is good to all; his compassion is over all he has made (Ps. 145:9).

His compassion is especially manifest to all who trust in him. David was a good man. Samuel described him as a man after God's own heart (1 Sam. 13:14). However, because of weakness, David abused his power as king and for selfish reasons cost the man Uriah his life (2 Sam. 11). Later, David greatly sorrowed over his error. Unable to right the wrong he had done, he suffered because of his actions. God did not take up for him in his wrongdoing. Yet, David learned something greater than all of this: He turned to God and found mercy greater than his own failings.

In the 51st Psalm he recounts his appeal to God following the episode with Uriah. He cries out: "Have mercy on me, O God, according to your unwavering love" (v. 1); "Create in me a pure heart" and "renew a right spirit in me" (v. 10). David resolves that he will teach others who err to return to the Lord (v. 13). He does not avert attention from his humiliation. Rather, he speaks openly of his experience so that others can learn of God's mercy. And, it is David who in the final verse of the 23rd Psalm brings us these words:

> Surely goodness and mercy will follow me all the days of my life, and I will dwell in the house of the Lord forever (Ps. 23:6).

If it could be said that God has a weakness, it would be his love for people. He is touched by all who will call upon him from a sincere heart. David sees God's goodness and mercy as following him — pursuing him — all the days of his life. Who would not desire this God as his shepherd?

They Sing That He Is the God of Truth

> I entrust my spirit into your hand; you have redeemed me, O LORD, God of truth (Ps. 31:5).

His word can be completely trusted and his faithfulness dictates that he will do what he says he will do. His truthfulness and his faithfulness are bound together.

> He who is the Glory of Israel will not lie or change his mind; for he is not a human being, that he should change his mind (1 Sam. 15:29).

This is a God who will not deny the truth. He will stand by one person who is right against the world when it is wrong.[12] Yet, part of the truth he wants people to learn is the great worth of love and mercy. He forever balances love and truth and his people must learn to do the same. It is not adequate for them to say that they will embrace one without the other. Part of truth is to love. And, part of God's love is love of truth. People may not perfectly attain to either one. It is certain, however, that they must always aspire to both.

This God not only instructs his people to *acknowledge* the truth; he also directs them to *love* it (Zech. 8:19). If we are really to be his people, we must love *all* that is true. To love him is to love his teachings. And let us never be mistaken: Truth can be known. If we are never able to say what is true, then by the same reasoning we can never say that anything is false. In such a world, truth and error fall together in confusion: a confusion from which we might never emerge. But God himself is the source of truth and he is its ultimate teacher.

To say that we cannot know truth is to limit God. And to his people, truth is something active — to be learned and lived:

> Teach me your way, O Lord, that I may walk in your truth (Ps. 86:11).

We Too Can Be His People

> Happy are the people whose God is the Lord! (Ps. 144:15).

David looks and sees God: He is David's shepherd. It is YHWH who wonderfully and completely provides for him. It is he who leads beside still waters; he who restores David. With him, there is need for no other as God.

We too are blessed if our God is the Lord. He can be our shepherd; our teacher. Let him teach us love, faithfulness, righteousness, mercy, and truth. Let him guide our steps. Let him be our strength.

> Have you not known? Have you not heard? The Lord is the everlasting God, the Creator of the ends of the earth. He does not faint or grow weary; his understanding is unsearchable. He gives power to the faint, and to him who has no might he increases strength (Isa. 40:28, 29, ESV).

Chapter Three

Notes

1. The Holy Bible, English Standard Version, "Preface," Crossway Bibles, Text Edition: 2007, ix. The NIV, NASB, NRSV and others provide similar explanations. In reality, two words are normally substituted for "YHWH" because it is customary to add the definite article to "LORD" when translating. In certain circumstances, (particularly when the name YHWH is in association with *adonai*, e.g. Gen. 15:2) some translations use "GOD" (all capital letters) to indicate the name. The name YHWH is sometimes referred to as the "Tetragrammaton," a term from Greek which references the four letters that compose the name in Hebrew.

2. That is the count offered by Ryrie. Charles C. Ryrie, *Ryrie Study Bible - Expanded Edition, New International Version* (Chicago: Moody Bible Inst., 1994).

3. This is according to Kittle. (That is the count disregarding particles.) B. P. Kittle, V. Hoffer and R. A. Wright, *Biblical Hebrew — A Text and Workbook* (New Haven, CT: Yale University Press, 1989), 410.

4. After referring to YHWH as God's "special or proper name," the NASB states, "It is known that for many years YHWH has been transliterated as Yahweh, however, no complete certainty attaches to this pronunciation." New American Standard Bible, "Principles of Translation," Lockman Foundation, 1995.

5. The tradition of not pronouncing YHWH continues to this day among Jews. A common practice is to verbalize *haShem*, "the name" (or other stand-in words) when reading the Hebrew Bible aloud. There was no directive in the Law of Moses or the prophets which prohibited the speaking or writing of God's name.

6. In the Septuagint (LXX), *kurios* (Greek for lord) was substituted for YHWH. Aramaic and Syriac versions used similar approaches. The Vulgate used *dominus* (Latin for lord). For a brief summary see: "YHWH," Tremper Longman III, ed., *The Baker Illustrated Bible Dictionary* (Grand Rapids: Baker Publishing Group, 2013), or The

Holy Bible, English Standard Version, "Preface," Crossway Bibles, Text Edition, 2007.

7. The Shepherd in this psalm is not the Messiah, but rather YHWH himself. It has been suggested by some that the 23rd Psalm may be Messianic. E.g. Harold Lindsell, ed., *Harper Study Bible — Revised Standard Version* (New York: Harper and Row, 1964), 790. While it may well be Messianic, it is a mistake in any event to see the Messiah as being the shepherd in this case. Clearly it is "YHWH" (v.1) who is the shepherd and if the psalm is Messianic, Messiah would be identified with the speaker/writer. The LORD then is the Messiah's shepherd. In chapter 11 of this book, the reader will find a consideration of the Messiah as chosen *by* YHWH to be a shepherd for the people.

8. The use of "holy, holy, holy" in addressing God (v. 3) is an emphatic which intensifies the declaration of God's purity and separation from all other beings. There is of course no indication of a Trinity here, as only the Father is being viewed and addressed.

9. It may rightly be said that God himself is the only one who is intrinsically good. He is good in a sense in which no one else can be compared (1 Sam. 2:2). On this point notice also the teaching of Jesus in Mark 10:18 and Luke 18:19.

10. God is kind toward the weak and resists their oppressors. He teaches that his people must be of that same heart (Ps. 82:3, 4; Jer. 22:3).

11. The patience of God towards humanity is with the hope that people would seek him. That is a theme found in both the Old and New Testaments (Jer. 29:13; Acts 17:27).

12. This is an often overlooked but important point in the story of Noah. That story reveals a God who is always vexed with evil, no matter who or how many people do evil. It shows by contrast that he would stand by one person who is of faith against everyone else when they are opposing the truth.

Chapter Four

He Makes Covenants

God said, "How I would set you among my sons ...And I thought you would call me, My Father, and would not turn from following me."

— God to Israel (Jer. 3:19, ESV)

What Does God Seek?

The true God is a God of relationships. Unlike the cosmic unknown of other religions, he desires connection with us. He tells Israel, "I thought you would call me Father." Just as human beings enjoy interaction and fellowship, he does as well. In fact, he made us so that we might intelligently relate to him. The Scriptures indicate that he created human beings "in his own likeness." We find then in our own desire for companionship a view into the heart of God. So what does God seek? He seeks us! He wants us to call him "Father"!

A Friend of God

> And the Scripture was fulfilled which says, "Abraham believed God, and it was counted to him as righteousness," and he was called God's friend (James 2:23).

The God who desires relationship with human beings has found a friend in Abraham. What greater honor could a person have than to be called a friend of our Creator? Abraham has that honor. And because they are friends, God makes a covenant with him:

> And God said to Abram, "As for me, this is my covenant with you: You will be the father of many nations. No longer will you be called Abram, but your name will be Abraham; for I have made you a father of many nations" (Gen. 17:3–5).

A way in which God interrelates with people is by covenants: He makes agreements with human beings.[1] His covenants contain promises of blessings. Abram is promised progeny — great numbers of offspring. This covenant is a unique bond between Abram and God. God even changes his name: He will no longer be called Abram but rather Abraham.[2]

The blessings of God's covenants often extend beyond the persons with whom the covenants are initially made. In the case of his covenant with Abraham, its provisions extend to his family and descendants.

God's agreement with Abraham comes from mutual love. Abraham is a man of faith and trusts in God. YHWH is drawn to him because of those very qualities. Nevertheless, the covenant does have ongoing conditions. Abraham is to "Walk before the LORD and be blameless" (vv. 1, 2). In turn, God will bless him and his children after him. The blessings upon Abraham overflow to others.

It is in similar fashion that God makes covenants with Noah, the children of Israel who came out of Egypt, King David and others. His greatest covenant of all, however, he reserves till last. It is the one he is working toward from the beginning. It is the covenant he makes with humanity through his Messiah — the Christ.

Finding Yourself in the Bible

Not being a descendant of Abraham, I never anticipated that promises God long ago made to him and his offspring would be of consequence to me. But it is here that all of us who are not children of Abraham find ourselves in God's plans. Notice that YHWH tells him:

> And through your offspring all the nations of the earth will be blessed, because you have obeyed my voice (Gen. 22:18).

It is the matter of extended blessings that makes God's covenant with this man of special interest to us. The blessings of the covenant with Abraham ultimately extend to people of all nations. Through his descendants many will be blessed.[3]

We who are not descendants of Abraham might ask, "How then shall these blessings come to us?" In the New Testament, centuries after Abraham and Sarah had died, the Apostle Peter sees the ultimate fulfillment of the blessings to the nations as coming through a particular one of Abraham's descendants: the one Peter calls "Christ" (Acts 2:38). The apostle speaks to his fellow Jews regarding him:

> You are the children of the prophets and of the covenant which God made with your ancestors, saying to Abraham, "Through your offspring will all peoples of the earth be blessed." When God raised up his servant, he sent him to

> you first, to bless you by turning each of you from your sinful ways (Acts 3:25, 26).

It is their connection to Abraham by which his descendants are blessed. As Jews they are heirs of the covenant God made with him. From Peter we further learn that it is by relationship to the Messiah, the Christ, that *all nations* will be blessed. Such is the nature of God's extended blessings: By the faith and obedience of one, many are benefited.

I still remember reading the Scriptures when for the first time I realized that the story of God's covenant with Abraham is not just a matter of early human history. Rather, it is something that affects me. As I read, I began to feel a sense of connection to Abraham — an ancient person of faith. And for the first time I found myself realizing that God's blessings to me are through him and a particular one of his descendants, the one that Peter described as the Christ — Jesus of Nazareth (Acts 3:20).

What does God seek? He desires relationship with human beings. And he wants that, not only with the descendants of Abraham, but people in all of the nations. That includes me! The God who created us wants to bless us. And through his promises to Abraham and his descendant the Messiah, he has made a way for that to happen. If I will connect with the Messiah, I will be blessed by God. I too can be an heir of God's covenant with Abraham. I too can be a friend of God. I can call him "Father."

Waiting for God's Messiah

The birth of the Messiah and the ultimate fulfillment of the promise of blessings to all nations were centuries into the future from Abraham. The nations would have to wait. What happened with Abraham's offspring while the nations were waiting? Much in every regard. Through those centuries, Abraham's descendants were a blessing to the nations. It was those descendants who held forth the knowledge of the one true God of heaven and earth. It is they who knew his name is YHWH. It is from them that true prophets came who spoke God's word. It is Abraham's descendants who preserved that word in the Scriptures.[4] That included the words of the prophets regarding the Messiah; his birth and the ultimate fulfilling of the promises that God made to Abraham.[5]

Moses Brought a Covenant

After the death of Abraham, his descendants settled in Egypt. There they grew into a numerous people. While Egypt was a favorable location, over time circumstances changed and they became forced laborers for the Egyptians. Because of God's care and love for the children of Abraham, and because of his promises to their fathers, he visited the people and delivered them from Egypt (Ex. 2:23–25). He sent them Moses who led them out and through whom he made a unique covenant with them. That covenant was a law: The Law of Moses.

> Blessed are those whose way is blameless, who walk in the law of the Lord. Blessed are those who keep his decrees, who seek him with all their heart (Ps. 119:1, 2).

They sang of his law — his Torah![6] The words cited above are the opening refrains of the 119th Psalm. It is the longest of the Psalms and all of its 176 verses celebrate God's word, his wisdom, his law. If we turn through the pages of human history, this is a rare thing: A nation singing songs about the law of their land. In ancient Israel they rejoiced and gave thanks to YHWH for the law he had given them. Moses said to the people:

> And what great nation is there that has statutes and decrees as righteous as this body of laws that I am setting before you today? (Deut. 4:8).

They were the people of YHWH, the one true God of heaven and earth. In this covenant, they would serve only him as God and keep the law that he gave them. As they did, he would wonderfully bless them (Deut. 30:16).

It was because of his love that he gave them this law. A nation cannot do well and prosper without order.[7] This nation had an order which was designed for them by God himself. And would we not expect that a law given by YHWH would be extraordinary? It was! This law excelled those of other lands. In it, his people learned to love the God who made them and at the same time love their fellow human beings.

Goodness and kindness were found in this law. The people were taught to care for one another. They learned not to hate their brothers and sisters in their hearts (Lev. 19:17). And they were to regard not only their kinsmen but their neighbors as well; for instance, one should not desire another's husband or wife. Neither should a person steal a neighbor's goods (Ex. 20:17). The thief would repay two-fold what had been stolen (Ex. 22:7). If a person came across another's animal, it was to be safely delivered back to its rightful owner (Deut. 22:1). If it was not known who the owner was, it was to be cared for until he or she was found (v. 2).

Kindness was to be shown to the poor and the foreigner. At harvest time, the people were to leave the gleanings of their crops for the needy. The corners of their fields were to be left unharvested. The poor and the wayfarer could always eat freely of the grain there (Lev. 23:22). People were to treat fairly those whom they hired (Lev. 19:13). The entire nation would rest on the seventh day of each week. Their servants and even their work animals rested on that day (Ex. 23:12).

Justice leapt in advances under this law. Here it was found that true justice was to be blind. They began to learn the great importance of impartiality. The wealth of a person was not to be considered in weighing legal responsibility (Lev. 19:15). The people were not to oppress the foreigner who dwelled among them (Ex. 22:21). Justice was to be *even* between the citizen and the non-citizen alike (Lev. 24:22). They were to never take advantage of widows or orphans (Ex. 22:22).

In this law, there was no human sacrifice. In the cultures of neighboring peoples was sometimes found the sacrificing of even children to their gods (Deut. 12:31). For Israel, the incident of Abraham and his willingness to sacrifice Isaac — but with God preventing him from doing so — had already made clear that human sacrifice would not be a part of the offerings made by this people (Gen. 22:1–13). Even the sacrifice of animals was not gratuitous. Those sacrifices served as necessary food for the families of Levites (Deut. 18:1) and for people who provided sacrifices (Lev. 7:11–16).

A Hard Law

It is no wonder that Moses said, "And what great nation is there that has statutes and decrees as righteous as this body of laws?" Yet while the Law of Moses was good, it was also harsh. Because of the hardness of people's hearts — because of the tendency to disregard God and to harm one's neighbor — the law had many provisions which existed solely as a response to evil. It sometimes provided for severe penalties. The penalty for certain crimes was death. Philip Yancey grasps the hardness of the times and helps us see Moses' Law in its historical context:

> The Hebrews lived in wild, barbaric times. Their laws, which may seem harsh to us, represent a great softening

> compared to their neighbors' laws. ... God had to work with people's moral condition at its given stage.[8]

The reality is that the law YHWH gave Moses, even with its harsh provisions, represented God's patience and love towards the people. Without that patience and love, all would have been destroyed because of evil doings. In this law, God met people where they were in order to lead them in the direction they needed to go. And who will sit in judgment of God? Some provisions of the law were hard. However, the people most affected by it — those who actually lived under its provisions — gave testimony to its benefits. Every time that the people sang the 119th Psalm, they sang these words:

> Oh, how I love your law! Those who love your law have abundant peace, and nothing can make them stumble (Ps. 119:97, 165).

A Great Stepping Stone — For a Chosen Few

There was an extraordinary drawback to Moses' law: It was given to only a very tiny fraction of human beings. It was not given to Adam, Noah, Abraham, Joseph or the other early fathers. It was not even given to all of Abraham's descendants. The nations which came from Abraham by Ishmael were not partakers of this law. Again, Moses in Deuteronomy 4:8 drew attention to the fact that other nations did not have such a wonderful law. What shall we say then of a law which did not include the vast majority of human beings?

In reality, the Law of Moses was a stepping stone to move a particular people towards a better time. Those people were the children of Israel who came out of slavery in Egypt: they and their descendants. The "better time" would be the day in which God's Messiah would be born and bring to them God's great and final arrangement with humanity.

This means that even with all of its advantages, the law that God gave to Moses was not for all people. And it was not for all time. God gave the law to Moses centuries after Abraham. When Moses read the law to the people in Deuteronomy, he himself said that it was not given to their ancestors:

> The Lord our God made a covenant with us at Horeb. The Lord did not make this covenant with our ancestors, but with us, all of us who are alive here today (Deut. 5:2, 3).

The Law of Moses was not the covenant that God had made with Abraham centuries before. Over and over again, provisions of the law would have made no sense with regard to their ancestors. Abraham, Sarah and others could not celebrate a Passover that had not yet taken place. They could not honor a priesthood of the sons of Aaron when Aaron himself had not even been born. There is not a single record in the Bible where Abraham or any of the fathers before Moses observed the Sabbath day. The Sabbath and other calendar observances of the law were uniquely given to those particular descendants of Abraham who came out of Egypt and to their children. There is no record in the Bible that Abraham, Isaac and Jacob observed the dietary restrictions of the Law of Moses.

Likewise, it was not God's plan that once this law began, it would never end. When it was given, the people were to observe its provisions *perpetually*, not just at their whims or convenience. It was to be kept continually throughout their generations *ad infinitum*.[9] Nevertheless, it was God's plan that in time this law would be superseded by the coming of Messiah and God's ultimate covenant with human beings.

God Makes a New Covenant

Moses was a forerunner and his law was a stand-in until the coming of the Messiah. It is through the Messiah that God would make his ultimate and final arrangement with the descendants of Abraham and all humanity. God himself showed the prophet Jeremiah (7th – 6th centuries BCE) his plans for a new covenant:

> "The day is coming," says the LORD, "when I will make a new covenant with the house of Israel and the house of Judah. It will not be like the covenant that I made with their ancestors in the day when I took them by the hand to bring them out of the land of Egypt" (Jer. 31:31, 32).

It was YHWH who told Jeremiah, "I will make a new covenant." No one could rightly oppose, dissolve or alter the covenant that God made with the people through Moses at Horeb (Deut. 12:32).[10] There was one, however, who had the right to dissolve that covenant: the God who made the covenant in the first place. And it was he alone who had the right to make a new arrangement: an arrangement that would not be like the one that he made with the children of Israel when they came out of Egypt.

God assured Jeremiah that he had justification for making a different covenant. He said it was "Because they broke my covenant" (Jer. 31:32). The earlier covenant was an agreement between *two* parties: God and the children of Israel who were in the Exodus. The people were to serve only YHWH as God, and keep the law he gave them by Moses. In turn, he would greatly bless them. For his part, YHWH would not break that covenant for "a thousand generations" (Deut. 7:9). However, by the testimony of God himself, they had broken it again and again — throughout their generations (Jer. 16:10–12).

The covenant which God foretold to Jeremiah would not only be "new" but also "better" — much better! The law that Moses brought to the people was wonderful. Nevertheless, it had severe limitations. As we have seen, it was given only to those children of Abraham who came out of Egypt and their descendants. The new covenant on the other hand is by the Messiah himself and extends to all peoples. Again, the Law of Moses was designed for the people of the Exodus and was beautifully suited to their agrarian society. However, God's new covenant by the Messiah focuses not on the elements of nature, but rather on the greater aspects of the human heart, the forgiveness of transgressions and a more direct, more personal relationship with God. Speaking of the new covenant, God told Jeremiah:

> "No longer will a man teach his neighbor or a man his brother, saying, 'Know the LORD,' for they all will know me, from the least to the greatest of them," says the LORD. "For I will forgive their inequity, and I will remember their sin no more" (Jer. 31:34).

In the New Testament, the writer of Hebrews reflects on God's declaration that he would make a "new covenant." The writer indicates that covenant *has come*. He tells his readers that the new covenant is superior to the old one: that it is founded on "better promises" than was the Law of Moses, and that it has a new mediator — the Messiah himself:

> But now Jesus has received a ministry which is more excellent, even as the covenant of which he is the mediator is a more excellent covenant, because it has been founded on better promises (Heb. 8:6).

The writer of Hebrews goes on to observe that the new covenant by Messiah will be the sole arrangement between

God and his people for all eternity (Heb. 13:20). There will not be two covenants in the age to come. The one that God gave by Moses had to give way to the superior one of the Messiah. The writer indicates that when God used the word "new" regarding the covenant of the Messiah, that made the one he had given Moses "old." In the day that God spoke to Jeremiah about a new covenant, time was passing by for the earlier covenant he had made through Moses:

> When God speaks of a "new" covenant, he has made the first one obsolete. When something is obsolete it is growing old and will soon disappear (Heb. 8:13).

Life in the Messiah

The supreme advantage of God's new covenant is that it brings a resolution to humankind's greatest problem: Death!

> For as in Adam all die, so in Christ all will be made alive (1 Cor. 15:22).

What the Law Could Not Do

When Moses came on the scene, the people had a much greater problem than slavery in Egypt. That problem was death. These people died! Before them, Abraham, Sarah and the greatest of their ancestors had died. When God gave the Law of Moses to those who came out of Egypt, he never told them that it would change the circumstance regarding death. Even Moses himself died (Deut. 34:5), leaving Joshua to carry on until he also died (Josh. 24:29). Neither Moses nor his law made provisions for resurrection or an unending life.[11] The Law of Moses wonderfully did what God intended it to do. However, that law was not for the purpose of addressing humanity's greatest problem: Death!

The Apostle Paul in the New Testament rightly observes that the death of an individual is not just the result of that person's wrong doing. It is also God's penalty against *all* of humanity for Adam's disobedience. Paul writes that the harsh reality is that even when people have no sin personally counted against them, they still die (Rom. 5:13, 14).

The Law of Moses significantly affected the lives of the people at the time. Keeping the law could change the quality of their lives. It could result in the lengthening of people's lives because of obedience (Ex. 20:12) or could shorten their lives because of disobedience (Ex. 21:12).

Moses' law was for the good of the people. However, with that good also came an undesirable consequence: It added to the reasons why people die. The law's great number of requirements[12] presented literally hundreds of opportunities to fail — to sin personally. The law did not resolve the underlying problem of death due to Adam's transgression. Because of human weakness and the tendency to err, its many provisions *did* add to the reasons that people die. It is for this reason that Paul writes:

> The sting of death is sin, and the power of sin is the law (1 Cor. 15:56).

So then what the law could not do was deliver those under it from death. The law never made a promise of unending life to those who would keep it.[13] Even if the Jews kept it perfectly, that would not undo the penalty of death which had long preceded the law because of Adam's disobedience. Again, Paul writes:

> If a law had been given that could give life, then righteousness would have come by the law (Gal. 3:21).

It would take the coming of a radically new arrangement to deal with death — the most severe of our human problems.

The Covenant of Life in the Messiah

> For the law of the spirit of life in Christ Jesus has set you free from the law of sin and death (Rom. 8:2).

God's new covenant does precisely what the Law of Moses could not do. With the coming of the Messiah, we now see the unveiling of God's ultimate plan for humanity. It is by the Messiah that YHWH sets all things right that have been askew since Adam erred in the beginning. It is the Messiah who leads us back to the harmony and peace that Adam and Eve had with God before their disobedience. Paul writes:

> Therefore, since we have been justified by faith, we have peace with God through our Lord Jesus Christ (Rom. 5:1).

Paul goes on to explain:

> For as through the disobedience of the one man [Adam] the many were made sinners, so through the obedience of the one man [Jesus] the many will be made righteous (Rom. 5:19).

God's final covenant with human beings hinges on our relationship to the Messiah and obedience to him. It is because of our connection to a man, Adam, that we are subject to death. Now, in God's greatest plan, it is connection to a man, the Messiah, by which we can be made free from death. The blessings of God upon the Messiah overflow to those who obey the Messiah.

> Blessed be the God and Father of our Lord Jesus Christ, who has blessed us in Christ with every spiritual blessing in the heavenly realms (Eph. 1:3).

The Messiah's Torah of Life

The Messiah's words, his teachings and commands, are the terms of God's new covenant. Jesus did *not* come to give the people the Law of Moses. They already had that. Jesus' mission was to bring God's new covenant. He did expect that his fellow Jews of the day would observe Moses' law (e.g. Matt. 23:2, 3). He himself was a Jew who was born during the term of the law. Paul writes that Christ was "born under the law in order to redeem those who were under the law" (Gal. 4:4, 5).

Both Moses and Jesus received words from God. However, what Moses received at Sinai was a law that was for a limited number of people, for a limited time and with limited benefits. What Jesus received was God's eternal and final arrangement with humanity which was for all people, for all time, and with the benefit of eternal life!

Jesus brought a "new commandment" (John 13:34). In this commandment, he raised the principle of "love for one another" to a new and higher level. Now the standard became the love with which Jesus loved his people (John 15:12, 17). Moses never spoke of this commandment.

That commandment is the foundation upon which God's new covenant is built. It begins with God's own love in which he "so loved the world that he gave his only begotten son" (John 3:16). It continues in that son who loved his fellow human beings so much that he gave his life for them (Matt. 20:28). The love of that son is then joined with the love that his people are to share (1 John 3:16). It is this ultmate love of God, the Messiah, and his people, that forms the basis for God's new and final covenant with humankind.

That love is a commandment, a law. It is the basis for the new Torah — the Torah of Messiah (Gal. 6:2). The New Testament is essentially an exposition of that love. Sharing in the unique love of God and of Christ is required in order for a person to be a partaker in the new covenant and to have eternal life (1 John 3:14, 15). And just as the love that Christ has toward God is conjoined with his obedience to God (John 8:28; Matt. 26:39–42; 1 Cor. 11:3), the love of Christ's people cannot be separated from their obedience to Christ — keeping his commandments (Heb. 5:9; John 15:14). And obedience to the Messiah's commandments leads to eternal life. Jesus said of the words that God gave to him:

> I know that his commandment is eternal life. Therefore, I speak just what the Father has told me to say (John 12:50).

Again, Jesus says:

> The words that I have spoken to you are spirit and they are life (John 6:63).

For people who have confidence in the leading of the spirit of God, they must recognize that according to the Bible, the spirit does not lead Christians to observe Moses' law. Rather, the spirit leads people to the new covenant of "life" in Messiah Jesus (2 Cor. 3:3–8; Gal. 3:1–5).

On the occasion above in which Jesus says that his words are "spirit" and "life," Peter makes this statement to Jesus:

> Lord, to whom shall we go? You have the words of eternal life (John 6:68).[14]

There were many teachers of Moses' law in the land. Yet Peter is recognizing that it is Jesus who has "the words of eternal life." Hence, the concern under the new covenant is not Moses' law but the words of Jesus and obedience to him:

> And having been made perfect, he became the source of eternal salvation for all who obey him (Heb. 5:9).

The New Testament is not a book filled with exhortations to keep Moses' Law. It is a book filled with exhortations to obey Messiah Jesus and keep his words. And *his* words will *never* pass away. It is Jesus himself who says:

> Heaven and earth will pass away, but my words will not pass away (Matt. 24:35).

Beyond Moses — To Messiah

Abraham and Sarah did not keep the Law of Moses. Moses was not even born for around two and one-half centuries after they died. His law did not come for nearly another century after that. Even Moses himself did not keep the law for the majority of his life. It was not given to him until he was about 80 years old (Ex. 7:7).

Abraham was declared righteous by God centuries before the Law of Moses and even before he was circumcised (Gen. 15:6). We see then that a person can be righteous in the sight of God by faith — *without* keeping the Law of Moses and *without* being circumcised. Paul rightly observes:

> Is this blessing only for the Jews, or is it also for uncircumcised Gentiles? Well, we have been saying that Abraham was counted as righteous by God because of his faith. But how did this happen? Was he counted as righteous only after he was circumcised, or was it before he was

circumcised? Clearly, God accepted Abraham before he was circumcised! (Rom. 4:9, 10, NLT).

The facts are that Abraham was righteous before God:

- Without circumcision
- Without the Law of Moses
- Without keeping the Sabbath and other calendar observances
- Without keeping the dietary restrictions of the law

The observance of the Sabbath was a unique sign between YHWH and the children of Israel when they became a nation. It was a beautiful observance of rest which symbolized the nation's unity with God. In the creation narrative in Genesis, God had rested on the 7th day. Now, this nation would rest from their labors on the 7th day of each week (Ex. 31:17).

This unique observance was reserved for the nation of Israel. It was a national day. Again, it was not given to Adam, Noah, Abraham or the other fathers (Deut. 5:2). It was not given to the children of Abraham who were descended from Ishmael. Even Moses did not observe the Sabbath through the majority of his life. For Gentiles to observe the Sabbath would have taken away from its uniqueness as a sign between God and the nation of Israel.

In the greater plan of God, the Sabbath, together with other calendar observances and dietary restrictions of Moses' Law, were all a "shadow" of a person. That person is the Messiah. By him, Israel and all of the nations will be given an unending rest and made clean and pure before God in all things (Col. 2:16, 17).[15]

Paul continues:

> For the promise that he would inherit the world did not come to Abraham or his descendants through the law but through the righteousness of faith (Rom. 4:13).

God never promised Abraham "a law." He did promise him that through his descendants all nations would be blessed. It was *not* Moses and his law through whom that would ultimately be accomplished. Rather, it is fulfilled through God's new covenant in Jesus. It is the Messiah's covenant in which God's ultimate moral code is revealed. It is in *his* covenant that true hope of unending life comes to humanity.

The Law of Moses embodied some things that remind us of God's dealings with Israel's fathers in times before the law. Likewise, there are things in the law which pointed forward to the Messiah and his great Torah. Even the 10 Commandments engraved on stones were an imperfect shadow of the Messiah's new covenant which is written by his spirit in the hearts of his people (2 Cor. 3:7, 8; Heb. 7:19).[16] We should never be mistaken: All of the things that went *before* the Messiah were intended ultimately to bring the Jews *to* the Messiah.

> Therefore the law was our guardian to lead us to Christ so that we might be justified by faith. Now that faith has come, we are no longer under a guardian (Gal. 3:24, 25).[17]

Now, the Messiah *has* come. He has given us God's great new covenant: the Torah of Life. Now, even the descendants of Abraham must come to God through the Messiah. Those who cling to Moses' law as their hope will ultimately die. Those who cling to the Messiah and his new law of life will live forever!

The children of Israel who came out of Egypt were wonderfully blessed. God delivered them, made them a nation and gave them a great law. They were further blessed to have had that law as a "stepping stone" to bring them to the Messiah and to God's new covenant. The Apostle Paul recognizes and respects that it was to these people that the Messiah first came, and that these people were intended to be the first to come to the Messiah (Rom. 1:16).

The law given to Moses was not God's first word, nor his final word, to humankind. Moses' law was a wonderful step forward. But it was indeed a stepping stone. It was a stride for a very small but important segment of humanity. The law was for the purpose of bringing the nation of Israel to God's Messiah and God's new and final covenant. Ideally, when they would arrive at the new covenant, it would be Israel which would then call the Gentiles to come to Messiah.

What Moses brought to the people was awesome. It was an amazing law with wonderful provisions. Yet both Moses and his law were a stepping stone to bring Israel to the Messiah. It is tragic for Jews today to stop on the stepping stone and not advance to God's ultimate and final plan. To stop there is to miss the greatest point of Moses' law. Jesus told Jews of his day:

> You search the Scriptures because you think that in them you have eternal life. But it is these very Scriptures that testify about me! Yet you refuse to come to me to have life (John 5:39, 40).

It is likewise tragic when Gentile Christians today are sometimes found attempting to observe Moses' law. They are unwittingly seeking to get onto a stepping stone that was never theirs to begin with. They do not realize that the Law of Moses itself forbade them as Gentiles from being a part of that covenant. The law even specifically forbade Gentiles from observing the Passover (Ex. 12:48). The Law of Moses was God's private arrangement with those children of Abraham who came out of Egypt and their descendants. It was not God's plan for us as Gentiles.[18] As Gentiles, we cannot begin observing the law of Moses without breaking it by doing so.[19] Gentiles were not allowed to participate in the Law of Moses.[20] Jesus never instructed Gentiles to keep the Law of Moses.[21]

It is by the Messiah that all peoples, Jews and Gentiles, must come to God. It is the new covenant, the new Torah with which God is concerned. YHWH has made Messiah to be Lord over *all* (Acts 2:36; 10:36). It is him we must hear; him we must obey. In one of the most important statements found in the Hebrew Bible, God instructs Moses about the coming Messiah:

> I will raise up a prophet like you from among their brothers, and I will put my words in his mouth. He will speak to them everything that I command him. It will come to pass that anyone who does not listen to my words which he will speak in my name, I will hold that person accountable (Deut. 18:18, 19).[22]

It is not by Moses that we will have peace with God. It is by the Messiah. It is not by Moses' law that we will come to unending life. Rather it is by the Messiah's Torah of Life. Jesus said:

> I am the way, and the truth and the life. No one comes to the Father except through me (John 14:6).

It is not Moses who is "the way," "the truth" or "the life." It is the Messiah. It is not Moses through whom we now come to the Father. It is through Jesus. The Messiah is that particular one of Abraham's descendants through whom all peoples of the earth will be blessed.

We as Gentiles are not a part of the covenant that God made with the children of Israel who came out of Egypt. We can, however, participate in the greater covenant that God made with Abraham long *before* the law. We can be partakers of that covenant by faith in the Messiah. He is ultimately the one by whom all of the nations will be blessed. Through the Messiah, Jews and Gentiles can find the resolution of matters that even predate Abraham. By Messiah we can all come to peace with God *and* everlasting life.

What God Seeks — We Can Give Him

It is truly wonderful! God desires relationship with human beings and has made a way for that to happen. It is in the Messiah's covenant that we find the ultimate terms for peace with our Creator (Rom. 5:1; Heb. 13:20, 21). By God's love and wisdom he has given us the opportunity not only to know him, but to have an unending life.

> For God so loved the world that he gave his only begotten son, that whoever believes in him shall not perish, but have eternal life (John 3:16).

The familiar words above are actually a summary of the new covenant. The terms of this covenant are that we must believe in — rely on and adhere to[23] — God's Messiah and keep *his* words. In doing so, we shall never perish but have unending life. That is God's great, ultimate and final covenant with humankind. John writes:

> And this is the testimony: God has given us eternal life, and this life is in his son. He who has the son has life; he who does not have the son of God does not have life (1 John 5:11, 12).

We as human beings do not have a choice as to whether we are born as descendants of Abraham. We do, however, have the choice of whether or not we will trust in Messiah Jesus. For all who do, they will be blessed with Abraham

(Gal. 3:9). Those who participate in the new covenant with Jesus Christ — whether Jews or Gentiles — are the ones whom God now counts as the true children of Abraham. They are the heirs of the promise:

> And if you belong to Christ, then you are Abraham's offspring, and heirs according to the promise (Gal. 3:29).

What greater blessing to the nations could there be than unending life? That blessing comes only through relationship with the Messiah, the most extraordinary one of Abraham's offspring. By him we can become the friends of God. In the Messiah, we can give God what he really seeks: We can call him "Father."

> For you are all children of God through faith in Christ Jesus (Gal. 3:26).

Chapter Four

Notes

1. The Hebrew word most often translated "covenant" is *berith*. The Bible in Basic English uses "agreement." God's covenants are generally agreements he makes with others in which the terms are set by him. While they contain promises, they are not always simply promises. Generally, a covenant can be "broken" by the parties (e.g. Lev. 26:15, 16). See *Brown-Driver-Briggs, Hebrew and English Lexicon* (Peabody, MA: Hendrickson Publishers, 2000), 136.

2. The meaning of "Abram" is "high or exalted father" with "Abraham" being "father of a multitude."

3. The promise of blessings to all nations/peoples is not to be understood as indicating universal salvation. There are those in Israel and among the nations who refuse to believe and thus are not partakers in the covenant or the blessings (Rom. 11:20, 21).

4. Romans 3:1, 2.

5. Acts 3:24–26.

6. The word "*torah*" means essentially "instruction" or "doctrine." It is used variously in the Bible to indicate any law or commandment. It is specifically used to refer to the Law of Moses as given to him by God at Sinai (Ex. 24:12). The word has also been applied to the five books of Moses as a whole (the Pentateuch). "*Torah*" is used to reference the Law of Messiah in Isaiah 42:4. The word is typically translated as *nomos* in the LXX, and the Greek New Testament uses that term when referring to the Law of Moses (Acts 13:39) and also when referring to the Law of Christ (Gal. 6:2; 1 Cor. 9:21).

7. While the children of Israel were in Egypt, they were under the dominion of the Pharaohs. When they became independent, they had no law. The law given to them by Moses served as an indivisible civil and religious code.

8. Philip Yancey, *The Bible Jesus Read* (Grand Rapids: Zondervan Publishing House, 1999), 12.

9. The Hebrew word *olam* is used regarding provisions of the Law of Moses. It is sometimes translated "forever." The word actually car-

ries a range of meanings from "long-lasting" to "perpetual" (ongoing) to "eternal." See *Brown-Driver-Briggs, Hebrew and English Lexicon* (Peabody, MA: Hendrickson Publishers, 2000), 761. With regard to the Law of Moses, *olam* has the significance of "ongoing" — "long lasting." The sense is "enduring" but not "eternal." For example, *olam* indicates only the remainder of a human lifetime with regard to slaves serving their masters (Ex. 21:5, 6). If the word is taken to mean "eternal," then it imposes provisions of slavery for all eternity (Lev. 25:45, 46). In Numbers 19:20–22 *olam* is translated "perpetual" (on-going) by the AV, NASB and NRSV. The NIV renders it "lasting."

10. Jesus tells the people that he did not come to destroy the law or the prophets. Rather, he came "to fulfill" (Matt. 5:17, 18). He *does* indicate that Moses' law *would* end and tells them when: it is when "all is fulfilled." It is Messiah who "fulfills" the law and brings God's new arrangement — the new covenant (Luke 24:44–47; Mark 14:23, 24; Heb. 10:15–22). It should be remembered that Gentiles are excluded from the law as long as the law stands. If the Law of Moses is eternal, and its jots and tittles will never end, then its provisions against Gentiles participating in it will never end. The greater hope for humanity, both Jews and Gentiles, is not at all to be found in the Law of Moses. It is found in the new covenant — the covenant of the Messiah.

11. The law's lack of a promise of eternal life may have given opportunity for the disputes between factions over the very concept of resurrection. The Sadducees insisted that there is no resurrection of the dead while the Pharisees held to a resurrection (Acts 23:8). Jesus presents them with a definitive scriptural answer to the question (Matt. 22:31, 32). However, even then his answer is taken from a passage which predates the law as given at Sinai. He quotes God's declaration to Moses in Exodus 3:15, 16. Likewise, the words, "shall live by them [the statutes]" in Leviticus 18:5, et al., fall short of being a reference to eternal life (note Deut. 6:2: "as long as you live — so you may enjoy a long life"). Paul clearly sees the words "live by them" (Gal. 3:12) as referencing the duration of a person's lifetime and not eternal life (Gal. 3:21). He indicates, regarding the righteousness that was under the law, that he had been "blameless." Yet he counted that as nothing so that he might "attain to the resurrection from the dead" through Christ (Phil. 3:6–11).

12. "613" is the traditional count of separate requirements of the Law of Moses. That count is generally traced to the medieval Jewish sage Maimonides (Moshe ben Maimon).

13. There is no reference in the Law of Moses that says keeping that law would result in eternal life. Jesus saw the keeping of the law by Jews as being a stepping stone which would bring them to him. They would in turn find eternal life through him (John 14:6). In Matthew 19:16–22, a Jewish man asked Jesus what "good thing" he must do in order to obtain eternal life. Jesus told him that if he wished to enter into life that he should keep the commandments. Jesus further told him to sell his possessions, give to the poor and "come and follow me." In this interaction, we see a picture of God's plan for the law as a stepping stone to bring the Jews to Christ and to eternal life *through him*. (Also note Luke 18:18–23; 10:26–28.) Again, a more complete statement of Jesus' words to the Jews regarding eternal life is: "You search the Scriptures because you think that in them you have eternal life. But it is these very Scriptures that testify about me! Yet you refuse to come to *me* to have life" (John 5:39, 40). When Jesus says, "I have come that they *may have* life" (John 10:10), it is Jews under the law who are the immediate subjects of his statement. Also note Galatians 4:4, 5.

14. English translations have long tended to render *zoe aionios* as "eternal life." Both the celebrated Anglican scholar N. T. Wright and New Testament scholar Anthony Buzzard move us forward in their recent translations of the New Testament. N. T. Wright renders the phrase, "the life of the coming age," i.e. the life of the kingdom. N. T. Wright, The Kingdom New Testament: A Contemporary Translation (New York: Harper Collins, 2011). That life, among other things, is of course unending in its nature and hence "eternal." Anthony Buzzard in his translation comments that the phrase *zoe aionios* is "much too vaguely translated as 'eternal life.'" He translates the phrase as "the Life of the Age to Come." Anthony Buzzard, The One God, the Father and One Man Messiah, New Testament (Morrow, GA: Restoration Fellowship, 2014), 246, N-46.

15. For an overview of the issues regarding Christians and the Law of Moses see, Anthony Buzzard, *The Law, the Sabbath and New Covenant Christianity: Christian Freedom Under the Teaching of Jesus* (Morrow, GA: Restoration Fellowship, 2005), http://www.21stcr.org/multimedia-2012/1-pdf/ab-sabbathbook.pdf.

16. Beyond Moses and the 10 Commandments, it is Messiah himself who brings us God's ultimate moral compass. In him is revealed the fullness of God's moral character. Messiah wonderfully models the character of God in the life he lives (John 14:9–11). It is for this reason that the Scripture says that we are "complete" in Messiah (Col. 2:10). In his teachings, Jesus was not revising the law or creating a

better version of it. Rather, he was laying out the terms for his new arrangement. The Law of Moses had helped prepare the people for Christ and led them in the direction of the New Covenant. Jesus explains and critiques provisions of the law in the light of God's greater covenant: the covenant that Jesus himself was now bringing to the people. This can be seen in his various, "but I say to you" teachings in Matthew 5:21–48 as well as other contrasts and distinctions he makes between the law and the new covenant (e.g. Matt. 19:8, 9; Mark 7:18, 19).

17. Translators propose a variety of possibilities for *paidagogos* ("guardian," above). The Amplified uses "trainer" with the sense of "guardian" or "guide." Translations tend to carry the idea of tutor (NASB) or even schoolmaster (AV). The better sense, however, is not so much "educator" but rather "guardian" or "supervisor." A pedagogue has the responsibility for delivering a child "*to* the teacher." Thayer defines it as "leader," "escort" — "a guide and guardian of boys." *Thayer's Greek-English Lexicon of the New Testament* (Grand Rapids: Baker Book House, 1977), 472.

18. There is some debate regarding the participation of the nations in the Feast of Tabernacles (Zech. 14) during the millennial reign. It is clear that whatever takes place in the millennial reign will be under Messiah's immediate direction and is not a matter of routine observance of Moses' law.

19. Misguided Gentile Christians, failing to understand the sufficiency of Messiah (Col. 2:10), sometimes propose to keep "parts" of the Law of Moses. To Moses, the law he gave at Sinai is indivisible. His requirement is that people keep the law *in its entirety* (Gal. 3:10; Deut. 28:15). According to the law itself, people are not given the option of keeping "part" or "parts" of it. The law is an "all or nothing" covenant between God and the Jewish people who came out of Egypt (Gal. 5:3). Likewise, the theory that there were two laws (or a "dual" law) is unscriptural. There was only one law given by Moses at Sinai. Moses knows nothing about a moral law versus a ceremonial law, etc.

20. This is not to disregard the fact that over time some Gentiles have converted to Judaism — become proselytes. The Apostle Paul strictly directs Gentile Christians not to do that (Gal. 5:2–4; 1 Cor. 7:18).

21. For Jesus to have encouraged Gentiles (other than proselytes) to keep the Law of Moses would have put him in opposition to the law itself. Jesus does not alter the fact that Gentiles are excluded from Moses' law.

22. Peter tells the Jews that the prophecy in Deuteronomy 18:15–19 is fulfilled in Jesus (Acts 3:22–26; cp. Acts 7:37).

23. To "believe" is *pisteuo* in the Greek New Testament. The word indicates more than just mental cognition or assent. To believe in Christ indicated commitment and obedience (Luke 6:46; John 3:36; Heb. 5:9). Thayer tells us that *pisteuo* is "conjoined with obedience to Christ." *Thayer's Greek-English Lexicon of the New Testament* (Grand Rapids: Baker Book House, 1977), 511.

Chapter Five

Monotheism — An Insufficient Truth

For I am God, and there is no one else; I am God, and there is no one like me.

— Isaiah 46:9

Monotheism is the belief that there is only one God.[1] That is true and of great importance. However, monotheism is an insufficient truth. People may believe that there is one God but have the wrong one in mind. It is a weakness of the term monotheism that while it tells us there is only one God, it does not in itself identify who that God is.

It is not the *concept* of monotheism that animates God's prophets of old. To them, it would not matter whether people believed in one god or not, if that one God is not YHWH. It is *him* that they celebrate. He is their Father (Deut. 32:6). Their monotheism is incidental to the eternal truth that *he* alone is God. Original monotheism is by definition about "the Lord."[2]

His First Priority

To God, the most essential of all truths is the truth about himself. Who he is and his sovereignty are the center of all that is right. He proclaims in the Scripture above, "I am God, and there is no one else; I am God, and there is no one like me." YHWH's first priority is *not* that human beings would know that there is only one God. His first priority is that all would know that *he* is God — *he* alone.

That priority is at the heart of God's relationship with people. How can human beings have a meaningful relationship with him if they do not know clearly who he is? Without the understanding that only he is God, they will search in vain to find truth elsewhere. They will not know to whom they should look for help; to whom they should give thanks. Without that understanding, all is futile; all is lost. The first priority is so essential, so fundamental, that all understanding of God must be measured by it. All right understanding of Scripture conforms to it. And for his people in the Bible, it goes beyond factual correctness. To know the one who alone is God is a matter of privilege. It is a tremendous honor that he is their God.

The Prime Directive

> You shall have no other gods before me (Ex. 20:3).

The Ten Commandments do not begin on a moral or ethical note as such. Rather, the first order of business in the commandments is related to God's sovereignty: They shall have no other gods before him.[3] The eternal truth that "he alone is God" now takes the shape of this crucial directive to the people: They shall serve *him* as God and no one else (Deut. 6:13; 10:20).[4]

To the people of the Bible, that decree is critical. If they keep all of the commandments but violate this one, keeping the others has little value. "He alone is God" is the principle upon which their faith and lives are built. That they are to serve only him as God is his most essential directive to the people. It is impossible to keep the first commandment while acknowledging anyone as God other than *him*.

Original monotheism was more than just a concept or ideal. It brought people to an unambiguous dedication to only one individual as God. That one was the Lord. While ancient Israel is often recognized as forwarding the cause of monotheism, that recognition by itself falls short. The nation's unique gift to the world was actually YHWH himself:

> So know this today, and take to heart, that the Lord, he is God in heaven above and on the earth below; there is no one else. Obey his statutes and commands which I am giving you today (Deut. 4:39, 40).

A New Monotheism?

True monotheism tells us more than that there is only one God. It also tells us that there is only one individual who is that God. As we have seen, that one is the Lord. He is their Father:

> But now, O Lord, you are our Father. We are the clay, you are the potter; all of us are the work of your hand (Isa. 64:8).

Over the course of time, humanity has seen the development of a different kind of monotheism. In this later view, original monotheism has been "stretched" from the essential truth that there is only one individual who is God, to the peculiar concept that multiple persons are one God. Here, the word "person" is used not to mean a human being, but rather any individual with a unique personality.

An example of this reasoning can be found at times in the Hindu religion. Hindus have traditionally worshiped many different individuals who have various names and personalities. However, we sometimes find Hindus viewing these as "manifestations" of the self-same God and declaring themselves to be monotheistic.[5] The prima facie lack of logic in this theory seems to elude them. Is such a "monotheism" really monotheism at all? It is difficult to see any practical difference between worshiping multiple gods and worshiping multiple persons or personalities who are called one God. Is not worship of a poly-personal God actually polytheism in disguise?[6]

We see then that the idea of a multi-person God is not logical. Neither is it scriptural. God's people in the Bible know nothing of a poly-personal Deity. They never speak of the concept of multiple persons as being one God. Neither do they speak of the one God as having multiple personalities or manifestations.

The God of the Bible is a perfect *one*. He is one perfect being who is one perfect God. He has one personality — His! He is almighty and with him there is neither room nor need for any other as God. God's people in the Bible bring us no other gods. Neither do they bring us other persons who share in Deity. Rather, they proclaim in three resolute declarations that God is only one person:

- There is no one besides him — Isaiah 44:8
- There is no one like him — 1 Kings 8:23
- There is no one who is God but him — 2 Kings 19:15

God — The Original Monotheist

> I am the Lord, your Holy One, the Creator of Israel, your King (Isa. 43:15).

Who would not desire to hear God speak? If he spoke to us, what would he say? What would he want us to know? Perhaps he would tell us that he loves us. Perhaps he would say that he wants us to love one another. These are matters of great importance. Both are true. Yet he would likely surprise us. There is something even more fundamental he wants us to know. He wants us to know who he is. He wants us to know him.

To know God as he really is, we must understand that he is a category of one. The individual speaking to Isaiah above says that he is the "Holy One" of Israel. No Scripture in the Bible refers to God as the "Holy Two" or "Holy Three." In the Book of Isaiah, he is referred to as the "Holy One" some 30 times. Rhetorically he asks:

> "To whom then will you compare me? Who is my equal?" says the Holy One (Isa. 40:25).

To whom can they compare him? No one else in the universe! YHWH is the original monotheist. He is not confused! Neither is he ambiguous. While the people of the nations quibble over how many gods there are or how many persons equal one God, he is certain: He alone is God. There is no question where he stands. The only question is, Will we stand with him? His people of old did:

> Now therefore, O Lord our God, deliver us from [Sennacherib's] hand, so that all the kingdoms of the earth may know that you alone, O Lord, are God (Isa. 37:20).

People are aware that the Bible teaches there is only one God. However, they are often not aware of how many times the same Bible speaks of only *him* — the LORD — as being that God. Why should we embrace the Bible when it says there is one God, and not equally embrace when it tells us there is only one individual who is that God?

Monotheism is an incidental truth on the way to the one God. However, if it brings us to anyone other than the LORD, it is not original monotheism. If it brings us to "persons," "personalities" or supposed "manifestations" of God, it is not the monotheism of the Bible. If monotheism is a bridge to God, then let us make sure that we have the right monotheism — the right bridge — the right God.

A Christian Dilemma

As we have seen, God's people of old steadfastly held to the absolute singularity of God. For them, when speaking of God, one equaled one, and that one was their Father. However, post-biblical Christian theology saw a departure from that uncompromising monotheism. Binitarian and Trinitarian theologies proposed a different understanding of God. Binitarianism is the belief that two distinct persons are the one God. Trinitarianism is the belief that three persons are one God.[7]

In the new monotheism, the simplicity of the prophets was displaced by a complex view of Deity in which one God is two or three persons.[8] Here, God's own spirit is often worshiped as a separate person of Deity, and the LORD's Messiah is honored not only as his greatest anointed king — but also as being God himself.[9]

Developed after the Bible was written, multi-person theologies proposed that two or three are the same Deity in terms of substance, yet different persons within that substance.[10] Confusing to even think about, the terms of such formulas are found in post-biblical literature and church creeds but not in the Bible itself. Clearly, this new definition of monotheism would be inconceivable to the Lord's prophets and his people of old. He told them that "he is God and there is no one else; he is God and there is no one like him" (Isa. 46:9). They believed him! Their faith began and ended on the point that their Father alone is God.

Over the centuries a poly-personal God has not held attraction for Orthodox Judaism. For the great majority of Jews, multi-person monotheism is an oxymoron. They have viewed it as syncretistic and a fatal compromise regarding the absolute sovereignty of the one who alone is God. Whether Hindu, post-biblical Christian, or other, all concepts of a multi-person monotheism have been rejected by faithful Jews.[11]

Judaism remains a devoted guardian of original monotheism. Theirs is a pure, uncomplicated view of the singularity of God. Scholars of various backgrounds sometimes refer to the "strict" monotheism of the Jews. But what then is "un-strict" monotheism? Can it rightly be called monotheism at all? The Jewish objection is clear: Does not multi-person monotheism — at its core — represent a departure from the Hebrew Bible? Does it not introduce others to be worshiped as God through a sort of theological back door? Is it not an attack on the sole sovereignty of the Father?

Christ and the earliest Christians were entirely devoted to absolute monotheism. Jesus and the apostles were all dedicated Jews. The New Testament was written by people who were strict monotheists. They all knew the Scriptures in which the Father had declared himself to be the only one who is God. Multi-person monotheism as a Christian concept developed in post-biblical times. In the second through the fifth centuries CE, Gentile Christians misinterpreted and re-interpreted the Bible in terms of multiple persons as one God.[12] Today, many Trinitarian scholars acknowledge that the Trinity is a post-biblical concept. For example, Baptist scholar Roger Olson and Episcopalian theologian Christopher Hall candidly write:

> The doctrine of the Trinity developed gradually after the completion of the New Testament in the heat of controversy ... The full blown doctrine of the Trinity was spelled out in the fourth century at two great ecumenical (universal) councils: Nicaea (325 A.D.) and Constantinople (381 A.D.) ... Both the practices and documents of the church finally led early Christian leaders to propose a trinitarian model of God, but the formation of this model took place over many years and in many contexts.[13, 14]

Trinitarian scholar William C. Placher in his *History of Christian Theology* admits that the Cappadocians, who were central to the development of Trinitarian theory in the 4th century CE, "were deeply influenced by Platonic [Greek] philosophy" and that "modern theologians often have a tough time restating their theory of the Trinity in plausible form apart from those Platonic assumptions."[15]

There are those who place absolute confidence in post-biblical church councils and Christian tradition. For them, it is not disconcerting that the doctrine of the Trinity was developed by theologians in the centuries after the Bible was written. However, it should be alarming for those who see the Bible as the inspired and best source for all matters of faith to find leading Trinitarian scholars speaking of this doctrine as "developing gradually after the completion of the New Testament" under the sway of men who were "deeply influenced by Platonic philosophy."

God is Not a Trinitarian

God is the ultimate authority in all matters. Who would know better than the Father himself if there are persons who share his Deity? For all who really believe in the Bible, the words of the God of the Bible should be definitive:

> For I am God, and there is no one else; I am God and there is no one like me (Isa. 46:9).

> There is no one other than me; I am the Lord, and there is no one else (Isa. 45:6).

True monotheism was not conceived by Israel. Rather, it originated with the God of Israel. His words are, "I am God and there is no one else; I am God and there is no one like me." He leaves no room for other persons who share in his Deity. Neither does he say anything about having multiple personalities or manifestations. Consider these words in Isaiah:

> For thus says the Lord — he who created the heavens, he is God, he who formed and made the earth, he established it; he did not create it to be void, but formed it to be filled with life — he says: "I am the Lord and there is no one else" (Isa. 45:18).

Six times in this verse God is spoken of in singular terms:

1. ***He*** created the heavens
2. ***He*** is God
3. ***He*** formed and made the earth
4. ***He*** established it
5. ***He*** did not create it to be void
6. ***He*** says "I am the Lord and there is no one else."

If we are to believe in the Bible, then we must worship *him* as God and *him* only. In fact, God is addressed with singular pronouns and verbs many thousands of times in the Scriptures.[16] We must not embrace any other person or persons as being Deity with him. We must not worship two or three and then say that "they" are the one God of the Bible. Neither can we rightly worship imagined personalities or supposed manifestations of God. To do so opposes the very words of God himself. He disallows all such reasoning:

> I am the LORD, and there is no one else; other than me there is no God. I strengthen you, though you do not know me, so that all may know; from the east and from the west, that there is no one other than me; I am the LORD, and there is no one else (Isa. 45:5, 6).

If we let *him* decide, then the answer is clear: The new multi-person monotheism does not stand the test of God's own words. The one who is the God of the Bible declares that apart from "me" there is no God. His words exclude any other from being God with him. And if the God of the Bible is not a Trinitarian, then why should I be?[17]

A Trilemma

Inept, Immoral, or the only one who is God

The God of the Bible and the Bible itself are inseparable. If the one speaking in the statements above is not the only one who is God, then both he and the entire Bible are discredited. We cannot look at the Bible as being a holy book or a book of ancient truths and at the same time disregard its words concerning him. From beginning to end, it declares *him*. Either it is a book of truth or it is worse than worthless: It is a book of lies.

That then leaves us with an extraordinary trilemma. There are three possibilities regarding the one who spoke to Isaiah in the statements above:

1. He is inept. There are other beings or persons who are God and he doesn't know it.
2. He is immoral. He is lying. There are others and he knows it.
3. He is the only individual in the universe who is truly God.

If he is inept or immoral, we must not serve him: He is not worthy to be called God. If we judge him to be true, however, then we need look no further — we have found God. And if he is God at all, then he is all of God there is. We must serve the Father as sovereign and him alone.

The famed C. S. Lewis proposed a now popular trilemma in which Jesus is said to have also declared himself to be God.[18] On the basis of that, it is argued that his claim must be true or else he is "a madman" or "something worse" (popularly, "mad, bad or God"). Lewis' proposal, however, has two critical flaws: First, his trilemma came too late. As we have seen, YHWH had already established that "he" is God and the only one who is. He is the Father of Israel (Ex. 4:22), and is the Father of Jesus Christ when Jesus is born (2 John 1:3). Second, Lewis' trilemma assumes that Jesus claimed to be God. That is incorrect. He never made that claim. Rather, Jesus affirms that his Father is the only one who is truly God and that he (Jesus) is the Messiah — the Christ:

> Father ... this is eternal life: that they may know you, the only true God, and Jesus Christ whom you have sent (John 17:3).

Jesus tells Mary Magdalene that his Father is in fact his God (John 20:17). The claim of Jesus regarding himself was that he is the Messiah, God's only begotten son (Matt. 16:16, 17).

God's first priority is not that he and one or two others together are God — it is that *he* alone is God. His prime directive is not that you shall have no other gods before "us." It is that you shall have none before "me." We must embrace the Father as the only one who is God, or renounce him as a fraud.

We are faced then with this trilemma:
The Father is inept, immoral, or the only
individual in the universe who is truly God.

Why I Am a Christian "Monotarian"[19]

I might be a Trinitarian, if it was not for God. It is *him* with whom I am at odds if I embrace multiple persons as one Deity. Again and again, I can hear him saying, "I am the LORD, and there is no one else" (Isa. 45:6). If I will not believe him, then why do I call him God? Either he is God alone or he is not God at all. We must never compromise the biblical definition of God. But have we already done so in the form of multi-person monotheism? Without the understanding that only *he* is God, it is impossible to know him as he really is.

The beliefs of Christian Monotarians stand in contrast to multi-person theologies. Christian Monotarians are strict monotheists. They hold to the original — biblical — monotheism of God's prophets and people of old. They believe that the Father of Israel — the Father of Jesus Christ — is the only one in the universe who is truly God (Isa. 64:4, 8; John 17:3);[20] that God's spirit is *not* another person of Deity but rather the Father himself at work in his presence and power (Matt. 10:20). They believe in Jesus as the LORD's Christ: his Messiah — the one whom he has made Lord of all (Acts 2:36; Ps. 2:2 cf. Acts 4:26); that he is God's only begotten human son; that he came into existence by a miracle in a young virgin by the name of Mary (Luke 1:35); that Jesus is our redeemer, our savior — but not our God (Acts 5:31; 13:23); that to truly follow Christ, we must serve *his* God (John 20:17).

As a Christian Monotarian I rejoice in the working of God by his spirit. I have found peace with God through his Messiah — his Christ (Rom. 5:1). He is the LORD's anointed (Ps. 2:2); his chosen king (Luke 1:32, 33); his miraculously begotten human son (Luke 1:35). Jesus, by relying on God, did not sin — yet he has borne our sins (Heb. 9:14). He trusted in God to the point of death; God raised him from the dead and seated him at his own right hand in heaven (Eph. 1:20). Nevertheless, the Messiah is not my God. Without reservation, my God is the LORD alone! It is YHWH whose spirit it is! It is YHWH without whom there would be no Messiah! I trust in God — I trust in his Christ. Who shall condemn me?[21]

I embrace the LORD alone as God of the universe. I believe in an uncomplicated singularity of God. I will accept no other gods and no other persons within Deity. I do not serve other personalities or supposed manifestations of God. I unreservedly hold to the original monotheism that God himself gave to his people in the Bible. His first priority is my first priority: "*He* alone is God." His prime directive is the basis upon which I live my life: "I will serve only *him* as God." It is critically important to God that we know who he is. Because I love him, it is also critically important to me.

> So they may know that you alone, whose name is the LORD, are the Most High over all the earth (Ps. 83:18).

Chapter Five

Notes

1. The word monotheism is derived from the Greek terms *monos* (only, alone) and *theos* (God). Both words occur in John 17:3.

2. It is interesting that the foundation of faith for the people of the Bible is not monotheism as such. The point of the Scriptures is that YHWH is God and the only one who is.

3. "Before me." The reference is not to priority. Rather, they shall have no other gods in his presence (*paniym* — before his face).

4. Jesus quotes Deuteronomy 6:13 and obeys that same command himself (Matt. 4:10; Luke 4:8).

5. One swami puts it this way: "Thus even though appearing to be many and different, they are actually so many personified expressions of the One and the same Supreme Reality." He goes on to say, "Each deity is, therefore, a personified expression of the One Supreme Divine Being." The swami explains that one substance can take many forms. Chidananda, Sri Swami, "Hinduism — Monotheism and Polytheism Reconciled," *Divine Life Society*, 2004, http://www:dlshg.org/discourse/may2002.htm. For an overview of modern Hinduism see C. J. Fuller, *The Camphor Flame: Popular Hinduism and Society in India* (Princeton, NJ: Princeton University Press, 2004).

6. It should be noted that Hindus often acknowledge that their belief is in multiple gods.

7. Oneness theology is a third view and represents a variation on the same theme. In Oneness, rather than persons, God is pictured as having multiple manifestations. It is often difficult to see, however, any real difference between multiple persons and the supposed manifestations.

8. Some Trinitarian scholars do not like the term persons on the ground that it does not adequately reflect the Greek word which was used in the post-biblical formation of the doctrine of the Trinity (one *ousia* in three *hypostaseis*). However, scholars do not propose any clear alternative and the use of "persons" is customary among Christians. At the root of the problem is that neither the word *hypostaseis*

nor any other Hebrew or Greek term that would rightly be translated "persons" is used in the Bible to refer to God. There simply is no use of the words "three persons (*hypostaseis*) in one essence (*ousia*)" in the New Testament. God is a single "self" — one individual — not two or three persons. There is in fact no place in the Bible where the word "three" is used to refer to the true God.

9. The people of the Bible never thought of God's spirit and his Messiah as being persons of co-Deity with the Father. The spirit of God was not understood to be a separate person from the Father, and the Messiah was seen as being his only begotten human son.

10. Without scriptural definitions for the new terms they employed, there were severe post-Nicaea debates regarding critical meanings. Notably, the meaning of the word "substance" in this context was wrestled over. The struggle centered on the subtle differences in the Greek terms *homoousios* and *homoiousios*. (Hence the adage, "an iota's worth of difference.") Other crucial terms also presented challenges, including *hypostasis* (Greek) versus *substantia* (Latin). Of course, the essential problem with all of this was that these post-biblical Gentile Christians were debating issues which were entirely foreign to both the Hebrew Bible and the New Testament. God's people in the Bible believed that God "just is" one.

11. While Judaism at large has rejected any form of multi-person monotheism, there is a contingent of Jews who believe in Jesus as the Christ (Messianic Jews). While wonderfully devout people, in embracing Jesus as Messiah they have also often crossed over from absolute monotheism to post-biblical multi-person monotheism. That is a tragedy to the entire Jewish community. With Trinitarianism as a barrier, Jews at large are unmoved by the witness of the Messianic contingency. Post-biblical theology proposing that Jesus is God has likely hindered many Jews from embracing him as God's Messiah. The author of this book has met some Messianic Jews who are Christian Monotarian. They have embraced Jesus as the Messiah while worshiping his Father as the only true God (John 17:3).

12. There are many writings which chronicle the development of multi-person monotheism in post-biblical Christianity. For a short overview of the Nicene Council (325 CE) see Peter Partner, *Christianity —The First Two Thousand Years* (London: Seven Oaks, 2002), 59 ff. For an enlightening history and review of issues surrounding that council also see Richard E. Rubenstein, *When Jesus Became God* (San Diego, CA: Harcourt, Inc., 2000).

13. Olson and Hall indicate that "Patristic trinitarian theology is grounded in a number of significant foundations." There they

include the Scriptures but also "early liturgies," "short creedal statements," "worship practices" and "the overarching rule of faith of the early church." Roger E. Olson and Christopher A. Hall, *The Trinity* (Grand Rapids: Wm. B. Eerdmans Publishing Co., 2002), 2, 15.

14. Dr. Dale Tuggy believes that Olson and Hall's assessment that "the full blown doctrine of the Trinity was spelled out" in the two fourth-century councils is to say too much. Tuggy indicates that "If we scour the documents of the First Council of Constantinople (381 CE), we will not see them using 'God' to refer to all three together." Tuggy does see the latter council as being "about the time" that the switch occurred. Dale Tuggy, personal correspondence, December 5, 2014. Also see, http://trinities.org/blog/10-steps-towards-getting-less-confused-about-the-trinity-8-trinity-vs-trinity/.

15. William C. Placher, *A History of Christian Theology* (Philadelphia: The Westminster Press, 1983), 78.

16. For a consideration of the four verses where it is sometimes argued that God is referred to with plural pronouns, see chapter 10 of this book. For an in-depth analysis of singular pronouns in the Bible with regard to God, see Dr. Dale Tuggy's article, "Divine Deception and Monotheism," *Journal of Analytic Theology*, Vol. 2, May 2014, http://journalofanalytictheology.com/jat/index.php/jat/article/view/jat.2014-1.030004192024a/232.

17. I have borrowed here (with adaptation) from the title of Anthony Buzzard's book, *Jesus Was Not a Trinitarian* (Morrow, GA: Restoration Fellowship, 2007).

18. C. S. Lewis, *Mere Christianity* (New York: Harper Collins Publishers, Harper Collins Paperback Edition, 2001), 52. Lewis' trilemma was not entirely his original work. Other apologists had used a similar device. E.g., R. A. Torrey (1856–1928) proposed Jesus to be either a "divine person, daring impostor, or a hopeless lunatic." Torrey, R. A., Sr., "Some Reasons Why I Believe in the Bible as the Word of God, A Sermon by R. A. Torrey, Sr.," Billy Graham Archives, undated.

19. I adopt the phrase Christian Monotarian here as it seems helpful to expressing my faith in God as a single individual and in Jesus as the Messiah, the Christ of God — but not himself God. The term "Monotarian" can be drawn from the Scriptures and particularly Jesus' declaration in John 17:3 that the Father is τον μονον αληθινον θεον. The first person I have known to use the term Christian Monotarian is my friend Pastor Mark A. Jones of Tennessee, http://hgcn.org/our-pastors.html. Sean P. Finnegan of New York has used the term

"Christian Monotheist" with the same intent, http://www.christian-monotheism.com.

20. This of course is not to disallow the use of the word "*God*" as an honorary title or appellation for certain people — Ps. 82:6, etc. See chapter 9 of this book for an exposition of the word when used in its honorific sense.

21. Christian Monotarians are biblically centered and embrace the Bible as the word of God. They believe in miracles, the virgin birth of Christ (Luke 1:34, 35), and that the man Christ Jesus was — by a miracle in Mary — literally God's only begotten human son (Matt. 1:20). Christian Monotarians believe that it was by depending on his Father that Jesus lived a sinless life (Heb. 4:15); did great miracles (Acts 2:22; 10:38); spoke the word of God (John 12:49, 50) and ultimately gave his life as a perfect sacrifice to God for the rest of us human beings (Heb 9:14; Rom. 5:6–10). They believe that Jesus was buried and then bodily resurrected by God (Rom. 10:9), was/is glorified at the right hand of God (Acts 5:31); that he will come again (1 Thess. 1:10) and raise from the dead those who trust in him (John 5:25–30; 1 Cor. 15:20–23).

In all of this, Christian Monotarians hold that Jesus, by the plan and work of God, was truly one of us: That he was the second Adam (Rom. 5:14). Just as God created Adam and made him a human being, likewise, God created his son Jesus in Mary as a *true* human being. Christian Monotarians believe that to bring salvation to the rest of humanity, Jesus himself had to be really one of us (Rom. 5:17–19): Not God, not a "God-man" — not an angel or "angel-man" — or any other kind of being. They believe that Jesus did not literally preexist his own conception in Mary and that language in the New Testament about his "preexisting" was intended to be understood as "types" (*tupos*) of the man Christ Jesus. Metaphorically, he was "bread" (John 6:35) a "rock" (1 Cor. 10:4) etc. They believe that our hope in Christ and of our resurrection is that he, as God's begotten human son, is genuinely one of us (Acts 17:31).

The term "biblical unitarian" typically refers to the same view of God as being only one individual. However, unitarians do not always embrace the same faith as Christian Monotarians regarding Jesus. As is the case at times among others who assert faith in Christ, some unitarians lean to rationalism at the expense of biblical faith and do not hold to his virgin birth, etc. Additionally, the term "unitarian" is often misunderstood by the public. Use of the term frequently leads to confusing "biblical unitarians" with "Unitarian Universalists" ("Universalism" or just "Unity"), which is an entirely different religion that is neither biblical nor Christian.

Chapter Six

Experiencing God By His Spirit

The earth was formless and empty, and darkness covered the face of the deep, and the spirit of God was hovering over the face of the waters.

— Genesis 1:2

The mightiest power in the universe comes upon an earth that is empty and without form. That power is the "spirit of God."[1] It hovers over the surface of the waters and brings the energy of creation to bear on the globe. Yet, look at another scene:

> Then Samuel took the horn of oil and anointed him in the presence of his brothers; and the spirit of the Lord came mightily upon David from that day forward (1 Sam. 16:13, NRSV).

Amazing! The same power that gave form to our planet now comes upon a lad in Judea. It is so mighty that it effected creation — yet, so gentle that it can affect an individual human life.

The Spirit of the Father

He who sits on the throne of the universe is present to work with his creation — he causes life to teem forth on the earth, and gives Israel's future king extraordinary knowledge, understanding and wisdom. These things happen because the spirit of the LORD is at work. God, who is the Father of us all, is able to be on his throne in the heavens and yet at the same time create life on earth or touch his servant David.

It is the presence of the LORD himself that comes upon David. Such coming of God's presence was something his people coveted and depended on. Notice this exchange between God and Moses about going into the land of Canaan:

> "My presence shall go with you, and I will give you rest." And Moses said to him, "If your presence will not go, do not send us on from here" (Ex. 33:14, 15).[2]

Who would not love to experience the tangible presence of God? David and Moses did. By that presence amazing things happened. If we today experience God directly, it will be by that same presence or spirit.

Two Ways the Father Works

Because of God's love, he works for the good of people. There are two ways in which he accomplishes his purposes in the world:

(1) Personal Action — He works directly. Here he extends himself personally. He moves by his "hand" (Ex. 7:5); his "outstretched arm" (Deut. 11:2); his "power" (Ex. 32:11); his "wind," "spirit" or "breath" (Job 26:13; 37:10). He speaks, and at his "word" light springs forth out of darkness (Gen. 1:3). These are not persons or emissaries. These attributes do not have their own unique personalities separate from the Father. Rather, they *are* God: aspects of the Father himself. What is accomplished by the spirit of God is rightly said to have been done by God. It is the Father in motion, God himself in action. How extraordinarily blessed is the person who experiences God in this way. This present chapter of our book and chapter 7 which follows take up the matter of God's direct work by his spirit and his word.[3]

(2) Through His Agents — He works through others. In chapters 8 and 9 of this book, we will explore another way in which God works: He equips and authorizes intermediaries. They are his angels, prophets, rulers and deliverers. These are separate entities from him. They have their own unique personalities. As his agents, he gives them authority to speak and act on his behalf. They themselves are *directly* affected by the presence of God. The work of God is then extended to others through them.[4]

While these agents are not God, he does identify himself with those he commissions. To reject someone God sends is effectively to reject God. To receive one God sends is by extension to receive him. What is accomplished by his intermediaries is often said to have been done by God.[5] It is he who authorized and empowered their work. Happy are those whom God blesses through his envoys. In chapter 11 we will come to his Messiah — his true human son. He is God's ultimate representative.

His Spirit is Him

> O LORD of hosts, God of Israel, you are enthroned between the cherubim; you alone are God of all the kingdoms of the earth. You have made heaven and earth (Isa. 37:16).

Hezekiah's words above bring us to the God of the universe. There is only one who is "enthroned between the cherubim." He is the LORD. He "alone" is "God of all the kingdoms of the earth." It is he who "made heaven and earth." Just as when Isaiah saw God (Isa. 6:1), Hezekiah also speaks of one throne and only one individual who sits on the throne. There is no throne for the "hand of God" or the "power of God." Neither is there a throne for the "spirit of God." These are not separate individuals from the Father. By his own hand, power, spirit and presence *he extends himself* to his creation. The spirit of God is the Father himself at work. New Testament theologian James D. G. Dunn in his important book, *Christology in the Making*, writes concerning the spirit of God:

> On this understanding, *Spirit of God is in no sense distinct from God*, but is simply the power of God, God *himself acting powerfully in nature and upon men*. ... Not merely of a power from God, but the power *of* God, of God himself putting forth efficacious energy.[6]

The idea that God's spirit is a separate person from the Father developed among Gentile Christians in post-biblical times. It became an essential element of the doctrine of the Trinity. Here again, the word "person" is used *not* in the sense of a human being, but rather of any individual with a unique personality. Complicated and confusing, the idea of God's spirit as a person in addition to the Father is unknown to people in the Bible. To them, the spirit of God is not a separate agent or person of co-Deity. Rather, it is the Father in action.[7] What has been done by the hand or spirit of God has literally been done by the Father himself.

The hand, arm, power, breath, spirit and word of a human being are not persons or different personalities as such. Neither are the various aspects of God.[8] The spirit of YHWH is literally YHWH himself. Anthony Buzzard puts it this way: "The spirit of God was not a different Person from God Himself, any more than the 'spirit of Elijah' (2 Kings 2:15) meant a person other than Elijah."[9]

That has also been and continues to be the orthodox Jewish understanding of the spirit of God. Orthodox Judaism disavows any notion that God's spirit is a person or individual with an independent personality from that of the Father. *The Dictionary of Judaism in the Biblical Period* indicates:

> Just as "spirit" was considered the essence of human life, so analogously the term "spirit" was used of the presence, activity and power of God.[10]

If we say that aspects of God are "persons," then how many "persons" might we find? How many shall we serve? To the people of the Bible, God's power or spirit are no more separate from the Father than are his "eyes" which are on the righteous, or his "ears" which are open to their cry (Ps. 34:15).

His people of old find that there is a personality in the spirit of God. However, it is the personality of the Father. If people resist the outstretched hand of God they have resisted God himself (Isa. 14:27). If they grieve his spirit, they have grieved him (Isa. 63:10; Eph. 4:30). To cause anguish to the heart or spirit of someone is to grieve the one whose heart or spirit it is. When people have grieved God's heart or his spirit, it is the Father himself that they have offended.

There is only one throne (Isa. 6:1). To say that God's spirit or any other aspect of him is a separate person from the Father is to say that the one on the throne is not the only one who is God. It is to say that there is another God-person who is with him; another who is like him.[11] Again, that violates his first priority:

> For I am God, and there is no one else; I am God, and there is no one like me (Isa. 46:9).

The spirit of God is not another who is "like" the Father — it *is* the Father in action. Again, he speaks to that matter in Isaiah the 40th chapter. Rhetorically, he asks:

> "To whom then will you compare me? Who is my equal?" says the Holy One (Isa. 40:25).

There is no one who is his equal; no one with whom to compare him. It is not "they" who are God. It is him. *He* is God and *he* alone.

There is no throne for the "hand of God" or the "power of God." There is no throne for the "spirit of God."

God's Spirit Has No Personal Name

We also see that the spirit of God is not another person from the Father in that it has no personal name. Just as our various features and exercises of our powers as human beings do not have personal names, neither do his. They are the "hand of the LORD" (Isa. 66:14); "his holy arm" (Isa. 52:10); "his mighty power" (Ps. 106:8). His spirit is "the spirit of God" (2 Chron. 15:1); "the spirit of the LORD" (2 Sam. 23:2) or "his holy spirit" (Isa. 63:10, 11).[12]

The Bible never says that terms like "spirit of God," "holy spirit," "the holy spirit," etc. are proper/personal names. No one in the Bible ever treated those terms as though they were.[13] The word "holy" is an adjective modifying the noun "spirit." That identifies the nature of the spirit that God has: It is holy! When the definite article is added, it points us to God's spirit as being one often referenced and at the same time unique.

In "YHWH," God himself has a personal name. Likewise, human beings, including the Messiah, have personal names. Even angels of God are known by name (Luke 1:19; Jude 1:9). Theologians who in the centuries after the Bible was written began construing God's spirit as a separate person of Deity from the Father, were left with the peculiar problem that the new "God-person" had no proper name. It was difficult to envision a nameless God. The problem was never adequately resolved and the tendency became to just treat words like "holy spirit," etc. as though they somehow were a name for this supposed person of Deity.

One Amazing Almighty

> He who lives in the shelter of the Most High will find rest in the shadow of the Almighty. I will declare of the Lord, "He is my refuge, my fortress; my God in whom I trust" (Ps. 91:1, 2).

God's Omnipotence

There is only one who is Most High — one who is Almighty. The psalmist tells us, "*He* is my refuge." If the Father is truly almighty, then he can do all things by his own power. While he uses his angels and human emissaries in his work with humanity, he needs no other as God. With the Father alone, all things are possible. If not, then he isn't truly almighty.

In the Bible, it is never the almighty "two" or "three" who are God — it is the almighty "one." The Father himself has an "arm" which he stretches out to his people. He has his own immeasurable power, his own spirit, hand, breath. What is it that needs to be done by God that he cannot do for himself? There is an absolute singularity in the omnipotence of God. It is the Father that we are limiting when we think that his spirit is another person of Deity.

A striking example of the fact that the spirit of God is the Father in action is found in the opening of Matthew's Gospel. Matthew writes that Jesus was begotten in Mary by God's spirit (Matt. 1:18, 20). To the people of the Bible, that is one and the same as saying that God fathered this child by the extension of his own miraculous power. What has been done by God's spirit has literally been done by the Father himself. Hence, Jesus never says that a "person" by the name of the "Holy Spirit" was his Father. Rather, he affirms that he is the son of God (Matt. 16:16, 17).

God's Omnipresence

Who then is everywhere present? Notice David's words:

> O LORD, you have searched me and you know me. You know when I sit down and when I rise up; you know my thoughts from afar (Ps. 139:1, 2).

Who is it who knows when David sits and when he rises? Who is it who knows his thoughts *from afar*? It is the LORD. The omnipresence of God is not achieved by his sending another person of Deity called "The Spirit." Rather, it is by the *literal* presence of the Father himself.

The wonder of God's spirit is not that it is another person from the Father: It isn't. The truth is more amazing than that. The wonder is that the Father is so mighty that he can sit on the throne of the universe and yet at the same time be moving upon the earth. By his own spirit, he can be in more than one place at a time. He really is Almighty!

> With the Father *alone*, all things are possible.
> If not, then he isn't truly almighty.

Whom Shall We Worship?

> But the LORD who brought you out of the land of Egypt with great power and an outstretched arm is the one to whom you must give worship. To him you shall bow down and to him make sacrifices (2 Kings 17:36).

To his people of old, worshipping anyone or anything as being God of the universe other than the LORD himself is unimaginable. They will magnify the one on the throne for his "great power and outstretched arm." But, the command is to worship the one whose great power and arm they are. It is to *him* that they shall bow down. They direct their worship to the LORD himself — *not* to his spirit as though it were another person. Notice these words from the 139th Psalm:

> Where can I go from **your** spirit? Or where can I flee from **your** presence? If I ascend to heaven, **you** are there; if I make my bed in Sheol, **you** are there. If I take the wings of the morning and settle at the farthest limits of the sea, even there **your** hand shall lead me, and **your** right hand shall hold me fast (Ps. 139:7–10, NRSV).[14]

David extols the one on the throne for his spirit, his presence. He marvels at the "hand of God that will lead him" and at God's "right hand that will hold him fast." Yet, David is not addressing worship **to** the "spirit" of God or **to** his "hand." All of the praise is to the one whose spirit and hand they are. In the Bible, people do not address worship to aspects or facets of God.

To his people of old, it would make no sense to give thanks directly to the "hand of God" or the "spirit of God." It would be like a man being handed a gift from a friend and then thanking "the hand" of his friend. What one's hand has done, the friend himself has done. The thanksgiving then is to the friend — the entire person — not to his "hand." Again, in the Scriptures, they thank God himself for what is done. They do not <u>directly</u> thank his "power" or his "spirit."

God's people of old bow to the Father on his throne. They bow to his kings and to his Messiah after he is born.[15] However, from Genesis to Revelation, neither angels nor human beings are ever said to bow before the holy spirit of God.

Likewise, no one in the Bible ever prayed to the "spirit of God." Just as praise and thanksgiving are directed to the one on the throne, so also are prayers and requests for help. This is the case even when the prayer is in regard to God's presence or spirit.

> Do not cast me away from **your** presence, and do not take **your** holy spirit from me (Ps. 51:11, NRSV).[16]

People in the Bible do not pray to God's spirit asking it to come or to remain with them. All requests are made to the one whose spirit it is. Again, it would be like desiring that a friend would hand you something, and then asking his *hand* itself to do it. The requests are made to the friend — the whole person — not to his hand.

An Apology to the Father

The doctrine of the Trinity came into existence in the centuries after the Bible was written. With that came liturgy, prayers and worship directed to the spirit of God. Most Christians today are not aware that there was no creedal statement on the spirit of God as a separate person of Deity until the Council of Constantinople in 381 CE. That creed set forward the post-biblical idea that God's spirit is to be worshipped and glorified as a person along with the Father and the Son.

Now, people sometimes express concern because there is a tendency for Christians to worship the "Spirit of God" with less passion or reverence than the Father. The concern is that the "Spirit" is being slighted. However, to the people of the Bible, such a concern is entirely backwards. It is the Father who is diminished when people worship his spirit as though it were a person in itself. It is the Father to whom we owe apologies.

God never directs anyone in the Bible to pray to "his hand" or to "his spirit." Most Christians find it awkward to pray to God's spirit. We are sometimes prompted to do so by modern Christian ministers.[17] Everyone should be aware that in the Bible itself, people did *not* pray **to** the spirit of God. Our tendency to shrink from praying to his spirit is actually scripturally well grounded. We should not allow ourselves as Christians today to be pressed into doing something that God's people in the Bible did not do.

In the same vein, God never commands anyone in the Bible to direct worship to his hand or to his spirit. No one in the Bible does. The commands are to worship God himself. They sing songs to God. They pray to him. When they worship God, they extol all of his attributes and virtues. They laud his mighty power and his holy spirit! But as they do so — they look upward. Their words are addressed to the one on the throne.

Jesus is our perfect example in all spiritual things. He leaves no room for doubt about the matters we have been considering concerning God's spirit. Jesus never prays to the "spirit of God." His prayers are to the Father. There is no example where Jesus is said to "speak" with God's spirit or have a conversation with "the spirit of God." He speaks to God himself. Let us as Christians follow the example of Jesus. Let our prayers and worship be to the God whose holy spirit it is. Let us pray to the Father as Jesus did (Matt. 6:9–15).[18]

Shall We Rob God?

> For my own sake, it is for my own sake, I will do this. How can I let my name be dishonored? I will not yield my glory to another (Isa. 48:11).

The One God speaks. He tells of his glory as sovereign God. Who is this one? It is the LORD (v. 1, 2). If we judge him to be true, then let us serve *him* as God and no other. Let us give him *all* of the glory due God Almighty. He has given glory to his angels. He has given glory to men. From the beginning, he had a great glory in store to give his Messiah after he is born. The glory of actually being the God of the universe, however, he shares with no one.

We have misused the concept of God's own spirit to create in our minds another "person" of Deity. No such person exists in reality. This idea has for centuries robbed people of a clear understanding of the absolute sovereignty of God. It has caused people unwittingly to give honor and glory that are due our Father to an imagined person of Deity.

We must not rob God. If we give honor to anyone or anything as being God Almighty other than the one who is saying to the prophet above, "I will not yield my glory to another," we have robbed him. We have given a glory that is his alone to someone or something else. God's spirit is not a separate person or personality to be worshipped. It is an exciting, extraordinary facet of the Father. God's spirit is Deity. However, that Deity **is** the Father. People in post-biblical times by their teaching and creeds made God's spirit into a separate person of co-Deity. In doing so, they divided the glory that is due our Father alone.

It is the Father that we are limiting
when we think that his spirit
is another person of Deity.

The Same One — Near and Far

It is an awesome divide. God sits in the heavens. We live out our lives upon the earth. As human beings we lack the strength and virtue to bridge the distance between ourselves and him. How can we know him? He answers that question for us:

> The Lord declares: "Am I a God who is only nearby, and not also far away? Can anyone hide himself from me in secret places so that I cannot see him?" says the Lord. "Do not I fill heaven and earth?" (Jer. 23:23, 24).

It is the same one who is both near and far. The distance between God and humanity truly is an awesome divide. Yet that distance has been bridged by God himself. By his spirit, the Father has reached out to us and works directly for his people. It is the exact same one who is nearby, far away, and fills heaven and earth. He is wholly sufficient. He alone is God.

Chapter Six

Notes

1. The Hebrew word for "spirit" here is *ruach*. It is used variously to indicate "breath" or "spirit" of man and other living beings (Gen. 6:17; 7:15, 22). It is also used to indicate the spirit of God (Gen. 6:3). In Genesis 1:2, the New Revised Standard Version and the Tanakh (Jewish Publication Society) both translate *ruach* with one of its most essential meanings, "wind."

2. The New Living Translation captures the sense, "I will personally go."

3. We do not have space in this writing to provide an exhaustive study of the word "spirit." For a range of uses of the word *ruach*, and further insights regarding pneumatology in the Hebrew Bible, see *The Brown-Driver-Briggs Hebrew and English Lexicon* (Peabody, MA: Hendrickson Publishers, 2000), 924-6. For a good overview regarding the spirit of God in the Old and New Testaments see Sean Finnegan's article, "An Unitarian View of the Holy Spirit," *21st Century Reformation*, http://www.21stcr.org/multimedia-2012/1-articles/sf-unitarian_view_holy_spirit.html.

4. Exodus 33 provides an example of the difference between God's own presence and that of his agents. God had told Moses he would send an emissary (his angel) to go before him (Ex. 33:1–3). Moses, however, desired that God would personally go with him in his presence (Ex. 33:14, 15).

5. This has led to people sometimes confusing God's agents with God himself. E.g. God speaking through an angel has led some to suppose that the angel himself ***is*** God. See chapter 8 of this book for more on this matter.

6. James D. G. Dunn, *Christology in the Making*, 2nd Edition (London: SCM Press, 2003), 133, emphasis his.

7. Or in the New Testament also Jesus (Acts 16:7).

8. It is recognized, of course, that aspects or attributes of God are at times personified. For example, God's wisdom is personified as a

woman in Proverbs 8:1ff. *Ruach* is typically translated in the Septuagint by *pneuma*.

9. Anthony Buzzard, *Jesus was not a Trinitarian* (Morrow, GA: Restoration Fellowship, 2007), 152.

10. "Holy Spirit," Jacob Neusner, William Scott Green editors, *Dictionary of Judaism in the Biblical Period* (Peabody, MA: Hendrickson Publishers, 1999), 298.

11. Of course, human beings are made in the "likeness of God" (Gen. 5:1) and therefore like him in some respects. That remains the case even after Adam's disobedience (1 Cor. 11:7). After the Messiah is born, he is the perfect human image of God (2 Cor. 4:4). Nevertheless, in a still greater sense, the true God is in a class by himself. In that regard, there is no one like him.

12. It is typical in our Christian translations to find "Spirit" capitalized when referring to the spirit of God, thus implying a separate person is intended. However, there were no upper/lower case distinctions in ancient biblical Hebrew or Greek and it is purely the translator's decision to capitalize. Translators typically do not capitalize other words which reference aspects of God (hand, arm, etc.). Doing so with the word "spirit" reflects a widespread bias in support of the post-biblical Trinitarian tradition of the spirit of God as being a separate person from the Father. When "spirit" is used with reference to the spirit of God, the King James Version has instances in which it is not capitalized (e.g. Gen. 6:3; Num. 11:29; Isa. 11:2; Micah 3:8). The NRSV and certain others tend not to capitalize spirit when translating the Hebrew Bible. The best Jewish versions of course do not capitalize the word spirit when referring to the spirit of God.

13. The reference in Matthew 28:19 does not present "Father," "Son" or "Holy Spirit" in themselves as being proper/personal names. My point is that the Father and the Son do have personal names whereas the spirit of God does not.

14. Emphasis added.

15. The reader will find a fuller consideration regarding worship of God's kings and of the Messiah in chapter 9 of this book.

16. Emphasis added.

17. Various examples of this are found in modern pop-theology. E.g., Benny Hinn, *Good Morning Holy Spirit* (Nashville: Thomas Nelson, 2004); Francis Chan, *Forgotten God* (Colorado Springs, CO: David C. Cook Publishing, 2009) and Robert Morris, *The God I Never Knew* (Colorado Springs, CO: WaterBrook Press, 2011).

18. Theologians have long struggled to convince the church-going public that they should pray to and worship God's spirit as though it were a person. Today their cause is better advanced by well-intended Christian song writers and musical artists. Those unsuspecting people are found using their considerable talents to persuade the public by songs that they should treat the spirit of God as a separate person. They could save the Christian community a great deal of error and confusion by modeling their songs about the spirit after songs (psalms) in the Bible. Again, those songs address worship to God, the One whose spirit it is (Psalm 139:7–10; 104:30; 143:10).

Chapter Seven

The Word of God

I have treasured the words of his mouth more than my necessary food.

— Job 23:12

God's word is the word of our Creator. It is the standard by which the words of all others must be measured. If we cannot trust the One who made us, all is lost! Why then would we imagine that we could trust anyone or anything else? His word is a connection to the very meaning of our human existence.

To the people of the Bible, God's word is the definition of truth. King David prayed, "And now, O Lord YHWH, you are God, and your words are truth" (2 Sam. 7:28). Jesus gives that same definition of truth in the New Testament, "Father ... Sanctify them by the truth; your word is truth" (John 17:17).

The one true God extends himself to creation by his spirit and shares his thoughts with us by his words. We as human beings come to know one another by our words. So it is that we can know God by his words. They are light to our minds. The psalmist writes, "The unfolding of your words gives light; it gives understanding to the simple" (Ps. 119:130).

A person's word is something that can be shared with others without being lost to the sharer. It is in that sense that God's word is "with" him and can come to be "with" us as well. It is spoken by the mouth of God (2 Chron. 6:4), and comes to his prophets (1 Sam. 15:10). In turn it is spoken or written by them (1 Kings 17:24); people can hear it, read it. As he imparts his word to us, we can know the mind of God.

His Word is Him

Just as God's spirit is him in his operation and presence, so is his word. By it he shares his knowledge, understanding and wisdom. To the people of the Bible, his word is the expression of his thoughts. In it are his will for us and his plans for all he does. And just as the word of a human being is not a separate person from that human being, neither is God's word a separate person from the Father. What God's word does is done by the Father himself. He acts by communicating — commanding.

As people, our thoughts are with us. We sometimes speak of a person "keeping her thoughts to herself." Yet one's innermost reasoning can be expressed by words. Our words begin with us, go out from us and have effect on those around us. They can benefit others and cause change in our world. Likewise, God's word is active. He declares:

> So will my word be that goes forth out of my mouth: It will not return to me empty, but it will accomplish what I desire, and succeed in the purpose for which I sent it (Isa. 55:11).

In the New Testament, we find again that God's word is dynamic:

> For the word of God is living and active. It is sharper than any two-edged sword, piercing even to the dividing of soul and spirit; joints and marrow. It is able to judge the thoughts and intentions of the heart (Heb. 4:12).

God's word is at times personified in the Bible. His wisdom is beautifully personified as though it were a woman[1] in Proverbs 8. This "woman" dwells with "prudence" (v. 12). It is said that God possessed her in the beginning (vv. 22, 30). But these are poetic statements about characteristics of God. Neither "wisdom" nor "prudence" are actually persons in themselves. God's voice, mouth, word and wisdom are never to be understood literally as persons in addition to the Father. Rather, they are expressions of the Father's own mighty power.

When we hear a person's voice or word, we rightly say that we have heard that person himself. What is said by one's voice has been said by him. It is an extension of that individual. When we converse with a friend, we do not afterwards say that we talked with his "voice" or spoke to his "word." Rather, we say that we spoke with our friend himself — the whole person.

So it is with God's word. In the entire Hebrew Bible there is no instance in which anyone is said to have had a conversation with "God's word" or prayed to it. No one makes requests to "the word of God." No one addresses thanks or sings songs to it. All of the requests, giving of thanks and even praise of the word are addressed to the Father on his throne — the God whose word it is:

> Your word is a lamp to my feet and a light to my path. Your word is very pure, therefore your servant loves it (Ps. 119:105, 140).

As we saw in chapter 6, God's spirit is the Father in presence to work. It is by his spirit that he shares his word with us. What is spoken by the spirit of God actually proceeds from the lips of the Father (Ps. 89:34, cf. 26). When the prophets speak by his spirit, it is the one on the throne that people hear. When they are moved to write by the spirit of God, it is the Father himself who inspires them.[2]

The Father Created by His Word

God's word is powerful beyond that of any other being. He spoke, and by his word creation came forth:

> The LORD merely spoke,
> and the heavens were created.
> He breathed the word,
> and all the stars were born.
>
> —PSALM 33:6, NLT

It was God's spoken word—his own personal word—by which he effected creation. It was the very "breath of his mouth." It was when the Father spoke in the beginning that light came:

> And God said, "Let there be light," and there was light (Gen. 1:3).

The Father did not send a person called "The Word" to cause light to be. Rather, it was by his command, his own intention or choice, that light came upon the world. In the New Testament, we find that same understanding of God's spoken word as the cause of creation:

> By God's word the heavens existed long ago and the earth was formed out of water and by means of water (2 Pet. 3:5).

It was by the "word of his command" (NRSV) that the heavens existed and the earth was formed. Yet the same powerful word by which God created the world can come upon human beings. God's word originates in his mind, is imparted to his prophets and revealed to us through them. Nevertheless, God's spirit or word being in or upon a person never means that person *is* God. Receiving the spirit of God or the word of God does not transfer to a person the quality of being God.[3]

Ultimately, God spoke by his Messiah after he was born. He was wonderfully moved by the spirit of the Lord and perfectly made God's word known to the people (Luke 4:18, 19). The Messiah so fully embodies God's word that he is called "The Word of God" (Rev. 19:13).

The Father did not send a person called "The Word" to cause light to be. Rather, it was by his own command that light came upon the world.

A Non-Biblical Word?

After the Bible was written, Gentile Christians, borrowing from their backgrounds in Greek philosophy, proposed a different kind of "word" from that of the Bible.[4] These post-biblical Christians thought in terms of a "Word of God" that was supposedly an ancient or eternal person who was with God in the beginning and helped him create the world.[5] However, concepts of God's word as a person were hopelessly flawed. They sent post-biblical Gentile Christianity on a trajectory away from the pure, absolute monotheism of the Bible. By the latter part of the 4th century, many concluded that not only was God's word a person, but so was his spirit and together with God himself, they are a tripersonal Deity. Thus, the true eternal God who is one individual with many attributes — including his own amazing word and spirit — was, over time, theologically transformed into an imagined three person God. From then until now, Gentile Christianity has divided its love and adoration between God and two other supposed God-persons.

But any notion of a person called the "Word" would be utter nonsense to God's prophets and people of old. Such a person did not actually exist in the Hebrew Bible. Any reference to a person called the "Word," whether as an ancient created being or as an eternal person, is conspicuously absent from the Old Testament. If such a being had existed, God's prophets and people of old would have spoken and written about him or her dozens — perhaps hundreds — of times. Yet in all of the Old Testament there is no reference to the existence of an actual being that they called the "Word."[6]

What we do find, from Genesis to Malachi, is God's spoken word — his personal communication. That is found around 400 times in the Old Testament.[7] It is the word of the Father himself that they write about. And just as God's hand, power and spirit had no personal names, neither did his voice, wisdom or word.

There was nothing that needed to be done by an imagined "Word-person" which the Father could not do by his own word. As we have seen, he can "send" his word — it goes forth "out of his mouth" (Isa. 55:11). By his word he speaks and even the elements respond (Ps. 33:6–9). He causes that same word to come upon his prophets: flesh and blood human beings. They in turn relate it to others. It is even said that he spoke through his prophets (e.g. 2 Kings 21:10). It is the Father then who causes the word by which he created the world ultimately to come to his Messiah after he is born. The Father perfectly embodies his word in him. It is in the Messiah that God's word is said to "become flesh."

John 1 — John Was a Jew

Post-biblical Gentile Christians famously imposed their idea of an ancient or eternal being called the "Word" on their interpretations of John's prologue (John 1:1–3, 14). As we have seen, out of the resulting confusion eventually came the now popular idea that John was indicating there are two who are the eternal God: God himself (the Father), plus the supposed eternal "Word" who was also fully God.

But for God's true people of old, it was easier to say, "The sun rises in the west,"[8] than to propose that there is anyone who is the eternal God other than the Father. John was a Jew. He was not a Greek philosopher. The language John uses in his prologue is not in and of itself philosophical or mysterious. The Greek term *logos* (word) is used over 300 times in the New Testament and is found in the synoptics.[9] It regularly indicates the spoken or personal word of God and of others. It is used similarly in the Septuagint.

John's understanding about God and his word was in harmony with his ancestors and the Old Testament — not with the Hellenistic Greek philosophy of the Gentiles. He did *not* quote Heraclitus, Plato, or other Greek philosophers. He did *not* quote Philo of Alexandria or other Hellenized Jewish philosophers who — with disastrous results — strove to reconcile Jewish religion with Greek philosophy.[10]

What John did quote was the Old Testament. When we look at it as source material for John's writings, we find that it repeatedly references God's own word — never a person they called the "Word." Again, in those Scriptures God's spoken/

personal word is noted around 400 times. That is opposed to -0- times for a person they called "The Word."

As a disciple of the Jewish Messiah, John's roots ran deep in the Old Testament. He was wholly dedicated to the absolute monotheism of his fathers. When reading John, anyone who does not have his Old Testament background fully in view will inevitably fail to grasp the meaning of his words. Like God's people before him, John's faith was anchored in the essential fact that only one individual is the God of the universe: YHWH himself. Jesus is not YHWH. It was in fact John who recorded Jesus' great declaration that his Father is the only true God and that he, Jesus, is the Christ, God's Messiah:

> Father ... this is eternal life: that they may know you, the only true God, and Jesus Christ whom you have sent (John 17:3).[11]

As John wrote his prologue, he knew the Old Testament Scriptures and was familiar with the hundreds of times in which God's word was referenced in them. John knew that it was by God's spoken word that he created in Genesis; his personal word by which he enlightened his people through the ages. John knew that in the entire Old Testament there is no instance of a person called the "Word."

With all of these things in mind, we can know two things with certainty regarding John: (1) When he is speaking of the one true God of the universe, it is the Father alone who is that God.[12] (2) When John is writing about God's word, he is not thinking about an ancient or eternal being in addition to the Father. He's thinking of the Father's own spoken word — his personal word.

This way of looking at the opening statements of John's Gospel is both scriptural and sensible: Scriptural in that the entire Hebrew Bible aligns with that view. It is sensible in that it does not contradict the essential principle that there is one eternal God and only one individual who is that God. Christians of John's day would have been comfortable with him writing about God creating the world by his spoken word. Likewise, they would have been entirely at ease with John writing that the Father is the only one who is truly God. On the other hand, those same early Christians would have been alarmed by the later notions of a second creator and the concept of a supposed person who was the eternal God along with the Father.

"With God"

As a Jew, John understood a principle which often eludes Gentile Christians to this day: In the Bible, aspects of a person are said to be "with" him or her. John knew the Scriptures in which God's wisdom is personified as a woman who was "with" him at the time of creation (Prov. 8). He also knew the Scriptures that taught God's word is with him; that it "goes forth out of his mouth," and accomplishes his purposes (Isa. 55:11).

Post-biblical Gentile Christians thought that if the word is "with God" (John 1:1, 2), that would mean that it must be a person. Quite to the contrary, such language was a way of expressing the relationship of an individual to his or her own characteristics. The Scriptures tell us that one may even commune or speak with one's own heart (Ps. 77:6; Eccl. 1:16). Yet one's heart is not a person in addition to the one whose heart it is. Likewise, God's word is not a person in addition to the Father himself. God's word was "with" (*pros*) God (John1:1) in the same sense that Paul wanted the word — the truth of the gospel — to remain "with" (*pros*) the Christians in Galatia (Gal. 2:5). A person is not indicated in either case.

The *Brown-Driver-Briggs Hebrew and English Lexicon* recognizes the concept of a person's own characteristics as being "with" (Heb. *im, et*) him or her. The lexicon specifies that this is a Hebrew idiom which is indicative of "a *thought* or *purpose* present with one ... operating in his mind."[13] So it is with God:

> With God are wisdom and strength; he has counsel and understanding (Job 12:13).

Wisdom and *strength* are "with" God. Yet these are not persons who reside with the Father. Rather, they are characteristics *of* the Father. Likewise, he "has" *counsel* and *understanding*. But these are also aspects of him. If characteristics of God are separate persons from the Father, then how many such persons might we find? If God's word is a person, then are his voice which is to be obeyed (Deut. 13:4) and his mouth (1 Kings 13:21) by which he speaks?

It is rightly said that wisdom, strength, counsel, and understanding are "with" God. It can also be said that they really "are" God.[14] These things are features or properties of his, not additional beings. They are him in the sense that they are ways that God eternally is. It is in that same way that God's word is *with* him and in reality *is* him. When the Scripture tells us "God's word is forever settled in heaven" (Ps. 119:89), it is not talking about a person with Deity, nor a created being. It is God's own personal word that is forever established there. The word of God is no more a separate person from the Father than the word of Jesus is a person in addition to Jesus or Peter's word was another besides Peter himself.

Likewise, John would be the last to propose that someone called the "Word" was involved with God in creating the world. As a faithful Jew,[15] John knew that the Father had declared in the Scriptures that he created alone — by himself:

> Thus says the LORD, your Redeemer, who formed you from the womb: "I am the LORD, who made all things; I alone stretched forth the heavens. I spread out the earth by myself" (Isa. 44:24).

And the Father did those things personally — not by an agent:

> This is what the LORD of hosts, the God of Israel, says: "By my great power and outstretched arm I made the earth; its people and the animals that are on it. I give it to whomever I please" (Jer. 27:4, 5).[16]

The Father created by his *own* "great power," his *own* "outstretched arm." He spoke, and at his word creation came to be. Again, that is why we call him "Father."

To attribute creation to anyone other than the Father is once again to "rob God." It gives honor to a supposed person which is due the Father alone as our Creator. John would be grieved to find people attributing to a theologically created being called the "Word" what the Father actually did by the power of his own spoken word. John would be mortified to find people using his writings in their attempts to make such a point.

In his prologue, John is repeating what the prophets of old had been saying about God's word down through the centuries. It is the same message we find from others in the New Testament. They too saw God's spoken word — his personal word — as the means by which he created:

> By faith we understand that the worlds were prepared by the word of God, so that what is seen was not made from things which are visible (Heb. 11:3).

"Made Flesh"

It was not an ancient or eternal being called the "Word" who became flesh — it was the Father's own word.[17] John did not come to bring a different definition of the word of God from that which had already existed among God's true people of old. Rather, he came to tell the world what God had now so excellently done with his word. John wanted everyone to know that the one true God has ultimately embodied his word in a particular human being—Jesus Christ! It is he who now speaks for God. John's essential message to the world is, "Let all humanity hear Jesus!"

In their confusion, Gentile Christians were effectively reading John backwards. When John wrote about God's word, he said that it was with him in the beginning and that it "became flesh" in the person Jesus Christ. Gentile Christians instead took the person of Jesus and transposed him onto God's word in the beginning.[18] But John did not say that "Jesus" or "the Son" or "Christ" was with God in the beginning. He does not say that "Christ" made the world or that "Christ" became flesh. He could have written exactly those things if they had been true. But it is not a being called "Christ" who became flesh in John's prologue. Rather, it was God's word which became flesh in Christ: God's human son.[19] Esteemed professor Colin Brown of Fuller Theological Seminary writes:

> It is a common but patent misreading of the opening of John's Gospel to read it as if it said: "In the beginning was the *Son*, and the *Son* was with God and the *Son* was God." What has happened here is the substitution *Son* for *Word* (Greek logos), and [by this backwards reasoning] the Son is made a member of the Godhead which existed from the beginning.[20]

It is not an ancient or eternal being named Jesus *who* became flesh.[21] It was God's spoken word which became flesh in the man Jesus. Jesus is not what God's word was in the beginning. He is what God's word became in the life of a human being.[22]

With the introduction of a supposed ancient or eternal being called the "Word," Gentile Christians were effectively creating a new Creator. What was really the Father's own spoken word was imagined to be a second person who shares with God the honor of being our Creator. This was unthinkable to God's true people of old. The cost of this change in theology was ultimately the unconscionable breaking away of post-biblical Christianity from the absolute monotheism of God's prophets, of Jesus himself, and his early disciples.

John's writings about God's word are wonderful. They are in agreement with the prophets of old who saw only one individual — YHWH himself — as being God. Rightly understood, John upholds God's first priority and his prime directive.[23] His writings bring the age-old mystery of God's word — its dynamics and power — to a culmination in Jesus, his only begotten human son. God's prophets and people of old would never have read John's writings and imagined that he was introducing an ancient or eternal person called the "Word."[24] It took Gentile Christians after the Bible was written to read that idea back into John.[25]

The real Jesus was born in the days of Herod the Great. God embodied his word in him so perfectly that it is said that God's word "became flesh" in Jesus. On the other hand, the imagined ancient or eternal "Word-person" who was supposedly a separate being from the Father was not created until the centuries after the Bible was written. "He" was the theological brainchild of Gentile Christians who were out of touch with God's prophets and his people of old.

> With God's word as a separate individual, Gentile Christians were effectively creating a new Creator.

The mystery of God's word is not that it was an ancient or eternal "second person" who resided with the Father. There was no such person. The mystery is not that such a one helped God create the world. The Father alone is our Creator. The mystery ***is*** that while God's word is "with" the Father, it "is" him — not another! The Father himself spoke and it was done! The wonder is that the Father could, by his *own* mighty word, cause creation, enlighten the lives of human beings, and ultimately bring his great plans for humanity to his Messiah after he was born. The marvel is that God would so fully and completely embody his word in this man that we can call him, "The Word of God." If it is the truth that we seek, we need look no further: We have found it in the life and teachings of Jesus!

Let Jesus Decide

> Then Jesus answered them, "My teaching is not my own. It is his who sent me" (John 7:16).

God receives his word from no one. It is the expression of his own mind. Jesus, on the other hand, receives his word from God. If we are to believe Jesus, he did not of himself have great knowledge and understanding. Rather, his wisdom was derived. As a true human being, he was taught the word directly by God. Luke picks up on this when he writes about Jesus growing in wisdom as a young man:

> And Jesus grew in wisdom and stature, and in favor with God and men (Luke 2:52).

Jesus never says that before he was born, he had been a person called the "Word." Neither Jesus nor John ever says that an ancient or eternal being known as the "Word" somehow came into Mary's womb and became a human being. Rather, Jesus received the word *after* he was born. He was taught by God from his youth.[26]

Jesus is called "The Word of God" because God's word was supremely made known to him — and then to all of humanity by him. He himself makes that clear when he speaks of his relationship to God's word. Even his teachings were not his own. They were the Father's:

- I do nothing on my own, but I speak only what the Father has taught me (John 8:28).
- I have not spoken on my own. The Father who sent me commanded me what to say and how to say it (John 12:49).
- The word you hear is not my own, but the Father's who sent me (John 14:24).
- Father ... the words which you gave to me I have given to them (John 17:8).

Jesus had to be taught by God. What kind of a "person" who is in and of himself the "Word" has to be taught "what to say and how to say it"? It eluded post-biblical Gentile Christians that their supposed ancient or eternal "person" called the "Word" was of "himself" totally lacking in any unique understanding and wisdom. If Jesus is fully divine, and as such omniscient, he would speak for himself. It would be pointless for the Father to try to teach an essentially all-knowing being.

By his own testimony, Jesus' life and experiences do not correspond to the idea that he was an ancient or eternal person who had extraordinary knowledge and was wise enough to create the world. By Jesus' own testimony, God's word and wisdom came to him as God taught him. Again, he states:

> I can do nothing on my own. I judge as God tells me. Therefore, my judgment is just, because I carry out the will of the one who sent me, not my own will (John 5:30, NLT).

What kind of a "person" who is in and of "himself" the "Word" has to be taught "what to say and how to say it"? (John 12:49).

Jesus and the New Creation

Jesus never says that he made the world in the beginning. Neither in the Gospel of John, nor in the balance of the New Testament, does he ever take credit for the creation of the cosmos. When Jesus speaks about creation, he indicates that only one created, and he attributes it directly to God:

> From the beginning of the creation that God created until now (Mark 13:19).

> Have you not read that *he* who made them at the beginning, "made them male and female" (Matt. 19:4).

For people to attribute the creation in Genesis to Jesus is a significant mistake. It would be like saying that "the Father died on the cross." To do that would be confusion and would give to the Father the honor that is due to Jesus as the only one who died for us. It is a similar dishonor to God when we say that "Jesus created the world." And just as it would not please God for us to say "the Father died on the cross," neither can it please Jesus when we ascribe to him all or part of the Father's honor for being our Creator.

Jesus was not involved in the creation in Genesis. As we have seen, the Father did that creating "alone" — "by himself" (Isa. 44:24). By one count, the Genesis creation is attributed to God, not Jesus, in at least 50 verses of the Bible.[27] Rather, it is Jesus through whom God is now bringing about a "new creation." There will be "new" heavens and a "new" earth in which dwells righteousness (2 Pet. 3:13; Isa. 65:17ff.). The new creation will be filled with people who are immortal — they will die no more. It is "in Christ" that this creation takes place.

> So, if anyone is in Christ, he is a new creation: the old things have passed away; look, everything has become new! (2 Cor. 5:17).

Jesus himself is the first of God's new creation of immortal human beings. He is the "firstborn from the dead" and will "never die again" (Col. 1:18; Rom. 6:10). God created the world in Genesis and then used Adam to bring forth the balance of the human race. Now God is using Jesus to bring forth a people of faith who will live forever in his eternal kingdom. Jesus is, so to speak, the second Adam. He is the firstborn in a great new family of God. The Apostle Paul tells the Christians at Rome that it is the will of God that they be:

> Conformed to the image of his son, so that he might be the firstborn among many brothers (Rom. 8:29).

It is this new life in God's new creation of which Jesus is the first. In this creation, Jesus is first in terms of both time and priority. He was the first to be raised from the dead never to die again. God has also determined that this man will forever be preeminent in his eternal kingdom. It is the "all things" of the new creation which God creates through Jesus.[28]

Jesus is due great honor. He is due the honor of being God's only begotten human son (John 1:14). He was born of a virgin (Luke 1:35), and filled with the spirit of God (Luke 4:1). The word of God was embodied in him as in no other before or since. It is Jesus who died for us (1 Cor. 15:3). But God raised him from the dead (Acts 5:30). After his resurrection, he was taken up into heaven and God caused him to sit at his own right hand (Acts 5:31). Jesus deserves all of the honor for being the one through whom God is bringing forth a new creation. All who are in Christ will live forever with him in God's eternal kingdom. Again, Paul writes to the Christians at Rome:

> And if we are children of God, then we are heirs, heirs of God and joint heirs with Christ, if indeed we share in his sufferings so that we may also share in his glory (Rom. 8:17).

The Living Plan of God

> These are my words that I spoke to you while I was still with you, that everything must be fulfilled which is written about me in the Law of Moses and the Prophets and the Psalms. Then he opened their minds to understand the Scriptures. —Jesus to his disciples (Luke 24:44, 45).

Jesus not only speaks God's word, but also uniquely fulfills it. This man is the living embodiment of the plan of God. God's great plans for humanity and our planet were foretold in words the Father spoke to the prophets of old. From the beginning, the center and focus of all of those plans was a man who would be born in time. That man was Jesus — God's Messiah — his true human son.

It is Jesus who ultimately reveals and fulfills God's plans for humanity. From birth to death, he was living out the words that God had spoken to the prophets ages before. In his resurrection, being taken up into heaven and seated at the right hand of God, this man was and is the living word of God. God's master plans for the redemption of human beings and of our planet have become reality in him.

We see this again in God's new covenant. Aspects of the covenant Moses gave the people was engraved on stones. However, God's new covenant is embodied in a man, Messiah Jesus (Isa. 42:6; 1Tim. 2:5; Heb. 8:6,7). It is by trusting in the person of Jesus that we participate in YHWH's great and final arrangement with humanity (John 3:16). Jesus and his teachings are the means by which human beings may enter into and be part of God's new creation (Eph. 2:10). In the Messiah we find the ultimate fulfillment of God's promises (2 Cor. 1:19, 20). The hope of unending life — life in the age to come — is in him (Rom. 5:17). God's plans for redemption and a new creation have become reality in this man. He was the plan of God — the word of God — in the flesh.

The Truth is Always Better

> The truth, whatever it is,
> is always better than error,
> whatever it is.
>
> — JDG

The truth is always better than error — even when error takes the form of cherished, time-honored traditions. As Gentile Christians, it is easy for us to be too comfortable with our own post-biblical church traditions and creeds. We cling to them tenaciously even when we must label them "mysteries" *because* they do not really make sense in light of the Bible. We have developed an ongoing romance with our own creation: a multi-person God. We must rather come to fall in love again with the one true God of the Bible. We must love the same one as our God, whom Jesus loved as his God (John 14:31; 17:3; 20:17). And we must come to love Jesus for who he really is: not God, but God's only begotten human son — our savior and Lord.

Over time, post-biblical Gentile Christians came to think of God's spirit and his word as individuals in addition to the Father. That was a catastrophic turn of events. The novel new way of looking at God's spirit and his word as persons became the building blocks for the doctrine of the Trinity. By the late 3rd century, we see people proposing a tripersonal God. Gentile Christianity has been living with the theological chaos of a supposed multi-person God, from then until now.

There is no understanding of God as multiple persons in the Hebrew Bible. God's prophets and people of old never speak of two or three persons as being the One God. Jesus and his disciples were rooted in the Old Testament Scriptures. They themselves were absolute monotheists. When rightly understood, John too was unswerving in his Jewish monotheism. We must be certain that when we say, "the word became flesh," we mean the same thing that John meant when he wrote it.

The Gentile notion of an ancient or eternal person called the "Word" is infinitely confusing and contradicts the most essential truths of God's prophets of old. Said to be a mystery, it is not a biblical one. Rather, it is a mystification created by post-biblical Gentile Christians. That mystery is the result of efforts to combine Platonic philosophical views with the Bible.

It is an entirely unacceptable mystery because it introduces a new co-creator of the world. In the minds of Gentile Christians, this "creator" eventually became a supposed second person who is fully God along with the Father. The incongruences between this and original Christianity have plagued us as Gentile Christians from then until now.

Without the influence of Greek philosophy and Hellenized Jewish Platonists, the notion of an ancient or eternal person called the "Word" would never have existed in Christianity. Yet on such flimsy grounds, Gentile Christians in the 2nd through the 5th centuries gradually led us into the nether-world of a multi-person God. The idea of God's spirit and his word as persons in addition to the Father goes too far. There was never sufficient scriptural reason to justify the idea of these as persons in themselves. It took a giant leap of non-biblical faith to get to God's spirit and his word as "persons." At the end of the day, two or three who are supposedly "one God" has never made logical or scriptural sense. It never can. It never will.

The idea that there is any person of Deity in addition to the Father is in total contradiction to God's first priority: *He* alone is God and there is no other but *him* (Isa. 45:5, 6). It is also a severe infraction of his prime directive: They must serve no other as the one true God but *him* (Ex. 20:3). The very notion of second and third persons who are supposedly God would have found YHWH's faithful prophets of old rending their clothes in protest.

The brilliance of the truth about God's spirit and his word is not in complexity but rather in simplicity. The truth is wonderful and easy. It is so understandable that any ordinary person can grasp it and benefit from it: God's spirit and his word are the Father himself — in action. That truth unambiguously holds to the eternal fundamental that there is one God and only one individual who is that God: He is the Father of us all (Mal. 2:10).

Perhaps we as Christians today have come far enough that we could recognize the spirit of God for what it really is: The spirit of the Father himself. Perhaps we could end the confusion of Jesus as a supposed second Creator and a God-person in addition to the Father. Maybe we could come to give Jesus the glory and honor that is really due him as the only begotten human son of God and the one through whom God is bringing forth a new creation.

Above all, perhaps we could return in our hearts to the original understanding that God is only one individual — the most extraordinary individual in the universe. Could we again celebrate the same one true God that Abraham, Sarah, Moses, Isaiah and a great host of others celebrated in their days? Could we come joyfully to uphold the great declaration of Jesus when he addressed his Father as "the only true God" (John 17:3)? Imagine how wonderful it would be if we took all of the glory and honor now being divided between God and two other supposed God-persons and gave it to the one to whom it really belongs: The Father himself!

Chapter Seven

Notes

1. God's wisdom in Proverbs 8 is a female. Note the feminine gender pronouns in Proverbs 8:1–3ff. "Lady Wisdom" is a leading character in Proverbs chapters 1–9.

2. God's spirit brings his word, and they are functionally interrelated (2 Sam. 23:2). However, in the Bible they are not generally thought of as identical characteristics of God.

3. John the Baptist (Luke 1:15), Elizabeth (Luke 1:41), Jesus (Luke 4:1), Stephen (Acts 7:55) and others were said to be "filled" with the spirit of God. That does not mean they are God.

4. The "word" of Greek philosophy was not the God of the Bible. It was an independent force or entity which supposedly "orders the world" and is said to "steer all things through all things." John Mansley Robinson, *An Introduction to Early Greek Philosophy* (Boston: Houghton Mifflin Company, 1968), 95. From these notions, Philo, other Platonistic Jews, and eventually post-biblical Gentile Christians evolved a "Word" *who* was supposedly another person from the Father and was to be honored as co-creator.

All of this is an affront to the God of the Bible who himself is the only power by which the world is "created" and "ordered." To make God's word something or someone other than the Father was unthinkable to God's true people of old. For them, the Father is the only one who created, and the only one who "steers" the universe. The word of God is neither a person in addition to the Father, nor an independent force. It is YHWH's own spoken word — his personal word.

5. In the fourth century, there were two major dissenting parties: (1) those who believed in an ancient created Word-person (Arianism) and (2) those who proposed an eternal, uncreated Word (pre-Trinitarianism). At the time of the Council of Nicaea (325 CE), both parties were entirely out of touch with the Jesus of the Bible who had to be a true *human being* in order to be the savior of *human beings* (Rom. 5:17–19).

Key leaders of the two camps were Arius and Athanasius who were both from Alexandria. Arius held to an ancient "Word" who, after he was created by God, was then involved in making the balance of creation. That unscriptural view is held today particularly by Jehovah's Witnesses. Athanasius led the way for the equally unscriptural and even more complicated philosophical theology that the "Word" was an eternal uncreated being in addition to the Father. That view eventually evolved to become the notion that there are two persons who are fully God. With the addition of God's spirit as a third person, the orthodoxy of post-biblical Gentile Christianity was born. Both approaches rob the Father of the glory that he alone is due as our sole Creator.

6. For a review of the genesis and evolving of post-biblical Logos Christology see Marian Hillar, *From Logos to Trinity: The Evolution of Religious Beliefs from Pythagoras to Tertullian* (Cambridge: Cambridge University Press, 2012).

7. That is around 400 times by my unofficial count based on a review of the New American Standard Bible and its use of "word" (singular). The term most often translated "word" from the Hebrew is *davar.* Its meaning is "word," <u>not</u> "person," or "spokesperson." Neither does it mean "man," "son," "angel," "god" or "God."

8. That is to borrow a line from George Martin. The fuller quotation is, "When the sun rises in the west and sets in the east."

9. It should be noted that "word" or "word of God" is often used as a synonym for the gospel of the kingdom (Matt. 9:35; 13:19; Mark 4:14; Luke 8:11).

10. Post-biblical Gentile Christians were particularly influenced by Philo. They lost sight of Jesus as a Jew and of the Jewishness of his early disciples, and were taken with Philo the Jewish philosopher. We find them reinterpreting Jesus and John in light of Philo and Plato.

11. Or, "You, Father, are the only one who is truly God." Also note John 5:44 where Jesus speaks of the Father as "the one who alone is God" (NLT, NRSV), or "Him who alone is God" (Amplified).

12. John of course uses *theos* to refer to the gods of the nations. On rare occasions (2 or 3 times), he uses the word "God" in its honorific sense for human beings. This is particularly of the Messiah (John 1:18(?), 10:33–36 and perhaps 20:28). For more on this use of "God" (from *el/elohim* and *theos*), see chapter 9 of this book.

13. *Brown-Driver-Briggs Hebrew and English Lexicon* (Peabody, MA: Hendrickson Publishers, 2000), 768. Also note Job 10:13: "I know that this was with you." NIV, "in your mind."

14. Prov. 23:7: "as a man thinks in his heart so is he" (Amplified, NASB).

15. Again, there were Hellenized Jews such as Philo who speculated on God creating only indirectly through intermediate "Powers." However Philo does not seem to have a clear and consistent view regarding that. In Philo, sometimes these "Powers" seem like agents who do God's bidding, and at other times just God's own personal powers.

16. Also note Job 9:8: "who alone stretched out the heavens" (NRSV).

17. "The word was God." To say that the word was the Father does not mean that the Father himself literally became flesh. Again, aspects of God can come "upon" or "into" people. That does not impart the quality of "being God" to those people. Jesus even goes so far as to say the Father dwells "in me" (John 14:10). Yet he never claims that he himself actually is the Father (God).

18. An example of the backwards reading of "Christ" into John's opening statements is found in The Living Bible paraphrase which gives, "There was Christ, with God." The Amplified adds "Christ" as commentary: "In the beginning was the Word (Christ)." It is not an overstatement to say that by eisegesis (reading into the text, rather than exegesis, reading what is actually in the text) there has been wide-scale corruption of John's words in the opening of the Gospel. If John meant to say "Christ" he could have said it. He did not.

19. Clearly, God did <u>not</u> speak in ages past by his son. The writer of Hebrews tells us that God "spoke to our ancestors through the prophets at many times and in various ways, *but* in these last days has spoken to us in a son" (Heb. 1:1, 2).

20. Colin Brown, D.D., *Ex Auditu*, 7, 1991, 88, 89.

21. It was perhaps one of the most foolish of theological errors when Gentile Christians in post-biblical times set out to find their missing person called the "Word" in the Old Testament. In the absence of clear examples of a person called the "Word," they began imposing their notion of "Word" back onto the lives of individual angels and men who lived in Old Testament times. Perhaps most desperate of all, they even confused their idea of a separate "Word-person" with YHWH himself. Thus, they found themselves proposing the impossible: that there are two YHWHs! Recognizing the weakness of these approaches, they have tended to retreat to the more convenient explanation that it was all just "a mystery."

22. The correct Jewish view can easily be seen from Scriptures like Proverbs 8, Isa. 55:11, etc. There are also grounds for this same understanding in the Apocrypha. Note particularly Ecclesiasticus 24 where wisdom/Torah is sent to pitch camp in Israel, and Wisdom 9, where God makes the world by his logos. Lady wisdom also reappears in both of those books.

23. It hardly seems necessary here to take up the Johannine Comma (the three heavenly witnesses of 1 John 5:7). There is a great mass of literature on that text and a broad consensus exists even among Trinitarian scholars that the reading of the Textus Receptus is not what John actually wrote at that point. Even the Roman Catholic American Standard Bible (1970) and the New Vulgate (1979) omit "the comma." Simply put, John did not speak of *logos* in that text.

24. For an overview of the question of preexistence in the writings of John see Dr. Dustin Smith, "John and Jewish Preexistence: An Attempt to Responsibly Set the Christology of the Fourth Gospel in its Proper Historical and Theological Matrix of Thought." http://www.21stcr.org/multimedia-2015/1_pdf/ds_john_and_jewish_preexistence.pdf.

25. This reading of the person of Jesus back into the beginning of John's prologue has been promoted through the bias of translators. For example, churchgoers today are often unaware that translators have taken liberties by capitalizing "word" in John 1:1, etc. The capitalizations give the reader the impression that a proper noun is indicated. Of course, in the Greek language of John's day there were no upper/lower case distinctions. Translators ignore their own inconsistency of capitalizing "word" here while not capitalizing it in the vast majority of its occurrences in the New Testament and in the Old Testament.

With regard to personal pronouns in John 1, if it is understood that God's word is a personification in John's prologue, then masculine personal pronouns could be expected even though a literal person is not intended (c.f. Prov. 8:1–3; "her," "she").

In any event, the use of masculine personal pronouns in John 1:2–5 by Trinitarian translators reflects a bias. The Greek *autos* could be translated "it" rather than "him" in these cases. Translators have created the inconsistency of rendering *autos* as "it" in reference to "word" in other cases in the New Testament (e.g. Luke 8:15, 21; Heb. 4:12, etc.). But for doctrinal convenience they translate it with masculine personal pronouns here. If John can be said to be his own best commentator, it should be noted that he uses neuter pronouns in 1 John 1:1–3 five times in the opening of the epistle (e.g. "that which was from the beginning").

It can be noted that not all translations have used capitalizations for "word" in John 1, nor have all used "him" to translate *autos*. Among those has been the venerable "Tyndale," which gives "word" and "it."

26. Nor is the young Jesus portrayed as regaining knowledge that he supposedly had in eternity before an incarnation. (That is the bizarre notion of some Trinitarian kenosis theorists.) The reader of Luke rightly infers that Jesus is learning all of these things for the first time.

27. Anthony Buzzard, *Jesus was Not a Trinitarian* (Morrow, GA: Restoration Fellowship, 2007), 75, n. 27.

28. Jesus is co-creator — not of the Genesis creation — but of God's new creation. 1 Corinthians 8:6 is best understood in light of the new creation. Paul is writing there to Christians and his statements in the verse do not refer to their mere mortal existence. Rather, Paul is pointing them to the much superior enterprise of the kingdom of God and eternal life through Jesus. Hence, it is "out of" (*ek*) God that all of these things exist and we now live for him (Rom. 6:13). But, it is "through" (*dia*) Jesus that we have this new existence and we have eternal life "through" (*dia*) him (hence, "in Christ," Rom. 6:10–12). Jesus himself says, "Just as the Father has life in himself, so he has granted the son also to have life in himself" (John 5:26). Jesus then is the way, truth and "life" for those who come to the Father through (*dia*) him (John 14:6).

Chapter Eight

By Prophets He Speaks — By Deliverers He Saves

> *I look to the mountains — Where will my help come from? My help comes from the* Lord *who made heaven and earth.*
>
> — Psalm 121:1, 2

To the people of the Bible, YHWH is their help. From his throne, he sees their plight. In his presence, he comes near. Yet his work with mankind is a partnership. It is human beings that he will help, and human beings will aid him in providing that help. They are his prophets and his deliverers.

Knowing God by His Prophets

"I would that all the Lord's people were prophets,[1] and that the Lord would put his spirit on them all!" — Moses speaking to Joshua at Taberah, Numbers 11:29.

Who would not like to talk with a true prophet of God? If we did, what would it be like? Immediately, we might think to ask him or her[2] about the future. Yet, a true prophet's first concern would likely be to talk with us about God. The prophet's message to us might be: "Know the LORD" (Hosea 6:3).

The Bible, at its heart, is not a history of great people. It is rather the story of ordinary men and women who serve the one who alone is God. In the Bible, people are not true prophets by their own choices or abilities. They do not prophesy by crystal gazing or a supposed "getting in touch with the cosmos." Rather, they are chosen and empowered by God for the benefit of his people. It is because of his love that he sends his prophets to them. They are his intermediaries. In his presence, he comes directly upon the prophets so that they can benefit others. Empowered by his spirit, they accomplish his purposes.

But how would we know a true prophet if we met one? Perhaps we would sense by the prophet's character or disposition that he or she is an extraordinary person. We might be awed that the prophet foresees future events that actually do happen. To the people of the Bible, however, those are not the most essential tests regarding who is a true prophet of God. For them, the critical question is: Does the prophet faithfully declare the Father alone as the only true God?

> If a prophet, or one who divines by dreams appears among you and gives you a sign or a wonder, and the sign or the wonder actually occurs, and he says, "Let us follow other gods" you must not listen to the words of that prophet or diviner by dreams. It is the LORD your God you must follow, him you shall fear. You will keep his commandments, his voice you shall obey, him only shall you serve, and you shall hold to him (Deut. 13:1–4).

Which god does a prophet speak of? If we are hearing a true prophet, it is YHWH — the Father alone. God's prophets are people living at different times and in different places. However, one thing is constant with them: Him! It is the one true God that they proclaim. People today who propose to speak the word of God are set against a sure measure: Do they proclaim the same God that his prophets of old did? It is impossible to be faithful to the word which they spoke if we do not hold to the same God they spoke of.

He Speaks Through Them — Literally

At times, God sends his word to prophets by angels (Zech. 4:4–6). On other occasions, he brings it to them more directly — by a dream (1 Kings 3:5), vision (Dan. 7:1) or a voice (1 Kings 19:12, 13). Yet at other times, God speaks through his prophets. David said:

> The spirit of the Lord spoke through me and his word was on my tongue (2 Sam. 23:2).

Some of the most wonderful of God's communications to humanity are through people themselves. He who made us can also speak through us. In such cases, a prophet is acting as an instrument of God. This was notably the case in the fulfillment of Joel's prophecy regarding the pouring out of God's spirit in the New Testament (Joel 2:28, 29 cf. Acts 2:4, 16–18, etc.).

There are occasions when God speaks directly to the people through a prophet and other times in which the prophet rehearses what God had previously revealed (1 Sam. 15:16). In either event, the words spoken by a prophet can be shocking. Imagine walking through an ancient city and coming upon a man speaking to a crowd. As we draw closer, we hear words like these:

> And I will take you as my people, and I will be your God; and you will know that I am the LORD your God (Ex. 6:7).[3]

Is this a human being claiming to be God Almighty? Not at all. It is an example of how prophets of God sometimes spoke in his name. If it is a true prophet we have come upon, then these are the words of God himself addressing people in the first person. After hearing a prophet on such an occasion, a person may rightly say, "I heard God speak" or "God said to me…" It is in fact God using a prophet to interact with people by their senses.

He Speaks Through His Angels

God also does amazing things through his angels.[4] He sometimes speaks through them. There are extraordinary examples in the Bible in which he carries on conversations with people through angels. On rare occasions, he even physically interacts with human beings by them.

None of this means that an angel in such a circumstance is literally God. That would be to confuse the Creator with his creation. Nevertheless, on such occasions people could rightly say that they had heard God speak or spoke "to God"; physically interacted with him; or that "God appeared" to them. Yet such events were God being present in spirit, working through the person of an angel.[5]

An extraordinary example of this can be found in the story of Moses at the burning bush (Ex. 3:4ff.). God speaks to Moses in the first person: "I am the LORD your God." Moses interacts with him by asking him questions and receiving answers. It is even recognized that God "appeared" to Moses in the bush (Ex. 3:16). Yet, from the very beginning of the story it is announced that it is an angel of God that is in the burning bush (Ex. 3:2).

Centuries later, Stephen affirms that it was "an angel" who actually appeared to Moses on that occasion:

> Now after forty years, an angel appeared to Moses in the wilderness of Mount Sinai, in the flame of a burning bush. It was this Moses ... whom God sent as both ruler and deliverer through the angel who appeared to him in the bush (Acts 7:30, 35).[6]

Note that Stephen does not say that God was an angel on this occasion, but rather that he did this "through"[7] an angel. It is a rather elementary mistake to think that because God dynamically interacted with someone through an angel, then the angel was literally God. It is tantamount to hearing God saying through a prophet, "I am the Lord your God" and concluding that the prophet himself is God. Likewise the popular fiction that angels in such cases were the Messiah in some supposed preexistent state is just as unfounded. The Bible never says that the Messiah appeared as an angel at any time in history.

He Showed His Prophets the Future

God gave his prophets of old understanding of matters that were past, present and even future. By his foreknowledge, he showed them things that were years or even centuries away. Much of what he shared with them were his own plans for times to come:

> "For I know the plans I have for you," says the LORD, "plans for your welfare and not for harm, plans to give you a future and a hope" (Jer. 29:11).

As God spoke to his prophets about the future, it was often in very graphic and sometimes present tense language.[8] It is much as a conversation I had with a friend who was going to build a house. He laid out his plans for me and with a sense of anticipation began to describe his future home. I still remember that he used active present tense language as he pointed out: "Here is my kitchen" and "Here is my dining room." Yet, he and I both understood that no one would prepare food in that kitchen or eat in the dining room till the plan became reality.

That is the way it was with God and his prophets. It was as though he would call them around him and unroll his plans. As he talked with them about future people and events, he often described them in present terms. Sometimes known as prophetic prolepsis, this is a way of expressing things that are not, as though they already were. God said to Abraham:

> No longer will you be called Abram, but your name will be Abraham; for I have made you a father of many nations (Gen. 17:5).

At that time, Abraham was not yet the father of *any* nations. He had only one son and that son was just 13 years old (Gen. 17:25). Yet God said to Abraham, "I *have made* you a father of many nations."[9] Even earlier, in Genesis 15:18, God had told Abraham, "I *have given* your descendants the land." In reality, at that time, he as yet had no descendants. But with God, such things are as good as done. Entire peoples existed *conceptually* in God's mind. When Abraham's descendants came into existence, it could be said that they had already existed in God's plans and foreknowledge.

Hence, the works of God exist in two ways: First, they exist in his plans and foreknowledge. Second, they come to exist literally as his plans are fulfilled. He says:

> I alone declare the end from the beginning, and from ancient times what is still to come. Whatever I plan will happen for I will do all that I please (Isa. 46:10).

As Christians, we have often failed to understand conceptual preexistence in the Bible.[10] This has sometimes led to people proposing that something being spoken about in God's plans and foreknowledge already existed literally. This is a mistake less often made by the Jews, who have tended to have a better grasp of conceptual preexistence than Christians. Professor E. G. Selwyn stated:

> When the Jew wished to designate something as predestined, he spoke of it as already existing in heaven.[11]

Things in the mind of God do not literally exist until his plans regarding them are fulfilled. Yet as we have seen, such conceptual preexistence was so definite — so certain, that he sometimes spoke of future people and events as though they already were. That concept is well understood and expressed by the Apostle Paul in the New Testament:

> As it is written, "I have made you a father of many nations." Abraham is our father in the sight of God in whom he believed: the God who gives life to the dead and calls things that are not as though they already were (Rom. 4:17).

They Saw the Messiah's Day

God foresaw his Messiah and events in his life. That was the case even though the Messiah did not come into existence until the days of Herod the Great. God let his prophets of old foresee his day and the goings forth of the Messiah were known about and anticipated ages before he became reality. They saw his day, but they saw it from a distance in time. They looked forward to the time in which he would come to be.

In post-biblical times, the notion of a literal preexistence of the Messiah invaded Christianity. It was thought that the Messiah first existed in some non-human form and then became a human being. While that idea has been popularized in post-biblical Christian theology, it was a notion foreign to God's people of old.[12] The prophets of old rightly understood preexistence as being in God's mind and plans, not literally or in reality. Notice this example where God is speaking to the prophet Jeremiah:

> I knew you before I formed you in the womb; before you were born I set you apart and appointed you to be a prophet to the nations (Jer. 1:5).

In his servant Jeremiah, God "knew" a man who did not yet exist. Before he was born, God "set him apart." In his plans, God "appointed him" to be a prophet to the nations. God is not speaking literally about some prehuman Jeremiah. Rather, these are the words of God telling the real Jeremiah what his plans for him had been before he even came into existence.

Likewise, the prophets looked into God's plans and saw the Messiah. They saw that he is the center of God's program for humanity and all creation. They saw that from the beginning, God had a destiny for him and for the nations through him. What Adam loses in the garden, Messiah wins back after he is born. As God's prophets viewed the plan, they saw his birth, and understood that God would set his spirit upon him and put his words in his mouth. They saw his death, resurrection and the great glory that God had in store for him: He is God's human heir of creation.[13] He will have the place of being the leader of all of God's people for eternity. Surely everyone should admit to the Messiah's conceptual preexistence. However, the tendency of too many of our Christian Bible teachers has been to accept uncritically later Gentile Christian theories about a supposed literal preexistence, rather than gaining a clear understanding of Jewish idioms.[14]

The Nonexistent — Preexistent Son of God

The notion of a literal preexistence of the Messiah fails when it is tested against the facts. The theory collapses for the most obvious of reasons: The Messiah was not literally there in the Old Testament. Prior to Jesus being born, there is no case where any of God's true prophets ever said that they met the Messiah or talked with him. They never said that the Messiah literally did anything in their times. The very word "Messiah" (Christ) means "anointed." But it is not until the New Testament that Jesus comes to exist and is anointed by God (Acts 10:38). The Apostle Peter makes clear that God "made" Jesus of Nazareth "to be" the Christ (Acts 2:36).

The prophets of old knew God by name. As we have seen, the Father is called YHWH over 6,800 times in the Old Testament. There is no record, however, that those prophets even knew what the Messiah's personal name was going to be.[15] In the New Testament, he is called by name over 900 times. Had the prophets in the Old Testament known him, they would have said so. They would have celebrated the fact that they knew him and would have called him by name — hundreds, perhaps thousands of times. They did not.[16]

God's prophets and his people of old did not know the Messiah because he was not there to be known. By prophecies and beautiful visions, they saw Messiah's day from a distance in time. But, they longed to see him and his great works clearly — personally. Jesus told the people of his day, "I tell you the truth, many prophets and righteous people longed to see what you see, but did not see it. They desired to hear what you hear, but did not hear it" (Matt. 13:17). The Apostle Peter who lived in the day of the Messiah says to the people:

> And all of the prophets who have spoken, from Samuel and those who came after him, foretold of these days (Acts 3:24).

In God's master plan, the Messiah was not an after-thought — He was in God's first thoughts. In his work to bring him into existence, God blessed others along the way. In a sense, the Messiah did not come to exist because of people in his lineage. Rather, God caused them to exist in order for him to be born. In the great plans of God, the Messiah preceded his own forebears. In that sense, he is before even Abraham — his own key progenitor.[17]

While the Messiah did not literally exist until the days of King Herod the Great, God did let his people foresee him in very graphic terms. In the promises of God, Abraham foresaw generations of his own descendants before they came to be (Gen. 17:4–6, etc.). He also saw the day of Messiah — the greatest of his descendants (Matt. 1:1; John 8:56). Abraham and the prophets saw the coming day of the Messiah and greatly rejoiced. They themselves believed in him from afar — from a great distance in time.[18]

By Deliverers He Saves

> For surely you are our Father, though Abraham does not know us and Israel does not acknowledge us. You, O Lord,

> are our Father; our Redeemer from of old is your name (Isa. 63:16).

It is the Father on his throne who is their Redeemer. Ultimately, there is no Savior but him (Isa. 43:11). Yet he often accomplishes his salvation by human deliverers.[19] He sends them to lead his people out in times of difficulty:

> Then in their time of trouble they cried out to you and you heard them from heaven, and in your great mercies you gave them saviors who saved them from the hand of their enemies (Neh. 9:27).

When the people are in bondage under Pharaoh, Moses leads them out (Ex. 3:10). Yet it is God who plans all of this and empowers Moses. It is YHWH himself who is their ultimate deliverer:

> Thus says the Lord, the God of Israel, "I brought Israel out of Egypt, and I delivered you from the hand of the Egyptians and from the hand of all the kingdoms that oppressed you" (1 Sam. 10:18).

Again, in the days of the judges, we find a time in which God's people depart from him and worship other gods; they fall under the control of a foreign king. When they turn to the Lord for deliverance, he has compassion on them and sends them a savior:

> But when the children of Israel cried out to the Lord, he raised up for them a deliverer who saved them, Othniel son of Kenaz, Caleb's younger brother (Judges 3:9).

Gideon is also a deliverer in those days. God commissions him to save the people:

> Then Gideon said to God: "If you will save Israel by my hand as you have said, look, I will put a wool fleece on the threshing floor. If there is dew on the fleece but the ground is dry, then I will know that you will save Israel by my hand, as you have said" (Judges 6:36, 37).

God also sends saviors in the days of the kings of Israel. He says to the prophet Samuel regarding Saul:

> Tomorrow about this time I will send you a man from the land of Benjamin. Anoint him to be ruler over my people Israel. He will save my people from the hand of the Philistines (1 Sam. 9:16).

Again, God saved his people through David:

> For the Lord has spoken of David, saying, "By my servant David, I will save my people Israel from the hand of the Philistines and from all of their enemies" (2 Sam. 3:18).

It is because of God's love that he sends deliverers — saviors. They are his servants to bring salvation to his people. When their work is done, the people greatly honor them. However, they will always know that the God who sends these saviors is the ultimate source of their deliverance.

God's Greatest Deliverer

In God's plans, his greatest and final savior is his Messiah. When he is born, God equips him and sends him to save the people. God prepares his Messiah and empowers him to deliver the people from their greatest enemies — sin and death. God says of him:

> By his knowledge, my righteous servant will make many righteous; and it is their iniquities that he bears (Isa. 53:11).

> God exalted him to his right hand as leader and savior so he might give repentance to Israel and forgiveness of sins (Acts 5:31).

God has sent saviors and deliverers. Above all, he has now sent his Messiah. Yet the Father alone is and always will be the ultimate Savior of the world:

> Look to me and be saved, all the ends of the earth; for I am God, and there is no one else (Isa. 45:22).

They Do "YHWH Things"

> Then Moses stretched out his hand over the sea, and through the night the LORD caused the sea to go back by a strong east wind and turned it into dry land, and the waters were divided (Ex. 14:21).

Who has seen such marvelous things? His prophets and deliverers do amazing works. Miracles, wonders and signs give credibility to the words they speak and bring success to their missions. Yet none of these works are done by their own abilities. Moses stretches out his hand over the water, but it is the "breath" (NIV, NLT) of the LORD that blows upon the sea and causes it to separate (Ex. 15:10).[20]

The sea parts at the raising of Moses' staff (Ex. 14:16). At the direction of the prophet Elisha, Naaman dips seven times in the Jordan River and is cured of leprosy (2 Kings 5:10–14). By Elijah, fire comes from heaven upon the sacrifice of the LORD (1 Kings 18:36–38). Another time, the prophet causes rain to be withheld from the land (1 Kings 17:1). On still another occasion, a woman's son is brought back to life (1 Kings 17:17–24).

These men and women of God do "YHWH things": things that we would expect only God to do. The works that they do can even rightly be said to have been done by God. Yet they themselves are not YHWH.

God's prophets and deliverers do amazing things. However, they do not act on their own. The God who sends them to his people also fully equips them for their missions. He equips them according to whatever deliverance is needed:

> Then he said to me, "This is the word of the LORD to Zerubbabel: 'Not by might, nor by power, but by my spirit,' says the LORD of hosts" (Zech. 4:6).

It is not by human might or power that Zerubbabel will succeed. Rather, it is by the active presence of God. It is by his spirit that wonderful works will be accomplished.

When the Messiah's day comes, God greatly equips him. He too does YHWH things. Like Zerubbabel, he does all his great works by the spirit of the LORD (Isa. 61:1, 2; cf. Luke 4:1, 18–21). Like Moses and others, he does miraculous signs (John 3:2; 11:47). His disciples also do great things (Acts 5:12).

The fact that God's prophets and deliverers do these amazing works does not mean that they themselves are YHWH. Neither are they God-men, or angel-men or some other kind of super-beings. Rather, they are people who are empowered by his spirit. They do all of their works by the spirit of God. That demonstrates that they are true human beings. If they were otherwise, perhaps they would have innate abilities and not need the working of God's spirit to do these things.

They Are His Human Agents

God's prophets and deliverers are his agents.[21] They speak his word, but do not originate it. He gives them power, and they come in his name. They act on his behalf according to the measure of authority that he gives them. To reject an agent of God is to reject God himself. On the other hand, to receive those he sends is to receive him.

What is done by an agent of God can rightly be said to have been done by God. *The Encyclopedia of Jewish Religion* indicates:

> Agent (Heb. *Shaliah*): The main point of the Jewish law of agency is expressed in the dictum, "A person's agent is regarded as the person himself" (Ned. 72B; Kidd, 41b). Therefore any act committed by a duly appointed agent is regarded as having been committed by the principal.[22]

Notice again the language regarding David in our earlier example:

> By my servant David, I will save my people (2 Sam. 3:18).

The people could rightly say that David was their savior, or that God saved Israel *through* David. Both are true. Such is the extraordinary relationship between God and his agents.

However, an agent should never be confused with his principal. An agent of God is by definition not God. The concept of agency in the Bible has never been well understood by many Christians. Angels, prophets and deliverers — including the Messiah — are all extraordinary agents of God Almighty. By misunderstanding their roles as his agents, people have at times erroneously proposed that God was an angel; that the Messiah was an angel or a "God-man" and other fantastic ideas. None of these things is true according to the Bible.

God's Greatest Agent

Moses, Joshua, Deborah, David, Daniel: names known and honored among human beings for thousands of years. These and many others are God's prophets and deliverers. But who shall be named the greatest among them? The prophets themselves have already answered that question: It is God's Messiah! By their testimony it is this man who is the center of all of God's plans for humanity and our planet.

They foresee his life and the spirit of God upon him (Isa. 11:2). They tell the people that Messiah himself will be a prophet of God (Deut. 18:15); that God will put his words in his mouth (Deut. 18:18, 19). They tell them that by his knowledge, he will make many righteous and bear their iniquities (Isa. 53:11). He will be God's ultimate prophet and deliverer. But his time was not yet. The prophets of old could only look forward to his day and the deliverance he would bring. But then his day did come! Happily, we live in that day. We now see the Messiah more clearly than the prophets of old did. We are highly privileged — and we greatly rejoice.

Jesus is God's apostle to us (Heb. 3:1), his special envoy and empowered representative. We now see more clearly than the prophets did that the Messiah was called by God to do greater things than even Moses. God gave Jesus the unique mission of bringing hope and salvation not only to the Jews, but to all of humanity. To accomplish the salvation of human beings, he had to truly be one of us — a real human being (Rom. 5:19). Yet because he really was one of us, by his own testimony he could "do nothing" of himself (John 5:30). Hence, God wonderfully equipped this man to accomplish things that were more extraordinary than anything done by anyone before or since.

By the power of God, Jesus healed the sick, raised the dead and did other amazing things (Acts 2:22; Matt. 12:28). God gave him unique authority to forgive the sins of his fellow men (Matt. 9:6–8; Mark 2:10; Luke 5:24). By the power of the spirit of God, Jesus lived a sinless life and then gave himself as a sacrifice for the sins of the rest of us. The writer of Hebrews indicates that Christ, "through the power of the eternal spirit offered himself to God as an unblemished sacrifice for our sins" (Heb. 9:14).

Because Jesus greatly pleased God (2 Pet. 1:17), God raised him from the dead (Acts 5:30), took him up into heaven (Luke 24:51), and seated him at his own right hand (Acts 5:31). So we see then that it is not an angel or a God-man who sits at God's right hand: it is one of us — a true human being (Heb. 10:12; Acts 7:56). God, by the power of his spirit, has made this man, even now, to be the head over the church (Eph. 1:20–22). He is the leader of the people that he has redeemed to God (Rev. 5:9). God has determined that Jesus will come again and establish his kingdom upon the earth (Matt. 5:5; 2 Tim. 4:1). By the incredible favor and power of his Father, this man will be doing amazing "YHWH things" for all eternity.

Chapter Eight

Notes

1. The word typically translated prophet from the Hebrew is *nabiy*. In itself it does not distinguish between a true or false prophet. In the LXX, *nabiy* is translated *prophetes* which is also the word as found in the Greek New Testament. It is the transliteration of that word which leads to the English "prophet."

2. It should be noted that both men and women were chosen by God to serve as prophets to the people (Ex. 15:20; Judges 4:4, etc.).

3. This example is of words which God directed Moses to say to the people (Ex. 6:2–7).

4. The Hebrew word which is typically translated "angel" in our versions is *malak* and generally refers to one who is commissioned as a messenger or representative — particularly a messenger of God. It is *aggelos* in the LXX and in the Greek New Testament. This led to the English transliteration of that word which is then anglicized as "angel."

5. For one to be an angel "of God" ("of the Lord") means by definition that one is not God. There are cases in which some interpreters have proposed angels to be actually God rather than God simply working through his messengers (e.g. Gen. 18:1–3; 31:11–13; 32:24–30). Such interpretations are unnecessary and go beyond the essential understanding that while God may remarkably appear in or through his creation, he is the Creator and never the creation itself. Much has been made of "theophanies" in which it is proposed that "an angel" is literally God on given occasions. Again, the easier and better understanding is that God appeared "in" or "through" his angel(s). Supposed "Christophanies" are entirely untenable. In that concept, it is proposed that an angel was actually a preexistent Christ. That is a non-scriptural and post-biblical idea. No Scripture in the Old or New Testaments ever says such a thing. That idea is in fact contradicted by Hebrews 1:1, 2 which indicates that God did *not* speak to the people in times of old by a son.

6. It is not certain that there was a particular angel who was always "the" angel of the Lord. Again, the often heard notion that "the angel

of the LORD" was literally "The LORD" himself makes little sense in that it requires that God sends himself as his own messenger. Likewise, the idea that an angel on occasion was a preexisting Messiah is unfounded. Neither the writer in Exodus nor Stephen in Acts imposes such an identification on the angel in the burning bush.

7. Literally, "by the hand of" the angel. My translation here agrees with the NIV, NLT and NRSV that the easier sense is that God sent Moses "through" the angel.

8. The language of the prophets which envisions future things as happening in the present tense or as already accomplished is sometimes referred to as prophetic or futuristic present. It is also known as prophetic "prolepsis," which is "the representation or assumption of a future act or development as if presently existing or accomplished." *Merriam-Webster's Collegiate Dictionary*, 11th Edition (Springfield, MA: Merriam-Webster, Inc., 2014).

9. It is odd that the NASB which typically prefers a more literal rendering wavers in this case and is one of the few translations to adopt a future tense for these words. Even the NIV holds to the more literal "have made you." The NASB does render the prolepsis correctly in Paul's quotation of the passage as recorded in Romans 4:17.

10. I prefer the term "conceptual preexistence" though "notional" or "ideal" preexistence are sometimes used to indicate the same thing.

11. E. G. Selwyn, *First Epistle of St. Peter*, 2nd Edition (Grand Rapids: Baker Book House, 1983), 124. Selwyn was dean at Winchester for some 29 years. He was the founder of the Christian academic journal *Theology*.

12. The idea of a literal preexistence of the Messiah took hold with post-biblical Gentile Christians who did not grasp the Jewish/New Testament understanding of conceptual or notional preexistence (Rom. 4:17). The idea of a literally preexistent Messiah remains foreign to orthodox Jews to this day. The moment that Christians accept the idea that the Messiah literally preexisted, they are launched into endless speculations as to when, where and as whom he existed. The fact that the Bible itself does not directly answer such questions should alert people that they are on the wrong path in this matter.

13. It is that glory which Jesus asks his Father for in John 17:5. In his prayer, he is fulfilling the Scripture in Psalm 2:8 where God said to the then future Messiah, "ask of me" and "I will give you the nations as your inheritance and the whole earth as your possession." Hence,

the incredible glory of the Messiah was that he would rule over the nations. Further, his people are joint heirs with him (Rom. 8:17) and thus partakers of that same glory (John 17:22; Rom. 8:17–21).

To be rightly understood, John 17:5 must always be viewed in the context of Psalm 2:8, 9; Romans 8:17–21, etc. The glory that Jesus had with the Father "before the world" was a glory in the great plan of God: glory in potentiality. It is similar to God saying to Abraham, "I have given your descendants the land," before those descendants actually existed (Gen. 17:18). Hence, Jesus had this glory with God before Jesus even came to exist in reality.

14. A more extensive consideration of the Messiah in the prophets will be found in chapter 11 of this book.

15. The phrase in Proverbs 30:4, "What is his name and what is the name of his son?" is not a reference to YHWH or YHWH's son. *The New Bible Commentary* rightly tells us that the statement references, "the hypothetical person who has scaled the heights to look on God and precisely measured His creation. Who is he — or (if he lived some time ago) where are the descendants of such a person?" *The New Bible Commentary*, Proverbs (Grand Rapids: Eerdmans Publishing Co., 1991), 569.

16. Post-biblical Gentile Christians were embarking on a proverbial "fool's errand" when they began searching for a supposed literally preexisting Christ in the Old Testament. This resulted in labeling men, angels and even YHWH himself as being "Messiah." Inevitably, these supposed sightings of the Christ in the Old Testament are not indicated by Jesus or his apostles as having actually been him. Again, when Stephen rehearses the matter of the burning bush before the council in Jerusalem, he never says that the angel in the bush was a preexistent Jesus (Ex. 3:2; cf. Acts 7:30, 35).

17. It is the easier and better understanding that when Christ speaks of being "before" Abraham, he is referring to his conceptual preexistence in the great plan of God and not a literal preexistence (John 8:58).

18. For an overview of the Jewish biblical perspective on preexistence see Dale Tuggy's interview of Dustin Smith, "Dr. Dustin Smith on preexistence in ancient Jewish thought," *Trinities* November 10, 2014, http://www.trinities.org/blog/podcast-61-dr-dustin-smith-on-preexistence-in-ancient-jewish-thought/.

19. The Hebrew word typically translated "savior" is *yasha*. It is applied to both God and men. The same word is sometimes translated "deliverer."

20. The word for "breath" in Exodus 15:10 is *ruach* which is the same word used in Genesis 1:2 for spirit. In both Exodus and Genesis, it is the one on the throne who "in presence" moves upon the waters.

21. The common Hebrew word for "agent" is *shaliah* which is comparable to *apostolos* in Greek. It indicates an authorized envoy or empowered representative.

22. *The Encyclopedia of Jewish Religion,* R. J. Z. Werblowsky, G. Wigoder, eds. (New York: Adama Books, 1996), 15.

Chapter Nine

Lords He Has Given — "Gods" He Has Made

He took the captains of hundreds, the nobles, the governors, and all of the people of the land and brought the king from the house of the Lord. The procession came to the king's house through the upper gate, and they seated the king on the royal throne.

— 2 Chronicles 23:20

Excitement! Pomp and ceremony! Such is the bringing of Solomon into his palace. He is the king of Israel. Because of YHWH's love for his people, he has given them rulers. He has given them lords.[1] They are to establish his love, faithfulness, righteousness, mercy and truth.

Serve YHWH and Serve His Rulers

> I am the LORD, your Holy One, the Creator of Israel, your King (Isa. 43:15).

The LORD God is their King. Yet he gives to his people men who rule on his behalf. The queen of Sheba tells Solomon:

> Blessed be the LORD your God, who has delighted in you and set you on his throne as king for the LORD your God. Because your God loved Israel, to establish them forever, he has made you king so you may rule with justice and righteousness (2 Chron. 9:8).

The throne belongs to the LORD. It is God himself who has placed Solomon on the throne. God's leaders owe their station to him. They are to follow him and govern on his behalf. As the prophet Samuel explains to the people:

> If both you and the king who reigns over you will follow the LORD your God — then it will be well (1 Sam. 12:14).

Moses tells the people, "You shall fear the LORD your God, serve him only and take your oaths in his name" (Deut. 6:13). Ultimately, they are to serve only the LORD. Yet to serve him truly, they must also serve those he appoints. To serve them does not divide allegiance. The people do not serve God's leaders as being God or persons who are thought to share his Deity. That would be a grave error. Rather, they honor them because it is his will that they do so. Honoring them ultimately brings glory to him who appoints them.

Those whom God makes to be rulers for the people are called "lords." They are not the LORD God; rather they are made lords by God. Notice a conversation between David and Saul while Saul is king in Israel. In it, David twice addresses Saul as his "lord." He also refers to himself as Saul's "servant."

> Saul recognized David's voice and said, "Is this your voice, David my son?" And David replied, "Yes, it is, my lord the king." And David added, "Why is my lord pursuing his servant? What have I done? What am I guilty of?" (1 Sam. 26:17, 18).

David's words to Saul recognize him as his superior. The word above for "my lord" in Hebrew is *adoni*. That word is estimated to occur some 195 times in the Hebrew Bible. As above, it most often indicates a king or other human superior. *Adoni* is never used for God.[2]

To refer to God's king as "lord" was day to day language in Israel. To do so was not in opposition to God. These are not competitors to the true God. They are his special agents, his servants for the sake of the people. David calls Saul *adoni* —"my lord"— because God made him David's superior.

They Are His Anointed Ones

> Then Samuel took a flask of oil and poured it on Saul's head and kissed him, and said, "The Lord has anointed you to be leader over his inheritance" (1 Sam. 10:1).

Saul is the first man to be king of Israel. It is at the direction of God that he and many others after him assume their role as kings. In dedication, oil is poured upon the heads of these men in an inspiring indication of God's blessings on them. By this anointing, they are consecrated to their office. Such a one may then be referred to as "the Lord's anointed." David says regarding Saul:

> The Lord forbid that I should do such a thing to my lord, the Lord's anointed, to lift my hand against him; for he is the Lord's anointed (1 Sam. 24:6).

God anoints those whom he will. People glorify YHWH when they esteem those he has chosen. It is his will that people serve them.

> To refer to God's king as "lord" was day to day language in Israel.

They Greatly Honor Them

Celebration! Singing and dancing! Women of the land come out from their towns with tambourines and songs of joy to welcome Saul and David! They sing a song of exaltation to them because of their exploits (1 Sam. 18:6, 7).

God does not give his glory to any other (Isa. 42:8). Why then do Saul and David receive such adulation and praise? God is "the King of all the earth!" (Ps. 47:7). Why then does Solomon sit on a throne with such splendor and majesty? (2 Chron. 23:20).

The glory of these kings is actually given to them according to the will of God. Notice how God had glorified David as king:

> O LORD, the king rejoices in your strength. His joy is great because you give him victory. For you meet him with rich blessings. You set a crown of pure gold on his head. His glory is great through your salvation. You bestow splendor and majesty upon him (Ps. 21:1, 3, 5).

It is God who has bestowed "splendor and majesty" on David; God who has "set a crown of pure gold on his head." YHWH does not share his place as God with anyone. He does not give the glory of being the sovereign of the universe to any other. But there is a great glory that he gives to those he anoints: those he makes lords.

People Bow to Them

> Come, let us worship and bow down, let us kneel before the Lord our maker (Ps. 95:6).

Bowing or kneeling before another is an extraordinary demonstration of honor or subjection. Doing obeisance can mean literally placing one's body on the ground before another. By doing these things people humble themselves before God. Yet they also bow before the Lord's anointed ones. Note another example from David and Saul:

> Afterwards, David rose up and went out of the cave and called out to Saul, "My lord the king!" When Saul looked back, David bowed with his face to the ground and did obeisance (1 Sam. 24:8).

To bow before an idol — a false god — would be a grievous wrong. It would imply that those bowing were subject to that god.[3] However, to bow down to one whom God has made lord is pleasing to YHWH.

Bowing before the Lord or before his anointed kings is not the only occasion for demonstrating such honor. An extraordinary example of bowing before a human superior is found in dreams that God gave Joseph when he was a young man. In the dreams, Joseph's brothers are seen as bowing before him (Gen. 37:5–11). Years later, those dreams are fulfilled in Egypt when his brothers bow before Joseph who has become a great ruler there. Speaking for his brothers, Judah calls Joseph *adoni*, "my lord" (Gen. 44:18–22). Joseph instructs them to tell their father that "God has made me lord of all Egypt" (Gen. 45:9).

The Scriptures are replete with instances in which the people of the Bible bow before others who are of high rank.[4] King Solomon shows such honor toward his mother:

> So Bathsheba went to King Solomon. … And the king rose up to meet her, and bowed down to her and sat down on his throne again. Then he had a throne set for his mother, and she sat at his right hand (1 Kings 2:19).

Solomon demonstrates great love and respect for his mother. He bows to her and shows her favor by sitting her at his own right hand. To sit at the right hand of a majesty is an extraordinary honor. It is *not* a place of equality with a sovereign. However, it indicates that exceptional glory has been bestowed upon a person.[5]

Worship the LORD and Worship His Kings

To worship means to give honor, reverence, or homage.[6] The people honor YHWH alone as sovereign of the universe. But as we have seen, they also honor the leaders he appoints. It is not "idol worship" to so honor them. It would only be wrong if they honored these leaders as being Deity. God's people should never honor anyone as being Deity except the Father himself.

The Hebrew word *shachah* is found often in the Old Testament and is frequently translated as "to bow," "make obeisance" or "to worship."[7] The word is used with regard to worshipping God:

- Worship [*shachah*] the LORD in holy splendor (1 Chron. 16:29).
- All the earth will worship [*shachah*] you (Ps. 66:4).
- All families of the nations will worship [*shachah*] before him (Ps. 22:27).

This same word, however, is often used regarding the honor given to God's kings. Notice these examples of people coming before David:

- Ornan bowed down [*shachah*] before David (1 Chron. 21:21).
- Abigail got off her donkey, and bowed down [*shachah*] before David (1 Sam. 25:23).

Translators have tended to selectively render *shachah* as "worship" when referring to God, and to find other terms (bow down, etc.) when it refers to his kings. However, that gives a false sense of distinction in the word. It is in fact the same Hebrew word in both circumstances.

Notice then this example of both God and the king being honored by the people:

> And all of the congregation blessed the Lord God of their fathers, and bowed their heads, and worshipped [*shachah*] the Lord and the king (1 Chron. 29:20).

Shachah here is translated "worship" the Lord *and* the king by the American Standard Version, Authorized Version (KJV), the Douay Version and a number of others.[8]

It would be a grave error to give such honor to the Lord's anointed ones if people were bowing to them as though they were Deity. These lords receive worship as the anointed ones of God — never as being God.[9] For one to be God's anointed means by definition that one is not God.

It is God himself who has decided that his kings shall receive such worship. The glory that he gives them exists in his plans for them before they take their place as monarchs. When people honor them, they are fulfilling God's plan: his will. When they worship those he anoints, it indirectly glorifies God himself.

Lord of Lords / King of Kings

> You, O king, are the king of kings. The God of heaven has given you the kingdom, power, strength and glory (Dan. 2:37).

It is an exceptional ruler indeed who may be referred to as "lord of lords" or "king of kings." Yet in the verse above, the prophet Daniel announces to Nebuchadnezzar of Babylon that he is the "king of kings." Nebuchadnezzar has triumphed over other monarchs of his day. They have become subservient to him. Daniel by the spirit of God reveals that it is God himself who has given Nebuchadnezzar this place and rule. The LORD later gives Cyrus of Persia rulership over great kingdoms. The Bible even refers to Cyrus as "the LORD's anointed" (Isa. 45:1). Cyrus rightly declares, "The LORD, the God of heaven, has given me all the kingdoms of the earth" (Ezra 1:2).

Such kings were crowned with many crowns. Not only did they wear the crowns of their native lands, but also the crowns of other lands which were now subject to them. Nevertheless, kings like Nebuchadnezzar and Cyrus did not accomplish God's purposes in crucial ways. They did not establish his righteousness upon the earth!

God's Ultimate Anointed King

God's greatest anointed one is the Messiah. In fact, the word "messiah" is from the Hebrew *mashiach* which literally means "anointed one." In both the Septuagint and the Greek New Testament *mashiach* is translated as *christos* which has come down to us in the words christ or Christ.[10]

Messiah is born centuries after kings like David, Solomon, Nebuchadnezzar and Cyrus. If God's people worshipped such kings (1Chron. 29:20, etc.), it would be incomprehensible that they would not worship God's greatest king — his Messiah. In fact, when he is born, his followers greatly honor him. They obey his words and prostrate themselves at his feet (Matt. 28:9). In time, all of the kings of the earth will bow to him. Those who honor the Messiah by extension give honor to the God who anoints him and makes him Lord and king (Acts 2:36; Luke 1:32, 33; Phil. 2:9–11).

He is the center of God's plans for humanity. God's ultimate plan for us and our planet is for righteousness to fill the entire earth. It is his greatest anointed one, *the* Messiah, through whom this will finally be achieved.

The Lord's Messiah is the *adoni* of all of God's people. For all time, the words to him from the lips of servants and kings alike will be: "my Lord."[11] Let the entire earth honor YHWH's anointed — his Messiah — his Christ.[12]

From the beginning, God has in store for him a glory that is greater than he bestows on any other ruler. And, by the determination of God, Messiah will rule forever. He will be Lord of lords and king of kings for all eternity.

"Gods" He has Made

> You are "Gods"; all of you are sons of the Most High (Ps. 82:6).

God speaks! In the verse above he addresses leaders of his people and reproves them (Ps. 82:1–5). Interestingly, he refers to them as "Gods." In doing so, he is giving special honor to these people. We have seen two uses of the word "god/God" in the Bible: (1) False gods, as in the gods of the nations, and (2) God, the true God of the universe. There is actually this third use found in the Scriptures. Here, the word "God" is a title of honor given to certain people. For clarity, the author in this book is using "God" or "god" (in quotes) when referring to the word as a term of honor for human beings.[13]

Such a title implies importance. These "Gods" ("gods") are people who have been given status and authority by God himself. They are his lords, kings, deliverers and judges. In the 82nd Psalm, they are rulers of the people.

Referring to these people as "Gods" ("gods") is not a statement about their nature. They are never gods in the sense of idol gods — the gods of the nations. Neither are they God in the sense of the sovereign God. They are just human beings. They live and die as other people do (Ps. 82:7). Here, the word "God" is being used as an honorary title. They are called "Gods" because of the special rank, authority and privilege given to them. The Hebrew word for "Gods" in Psalm 82:6 is *elohim*.[14]

Such is the case with Moses. God chooses Moses to deliver his people out of Egypt. He empowers him for that task and sends him on the daunting mission of demanding that Pharaoh release the people. God says to Moses:

> See, I have made you "God" to Pharaoh; and Aaron your brother shall be your prophet (Ex. 7:1).

Similarly, human magistrates are referred to as "Gods" in Exodus the 21st and 22nd chapters. There, the people are instructed to bring issues before the authorities. Often translated as "judges," the title given to those authorities in the Hebrew language is literally *elohim* — "Gods" (Ex. 21:6; 22:8, 9).[15] Citing Exodus 21:6, *Brown-Driver-Briggs Hebrew and English Lexicon* tells us that this use of "God" is for:

> Rulers, judges, either as divine representatives at sacred places, or as reflecting divine majesty and power.[16]

These "Gods" ("gods") are never the one true God, YHWH. Neither are they demigods or the gods of the nations. We can apply three tests which tell us those things with certainty:

1. These are sons of God (Ps. 82:6) — The gods of the nations, on the other hand, are his enemies. Likewise we know that they are not God for the same reason. Those who are sons of God are not God.
2. They are *made* "Gods" (Ex. 7:1) — They derive their station, authority and power from him. He derives his authority and power from no one. These are "Gods" because he declares them so (Ps. 82:6). Moses was "God" to Pharaoh because YHWH made him that.
3. These "Gods" have a God (Ps. 82:1) — The sovereign God of the universe has no God. These "Gods" do *his* will. They are subject to him. He is subject to no one.

It is not wrong to call human beings whom God has exalted "lords." Neither is it wrong to call them "Gods." If it were, he would not have done so himself. It would be wrong to honor these "Gods" as though they were God or as divine persons alongside the Father — there are no such persons. However, when the people rightly honor them, it brings glory to God himself. It is he who gives them their extraordinary position.

While this third use of the word "God" is not frequently found in the Bible, it is wonderful! Today, such language may at first strike us as odd. However, it was more common to the people of the Bible. Consider — through the centuries when people sang the 82nd Psalm, the words coming off their lips literally referred to human rulers as "Gods."

These "Gods" are people: not God-men or angel-men. They are true human beings in places of special honor.

Messiah Is Called "God"

> Your throne, O "God," will endure forever. The scepter of your kingdom will be a scepter of justice. You love righteousness and hate wickedness. Therefore has God, your God, anointed you with the oil of joy beyond your fellows (Ps. 45:6, 7).

After he is born, the Messiah is also given the honor of being called "God." The 45th Psalm cited above is widely agreed to be prophetic — looking from the day of the prophet forward to the day of the Messiah.[17] If such leaders as Moses and rulers in Israel were called "Gods," then it would be surprising if the Messiah would not be honored in that way.

When the Messiah's day comes, his people call him "Lord" and "Christ." It is estimated that Jesus is called "lord" (*kurios*) around 400 times in the New Testament. He is even more often referred to as "anointed" (*christos*). That word is used for him around 550 times. Those are key Messianic terms for one whom God makes king. That this is the meaning intended by the people of the New Testament regarding Jesus is made clear in Peter's statement to the multitude on the Day of Pentecost that "God has made him both Lord and Christ" (Acts 2:36).

On the other hand, the use of "God" (*theos*) is very rare in the New Testament when used for the Messiah. It is used regarding him only 2 times for certain.[18] That those uses are in the honorific sense of the word "God" is witnessed by the rarity with which they occur[19] and by the fact that the word

God (as *ho theos*, literally, "the God," translated as God) constantly references the Father. It is used for the Father over 1,300 times in the New Testament.

The rare occasions when "God" is used for the Messiah do not indicate or imply that he is the God of the universe. Rather, the God of the universe is *his* God. In the 45th Psalm itself, we find it is said of the king, "God has blessed him forever" (v. 2). It is the God *of* Messiah who anoints him with the oil of joy beyond his fellows (v. 7).

The Expositors Bible indicates regarding the use of "God" (*elohim*) for the Messiah in Psalm 45:

> The designation, therefore, of the king as Elohim is not contrary to the Hebrew line of thought. It does not predicate divinity, but Divine preparation for and appointment to office. ... August, then, as the title [*elohim*] is, it proves nothing as to the divinity of the person addressed.[20]

Isaiah 9:6

Another passage of interest with regard to the Messiah being called "God" is Isaiah 9:6:

> For to us a child is born, to us a son is given; and the government shall be upon his shoulder, and his name shall be called Wonderful Counselor, Mighty God, Everlasting Father, Prince of Peace (Isa. 9:6, ESV).

While this verse is not quoted by anyone in the New Testament, it is widely agreed to be prophetic regarding the Messiah. Often celebrated by Christians today as a declaration that the Messiah is God Almighty, there are a number of reasons that is *not* the case:

<u>*El not Elohim*</u> — A somewhat lesser word for God is used in this passage than is the case even in Psalm 45.

In Isaiah 9:6, the word for God is taken from *el* rather than the more preeminent word *elohim*.[21]

Mighty not Almighty — Messiah in this case is not referenced by the adjective "almighty" (*shaddai*) but rather by the lesser term "mighty" (*gibbor*). *Gibbor* occurs around 150 times in the Hebrew Bible and seldom refers to the LORD God. Rather, it is the word preferred for men of valor, great warriors, etc. and is the term applied to David ("mighty") in Psalm 89:19ff.[22] It is significant that *shaddai* (almighty) is not found in Isaiah 9:6. *Shaddai* in all of its 48 or so occurrences refers to the LORD God. The title "Almighty God" (*El Shaddai*) is not applied to the Messiah in the Scriptures.

Made "Father" to God's People — The reference to the Messiah as "father" is also a venerable recognition. He is not to be understood as their father in a genetic sense as is Abraham. Rather, he is one who is "made" to be father as governor of the people. Isaiah himself picks up on this understanding of Messiah as father a chapter earlier when in spirit he foresees Messiah speaking and saying:

> Behold, I and the children the LORD has given me are for signs and wonders in Israel from the LORD Almighty (Isa. 8:18).

The writer of the Book of Hebrews in the New Testament affirms that Isaiah 8:18 is a prophecy about the Messiah and his people (Heb. 2:13). Messiah is a father in governance and oversight. It is the children that God has *given* him of whom he is the father.

It was in that same sense that Joseph was "made" father in Egypt. Joseph says that:

> God has made me a father to Pharaoh, lord of his entire household and ruler of all Egypt (Gen. 45:8).

Father "Forever" — The term sometimes translated "everlasting" in Isaiah 9:6 is from the Hebrew word *ad* and indicates that Messiah will unendingly (in perpetuity) be "father" to God's people. He will never be replaced by any other ruler. Isaiah 9:7 states that "there will be no end to his government and peace." Because God has decreed it, the kingdom and rule of Messiah will endure forever (Luke 1:32, 33). To be an "everlasting" father means he will be a father who "lasts forever."[23]

Prince not King — It has also been noted that for Jesus the somewhat less auspicious title "prince" (*sar*) of peace is used rather than "king" (*melech*). *Sar* indicates a "chieftain, chief ruler, official, captain or prince."[24] The word *sar* is not used for God in the Bible.[25]

All in all, Isaiah 9:6 is best understood in keeping with its context. It is Messiah's rulership in God's kingdom which is being addressed in this passage (Isa. 9:7). It is in his role as ruler of that kingdom that he will fulfill all of the things that God causes him to be: "wonderful counselor," mighty "God," "enduring Father," and "prince of peace."[26]

In Isaiah 9:7 we see that this ruler will sit upon "the throne of David." And in that verse we also see that none of this will be accomplished by the ruler himself. Rather, it is the "zeal of the Lord" that will perform these things.[27]

One God Over All

The Lord Most High is awesome,
a great King over all the earth! (Ps. 47:2).

Lords he has given — "Gods" he has made! His people shall serve YHWH *and* those he appoints over them. They shall honor his chosen leaders in extraordinary ways. They shall honor his Messiah as his chief leader through all eternity. That is the will of God. His leaders receive glory according to his certain plans for them. Yet, all of these lords and "Gods" have a God! It is YHWH! He is forever the one above all.

Chapter Nine

Notes

1. The word most often translated "lord" from the Hebrew is *adon* in its various forms. The essential meaning is "lord, master, owner." In the LXX, it is typically translated *kurios* which is also the word commonly found in the Greek New Testament. For more on *adon*, see *Brown-Driver-Briggs* (or other) *Hebrew and English Lexicon* (Peabody, MA: Hendrickson, 2000), 10.

2. A Hebrew word reserved for referring to the LORD God is *adonai* (ah-doh-nigh) whereas *adoni* (ah-doh-nee) is used for non-Deity lords or superiors. In the Hebrew Bible, *adoni* refers to human superiors with exceptions being certain cases in which angels are being addressed (e.g. Josh. 5:14; Judges 6:13; Dan. 10:16). It is important to note that in Psalm 110:1, the phrase is "YHWH said to *adoni*" which means that the Messiah is identified as being a non-Deity "lord." By one count, adonai occurs 449 times in the Hebrew Bible and regularly refers to YHWH, while adoni occurs some 195 times (including Ps. 110:1) and never refers to the LORD God. For a fuller consideration regarding the Messiah as being *adoni* and not *adonai*, see Anthony Buzzard, *Jesus was not a Trinitarian* (Morrow, GA: Restoration Fellowship, 2007), 85ff.

3. This is of course what is at stake in the famous story of the three Hebrew children who refuse, even upon pain of death, to bow before Nebuchadnezzar's golden image (Dan. 3:28).

4. Abraham gives honor to the people of the land in which he sojourns by bowing before them. When his wife Sarah dies, he entreats them for a place to bury her. It is a beautiful story in which Abraham twice bows to the ground before the people (Gen. 23:1–12). Such honor is given at a time when Jacob and his brother Esau have been estranged and Jacob determines to make reconciliation. As Jacob approaches his brother, he bows himself to the ground before Esau seven times. In turn, Jacob's wives and children also honor his brother by bowing before him (Gen. 33:1–8).

5. David foresaw the day in which God would seat the Messiah at his right hand (Ps. 110:1). While this is an incredible honor, it is

important to recognize that the Messiah's glory, together with his accompanying authority, are *given to him* by God (Matt. 28:18). For Messiah to be seated at God's right hand means that he himself is *not* God. He will in fact be subject to God forever (1 Cor. 15:27, 28).

6. While use of the word "worship" is now often limited to describing honor given to God, that is not the case in the Bible. The *ISBE* indicates that worship is: "Honor, reverence, homage, in thought, feeling, or act, paid to men, angels, or other 'spiritual' beings ... but specifically and supremely to Deity." "Worship," *International Standard Bible Encyclopedia* (Grand Rapids: Eerdmans, 1955), 5:3110.

7. It is the word *shachah* that is found in the foregoing examples of people bowing before God as well as persons of honor.

8. A survey of translations of 1 Chronicles 29:20 finds a number of them rightly reflecting that the "worship" there is to both God *and* the king. The NASB deals variously with the word *shachah*, tending to translate it as "worship" when it refers to the true God or (negatively) to the gods of the nations. It then tends to avoid the word "worship" when *shachah* is used with reference to human beings. The failing of that approach is particularly evident in 1 Chronicles 29:20 where the NASB translators recognize that *shachah* refers to both God *and* the king. However, in translation they then retreat to the use of "did homage," avoiding the word "worship" in that case.

9. There are examples in the Scriptures where both people of honor and angels accept obeisance and other forms of worship from human beings. The kings of Israel including the Messiah accept such worship. There are also examples in the Scriptures in which people as well as angels refuse such worship. They do not refuse it because it is reserved only for Deity, but rather because of their own lack of authority and position.

10. Note the transliteration *messias* in the Greek New Testament in John 1:41; 4:25.

11. Additional notes on the words LORD and lord: As discussed in chapter 3 of this book, in the Old Testament, the word LORD (all capitals) is used as a stand-in for the name YHWH in most English translations. In this book, the author uses LORD synonymously with YHWH and reserves it for referencing God himself.

In both the Old and New Testaments, there is also the "normal" use of the word "lord" which refers generally to masters, owners, kings, rulers, etc. The word in that sense applies to human superiors including the Messiah and at times also refers to God himself (he too is "lord" in that regard, e.g. Lam. 3:58).

In the New Testament, the term "lord" (Greek kurios) is used to refer to various ones from a person thought to be a gardener (John 20:15), to a civil authority (Matt. 27:63), the Messiah (Acts 2:36) and occasionally to God Almighty (Acts 17:24, 27–31, etc.).

Capitalization of words used for Jesus: Translations customarily capitalize "Lord," "King," "Christ," "Messiah" and some other words when they refer to Jesus. When translators intend those capitalizations to indicate that he is deity, it reflects a religious bias and is inappropriate. Capitalizations of such words by the author in this book may be taken as indicating special honor to our savior, but should not be seen as indicating that Jesus is God. (As regarding the text of Scripture itself, the Bible reader should always remember that there were no upper/lower case distinctions in the biblical Hebrew or Greek of Bible times.)

12. The Messiah is appointed by God to be our ultimate Lord for all eternity. He is "Lord of all" (Acts 10:36). Nevertheless when it is said he is Lord of all, it is understood that there is one exception — the God who makes him Lord is not under him (1 Cor. 15:27).

13. In the present book, normal conventions are used by capitalizing the word God when referring to the God of the Bible. The lower case is normally employed when referring to other gods. Translators of the Bible have been somewhat uncertain about how to indicate the less frequent but important third use of the word — as an honorary title referring to those exalted by God (judges, rulers, the Messiah, etc.). In Psalm 82:6, diversity of translation includes use of the lower case (gods) in the NRSV, AV (KJV), etc., uppercase (Gods) in Youngs Literal Translation, Rotherham, and lower case with quote marks ("gods"): NIV, New Century, etc. The present book employs either "Gods" or "gods" when referring to such exalted persons.

14. The Hebrew word used in Psalm 82 and Exodus 7:1 with regard to people being called "God(s)" is *elohim*. *Elohim* refers frequently to the one true God of heaven and earth and on rare occasions (as here) to people of great honor and position. It is also used for the false gods of the nations. The *ISBE* states: "[*elohim*] is therefore a general term expressing majesty and authority." The encyclopedia also sees Judges 5:8; 1 Samuel 2:25 and Psalm 58:11 as examples of the use of *elohim* to refer to honorable persons. "God, 3. The Names of God," *The International Standard Bible Encyclopedia* (Grand Rapids: Eerdmans, 1955), 2:1254. Also note Psalm 58:1 which is a similar case. In that example, *el* is used rather than *elohim*.

15. Translations are divided between rendering *elohim* in these passages as "Gods," "gods," "judges" and "God." It should be noted that while many translations render *elohim* as "judges" in Exodus 21:6 and 22:8, 9 (NIV, AV, etc.), *elohim* is not normally defined as meaning judges and typical Hebrew words for "judge(s)" are not in the text of those verses. Those words are *paliyl* (e.g. Job 31:11) and *shaphat* (e.g. Num. 25:5).

16. *The Brown-Driver-Briggs Hebrew and English Lexicon* (Peabody, MA: Hendrickson, 2000), 43.

17. The writer of Hebrews quotes Psalm 45:6, 7 in Hebrews 1:8, 9 and sees the Psalm as being Messianic.

18. Raymond Brown, the noted Roman Catholic scholar, concludes with regard to Messiah being called God that there are "three reasonably clear instances" in the New Testament. There are five others that he thinks have "probability." Raymond E. Brown, *An Introduction to New Testament Christology* (New York: Paulist Press, 1994), 189.

Trinitarian scholar Alister E. McGrath notes Brown's "three clear instances" and argues (against himself I think) that there were so few instances because of the New Testament writers' "background in the strict monotheism of Israel" and the idea that "anyone could be described as 'God' would have been blasphemous within this context." It seems to me that we could hardly make our point on that matter better than Dr. McGrath here makes it for us. Alister E. McGrath, *Christian Theology — An Introduction,* 4th Edition (Malden, MA: Blackwell Publishing, 2007), 280, 281.

19. It should be noted that some supposed instances of Jesus being called God do not hold up at all. In Romans 9:5, the last part of Paul's statement should not be seen as indicating that Jesus is God in any sense. That would be very awkward for Paul and completely disregards his context. Rather, his last phrase should be understood as another of his short doxologies addressed to God himself (Rom. 1:25; 11:36 and 2 Cor. 11:31). There is no difficulty with Paul's statement so long as context is observed. In Romans (and otherwise in Paul's writings) context finds Christ and God as two individuals — not one (e.g. Rom. 1:7, 8; 5:1). The NIV, Holman (HCSB) and some others recognize that there are at least three different translations which are possible in this verse — two of which do not make Christ God (see HCSB translation footnotes). For more on Romans 9:5, see Anthony Buzzard and Charles Hunting, The Doctrine of the Trinity — Christianity's Self Inflicted Wound (New York: Inter-

national Scholars Publications, 1998), 281–283. Also note, http://www.21stcr.org/multimedia-2015/1_article/ab-romans_9_5.html.

Context is also the key with regard to the so-called "Granville Sharp Rule." Sharp's grammatical theorem works only if one begins with the presupposition that the words "God" and "Christ" describe one being in certain verses. However, context disallows that possibility in every case in which the rule is supposed to apply (e.g. Eph. 5:5 cf. Eph. 1:3; Titus 2:13 cf. Titus 1:1; 2 Pet. 1:1 cf. 2 Pet. 1:2). Likewise, many exceptions must be invoked for Sharp's rule to work. To that it must be said that a rule with significant exceptions is not really a rule. David Maas rightly observes that Mr. Sharp's "discovery" of this supposed rule was "self-serving and self-validating." For overviews of the fallacies of Granville Sharp's rule, see David Maas' full comments in "Does Peter Call Jesus God in 2 Peter 1:1?" http://www.21stcr.org/multimedia-2015/1_article/dm_does_peter_call_jesus_god_in_2peter_1_1.html. Also see Anthony Buzzard and Charles Hunting, The Doctrine of the Trinity — Christianity's Self Inflicted Wound (New York: International Scholars Publications, 1998), 279–281. Also note, http://www.21stcr.org/multimedia-2015/1_article/ab-does_nt_call_jesus_god.html.

At the end of the day, nothing definitive regarding Christ being God should be attached to such doubtful grammatical issues as are found in Romans 9:5 and Scriptures supposedly covered by the Granville Sharp Rule.

20. A. Maclaren, *Expositor's Bible: The Psalms,* Vol. 2, W. R. Nicoll, ed. (London: Hodder and Stoughton, 1891–1894).

21. While *el* is used for YHWH, like *elohim* it is also used for gods of the nations (e.g. Judges 9:46; Ps. 44:20) as well as men of honor (e.g. Ps. 29:1; Job 41:25).

22. Martin Luther in German picks up on the sense of "warrior" or "champion" and translates *gibbor* as "mighty hero" (*mächtiger Held*).

23. The Bible in Basic English catches the sense of *ad* in Isaiah 9:6 with "Father forever." There is no statement here regarding a literally preexistent Messiah. The Scripture is pointing to the future. He will be "enduring" as the "unending" father of God's people.

24. *The Brown-Driver-Briggs Hebrew and English Lexicon* (Peabody, MA: Hendrickson, 2000), 978.

25. The word *sar* occurs over 360 times in the Hebrew Bible and references one who is distinct from, and less in rank than a king (Jer. 25:18; Neh. 9:32; 2 Chron. 30:2). In the case of Isaiah 9:6, Messiah

is then pictured as *sar* (prince) under God himself who is *melech* (king — Isa. 6:5).

26. The use of definite articles in these phrases in Isaiah 9:6 by the AV (and some others) is unwarranted.

27. The words in Isaiah 9:6 (*Pele-Yo'etz El Gibbor Avi-'Ad Sar-Shalom*) are likely an extended Hebrew "sentence name." The name contains characteristics of the Messiah. Some have seen it as describing YHWH himself. In my opinion, that is very unlikely due to the diminutives in the name (*el* not *elohim; gibbor* not *shaddai* and *sar* rather than *malech*). This language is then better suited to the Messiah than to YHWH. If 9:6 were to be understood as being a name describing YHWH, then here the Messiah bears an honorary title which is descriptive of his God. There are many such names in the Bible including some in Isaiah. Particularly note the case just earlier in Isaiah 8:3, *Maher-shalal-hash-baz,* and of course *Immanuel* in Isaiah 7:14. Matthew confirms *Immanuel* as being a title which the Messiah bears in honor of his God (Matt. 1:23). That honorary title recognizes that God causing the Messiah to be born and commissioning him to be savior is a living, breathing testimony to Israel that "God *is* with us." (The elliptical verb in Matthew's translation is rightly expressed by Holman's Christian Standard Bible, New Revised Standard Version, New Living Translation, New Jerusalem Bible and a number of others.).

Chapter Ten

God on Trial

God is not a man, so he does not lie; he is not a human being, so he does not change his mind.

— Numbers 23:19

Has He Misled Us?

We have seen the proclamations of the Father. By his word, he excludes all others from being God. His prophets and people of old unyieldingly hold that he is the only individual in the universe who has ever been or ever will be God. That the Father is the only true God is the faith of the Messiah when he is born (John 17:3). It is also the faith of the earliest Christians (Eph. 4:6).

In post-biblical times, however, Christians began straying from the absolute singularity of God. They doubted that all of who God is rests in the one on the throne. In spite of his declarations, they thought they found other "God-persons" along with the Father. Binitarianism is the belief that there are two divine persons who together are one God. Trinitarianism proposes three. In these approaches, God's spirit and/or his Messiah are worshiped as divine persons in addition to the Father.

Has he misled us? Has the Father appropriated to himself all of the glory that is due God, when part of that honor belongs to one or two others? If he is not the only one who is God, then he is found to be untrue. We must resolve this matter.

In this chapter of our book let us view, as it were, God in the witness stand. Let us hear his testimony. What will our Father say about himself? Is he a reliable witness? And what will he say about objections that some people have raised who insist that there are one or two other persons who are also God?

He Testifies

> "To whom then will you compare me? Who is my equal?" says the Holy One (Isa. 40:25).

It is not the Father and others who together are the one God. It is he and he alone. He has no equals and there is no one with whom to even compare him. He alone is almighty. YHWH is the Holy One — the only One! He testifies again:

> I am the LORD, and there is no one else; other than me there is no God. I strengthen you, though you do not know me, so that all may know; from the east and from the west, that there is no one other than me; I am the LORD, and there is no one else (Isa. 45:5, 6).

In those powerful words, he proclaims that there is one God and at the same time precisely how many persons compose that God. He tells us that from the rising of the sun to the place of its setting:

1. **I** am the Lord
2. There is no one else
3. Other than **me** there is no God
4. **I** strengthen you
5. Though you do not know **me**
6. There is no one other than **me**
7. **I** am the Lord
8. There is no one else

His first priority is that "I alone am God." The prime directive is not that people should worship no other as God but "them." Rather, it is that they must worship no other as God but him. And he is absolutely certain:

> For thus says the Lord — **he** who created the heavens, **he** is God, **he** who formed and made the earth, **he** established it; **he** did not create it to be void, but formed it to be filled with life — **he** says: "*I am the Lord and there is no one else*" (Isa. 45:18).

Immediately after his declaration above that "*I am the Lord, and there is no one else,*" he tells them, "*I speak the truth*" and "*declare what is right*" (v. 19). The truth he is declaring is the truth about himself.

If we believe him at all, we must believe that he is all of God there is! The Father excludes every other being in the universe from being sovereign God. He excludes the deities of the nations. He prohibits the concept that there are any persons who share his Deity with him. This one individual insists that he alone is God.

Cross Examination / Four Questions

Genesis 1:26

You said at creation, "Let us make man." Didn't you and one or two others do the creating? Are there not other persons who share your Deity and are also fully God?

God Answers...

Thus says the LORD, your Redeemer, who formed you from the womb: "I am the LORD, who made all things; I alone stretched forth the heavens. I spread out the earth by myself." — Isaiah 44:24

The Father himself settles the matter: He alone created. He personally made the world and all that is in it. That is why we call him our Father. It is his own mighty power that has brought all things to life both in the heavens and upon the earth. Being our Creator is his glory — his alone. He will not share this honor with any other.

In Genesis 1:26, only one is identified as being God. It is the one speaking, "Then God said, 'Let us make man.'" In the next verse it is affirmed that the creation of man is actually accomplished by the one who is speaking. It is "he" who creates man and in "his" image:

> So God created man in *his* own image. In the image of God *he* created him; male and female *he* created them (Gen. 1:27).

It is rightly understood that the Father is speaking in Genesis 1:26. It is then the Father who is creating throughout the first chapter of Genesis. The same one who speaks does the creating. The phrase "God said" occurs some 10 times there.[1] There is no indication that a different one is speaking in any of those cases.

By the speaking of his word, light springs forth: "And God said, 'Let there be light!'" (v. 3). By that same one, mankind is made (v. 27). The Genesis creation narratives do not say that God is multiple persons. No one in the entire Bible makes such a point regarding the words, "Let us make man."[2]

To whom then is God speaking? The answer is found when we understand that by the time he is saying those words he has already created wonderful heavenly beings. They "shout for joy" as he lays the earth's foundation (Job 38:4–7). As he speaks the words, "Let us make man," we are viewing a scene from that creation. In it, God is graciously addressing his heavenly court. It is God himself who will do the actual creating while they rejoice at the work of his hands!

It is often not known by Christians today that the best of even Trinitarian scholars do not make a case for a multi-person Godhead based on the plurals found in Genesis 1:26. For example, the *NIV Study Bible* is not drawn to the conclusion that this is an interaction between members of a Godhead. Rather, it indicates:

> God speaks as the Creator-King, announcing his crowning work to the members of his heavenly court.[3]

The evangelical *Word Biblical Commentary* makes these observations:

> It is now universally admitted that [a suggestion of the Trinity] was not what the plural meant to the original author. … "Let us create man" should therefore be regarded as a divine

announcement to the heavenly court, drawing the angelic host's attention to the master stroke of creation, man.[4]

Again, God tells Isaiah that the amazing work of creation was actually accomplished by him personally:

> I made the earth and created man upon it. My own hands stretched out the heavens. I commanded all of their host (Isa. 45:12).

Who Rested?

How many did the work of creating is again made clear when we see how many rested from that work:

> And God looked at everything he had made and saw that it was very good. And it was evening and then morning, the sixth day. So the heavens and the earth were finished and everything in them. By the seventh day God had completed his work of creation, so he rested on the seventh day from all of his work (Gen. 1:31; 2:1, 2).

It is "he" not they who sees that all he has made is good; "he" who completes the work. It is "he" who rests from the work.

How Many Did Adam Know?

In mankind, God creates a being with whom he can interact and have true fellowship. When Adam and Eve commune with their Creator in the garden, it is with only one that they speak. It is him they know — not them.

> They heard the LORD God walking in the garden in the cool of the day, and the man and his wife hid themselves from the presence of the LORD God (Gen. 3:8).

The one Adam knew as his Creator is the same one that Malachi declares to Israel:

Have we not all one Father? Has not one God created us all? (Mal. 2:10).

"Let us make man" are wonderful words spoken by God at the time of our creation. However, they are not words in which God is speaking to other divine persons. There are no such persons. As we saw in chapter 6 of this book, the spirit of God is not a person in addition to the Father. It is the Father himself, active in presence and power to work. Again, God's Messiah is not even born for millennia following these events. After he is born, God will bring forth a *new creation* through him.[5] However, the creation in Genesis is accomplished by our Father alone. Like the heavenly beings of Genesis 1:26, let us too rejoice and forever celebrate that we are the work of his hands.

Elohim

The Hebrew word *elohim* is sometimes used to reference the true God. It is plural in form. Doesn't that mean the word God implies more than one person?

God *Answers...*

Remember the former things of old. For I am God *[Elohim]*, and there is no one else; I am God *[Elohim]*, and there is no one like me. — Isaiah 46:9

His testimony is unequivocal. He states, "*I* am *Elohim*, and there is no one else." *He* is *Elohim*, and there is no one even like him. When the word *elohim* is used to refer to the true God, it indicates a "him" — never a "them."

Plural in its *form,* the word *elohim* has two uses in the Bible: (1) It can mean a plurality of beings and commonly refers to the gods of the nations. (2) It can refer to the plurality of *qualities, power* or *greatness* of a single individual. It is in that sense that Moses who is only one person is declared an *elohim* in Exodus 7:1. When referring to a single individual, the word is normally accompanied by singular verbs. That is the way in which *elohim* is used when referring to the true God of heaven and earth.[6] The *NIV Study Bible* indicates that the use of *Elohim* in Genesis 1:1:

> [*Elohim*] is plural but the verb is singular, a normal usage in the OT when reference is to the one true God. This use of the plural expresses intensification rather than number and has been called the plural of majesty, or of potentiality.[7]

In *A Dictionary of the Bible,* Dr. William Smith writes:

> The plural form of Elohim has given rise to much discussion. The fanciful idea that it referred to the Trinity of persons in the Godhead hardly finds now a supporter among scholars. [*Elohim* when used of the true God] is either what grammarians call the plural of majesty, or it denotes the fullness of divine strength, the sum of the powers displayed by God.[8]

The word *elohim* never indicates multiple persons when referring to God. That can readily be understood by these facts:

1. The Father himself testifies that *he* is *Elohim* and there is no one else who is (Isa. 46:9).
2. No one in the Bible ever says that the word *elohim* indicates persons when used with reference to God Almighty.

3. Accepted versions of the Bible do not translate the word *elohim* as "persons" or "Gods" when referring to the true God of heaven and earth. The word *elohim* in such cases is routinely and rightly translated "God."

Hezekiah affirms the testimony of God. He tells us again exactly how many persons compose this *Elohim*:

> And Hezekiah prayed before the Lord, and said: "O Lord, God of Israel, who are enthroned between the cherubim, you are God [*Elohim*], you alone, of all of the kingdoms of the earth. You have made heaven and the earth" (2 Kings 19:15).

You are *Elohim*, you alone! The word "you" is singular in Hezekiah's statement. He is addressing only one individual. Hezekiah also confirms again that it is that same individual who "made heaven and earth." Only one is *Elohim*. Only one created. He is our Father!

One in Unity?

When the Bible says that God is "one," doesn't that mean two or three persons united as one God?

God Answers...

I am the Lord, your Holy One, the Creator of Israel, your King. — Isaiah 43:15

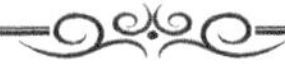

How many does it take to make one? The Father himself steps to the edge of space and time and testifies, "I" am your

Holy One! God is not multiple beings in unity. Only one individual is God, so unity is not even in question. Again, remember his words:

> "To whom then will you compare me? Who is my equal?" says the Holy One (Isa. 40:25).

The words "Holy One" above are from the Hebrew *qadosh*. It is singular here and indicates one individual. Some 30 times in Isaiah he is spoken of as the "Holy One." It is not, "we are your holy ones" nor "we together are your holy one." It is he alone! There is no one to whom he can even be compared; no one who is his equal! Hence, the declaration of God to Moses from the burning bush is that he is the only one who is truly God. It is not the great "We Are" who speaks to Moses; it is the great "I AM" (Ex. 3:14).

Likewise, the Hebrew word *echad* means "one." Nevertheless, it has been particularly misused by some multi-person enthusiasts. They propose the non-scriptural idea that *echad* indicates a "compound one."[9] They then ask the public to believe that when the Bible speaks of God as being "one" (*echad*) it really means that God is composed of multiple persons. The idea has no basis in etymology or the Scriptures.

That entire line of thought is a desperate reach to find a way around the great corpus of Scripture which declares that there is only one who is God. In their proposal, theorists are seeking to redefine the word "one" itself. While blatantly unsound, this idea has become a fad in recent "pop" theology.[10]

Anthony Buzzard correctly appraises the misuse of the word *echad*:

> *Echad* occurs 970 times in the Hebrew Bible and it is the number "one." It means "one single." ... It is nonsense to suppose that the word "one" has altered its meaning when it modifies a compound noun. ... On this amazing piece of

> verbal trickery [some] Christians have been persuaded that in the phrase "one God" the word "one" imparts some sort of plurality to the word God. This is completely unfounded. It is plainly false.[11]

The word *echad* is not complex or mysterious. It means "one."[12] It is indicative of "one" as opposed to two or more. As an adjective, it can modify nouns that are in themselves either singular or collective. For example: one woman (singular), or one group of women (collective). The word one itself, however, is always singular.

YHWH is an individual, not a group of individuals. It is "he" who is the Holy One (Isa. 55:5; 60:9). Notice typical uses of *echad* in the Bible when referring to one person:

> How can you resist *one* [*echad*] officer? — 2 Kings 18:24
> Send *one* [*echad*] of the priests you took. — 2 Kings 17:27
> Seventy years, the lifetime of *one* [*echad*] king. — Isaiah 23:15
> Abraham was only *one* [*echad*] man. — Ezekiel 33:24

There is one officer, one priest, one king. Abraham was one man. He was not a group of men in unity. Even the casual Bible reader can establish for herself that the word *echad* means simply "one" by observing parallel uses of the word in Malachi 2:10:

> Have we not all one [*echad*] Father?
> Has not one [*echad*] God created us all?

It is inconsistent to argue that *echad* means multiples when referring to "God" but not when referring to "Father." The absurdity of the idea that "one" means more than one person is evident.

In summary, we understand that only one individual is God by five facts:

1. No one in the Bible ever makes the point that the word "one" means multiple persons when referring to God. Such an idea is extra-biblical.
2. God himself indicates that "he" is the Holy One. He testifies that there is no one to whom *he* can be compared — no one who is *his* equal (Isa. 40:25).
3. Accepted versions of the Bible do not translate the word *echad* as "multiple persons" or "persons in unity."
4. The word *echad* is used with singular verbs. We regularly find "one is," not "one are."
5. The idea that the word *echad* means a "compound one" is not linguistically proper. One means one! If there is plurality in a statement, the plurality does not reside in the word "one," but in the collective noun that it may modify.

Only one is God! No verse in the Bible says that God is a group of persons with Deity operating in unity. God *is* in unity with his people — his kings — and in complete unity with his Messiah after he is born (John 10:30). But he is not in unity with anyone who is God. "He" alone is God. Neither does anyone in the Bible talk about the post-biblical philosophical notion that God is two or three persons who are all one "substance"![13]

It is not the great "We Are" who speaks to Moses; it is the great "I AM."

How many does it take to make one? In the case of God Almighty, sole sovereign of the universe, it takes exactly HIM! This One is so great, so perfect and so completely able to meet all of our needs that multiples of him could not be greater than he already is. That which is perfect cannot be made better.[14]

It's a Mystery!

Aren't you too mysterious for human beings to understand? Isn't all of this just a great mystery that no one can comprehend?

God Answers...

Let him who would boast take his boast in this, that he understands and knows me, that I am the Lord.
—Jeremiah 9:24

He himself testifies that his people should glory in that they "understand" and "know" him. The truth of how many compose the one God is not a mystery! It is knowable and is known to ancient Israel. Israel knows with absolute certainty: It is one! Moses says to the people:

> To you it was shown so that you might know that the Lord, he is God; there is no other but him (Deut. 4:35).

The inherent difficulties in multi-person theology have driven some adherents to propose that the idea is simply a "great mystery" and can't be understood. No one would argue with that assessment. Surely it would be an incredible mystery that in the Bible there is one affirming that only "he" is God while at the same time there are one or two other persons who share his Deity. This mystery, however, exists only for those proposing a multi-person God.[15]

God is indeed the most spectacular being in the universe. He is truly unfathomable! We are finite—looking to the one who alone is infinite. Anyone who claims to fully comprehend him is surely deluded. Yet the most complex being in the universe is simple to understand in this regard: There is only one of him!

The fact that only one individual is God is directly, clearly and repeatedly addressed in the Bible. On the other hand, the contradictory concept that multiple persons are the one God is never directly stated or specifically addressed. That idea is a construct. If we are to believe in a mystery, it should be one that the Bible straightforwardly identifies and describes. Otherwise, how will we know that it is a mystery from God? How will we know that it is not simply confusion or misunderstanding that has been labeled "a mystery"?

Appeals for people to accept the idea of multiple persons as one God "by faith" also point to the extraordinary weaknesses of the theory. Why should we strain to have faith in a concept that must be labeled "a mystery" *because* it contradicts what the Bible forthrightly says?[16] How many the one God is, is not a mystery at all. Why not let go of the contradictory multi-person "mystery" and embrace the clear revelation that only one individual is God? All of our faith toward God is due to the one of whom it is said, "There is no other but *him*" (Deut. 4:35). This too was Jesus' belief (John 17:3).

Let *our* appeal be that all would have the same faith in the same God that his people of old did. That faith is: Only one individual is God and "he" is all of God there is. Let us tell the world that our Father is perfect and that to imagine there are any other persons with Deity can only diminish him in the eyes of his own creation. It can only dilute the honor that is due him alone as God.

Now We Must Decide

What shall we do with him? There is no middle ground. We must believe that he is the only one who is God, or reject him as a complete fraud. And again, if we reject the God of the Bible, we must reject the Bible itself.

His testimony is certain. He affirms on the basis of himself as God Almighty that "I am the Lord and there is no one else" (Isa. 45:18). His answers to questions are decisive; his credibility unparalleled. If anyone in the universe understands what was meant by, "Let us make man" — it is him. He is the one who said those words. Yet he tells us conclusively that he alone created (Isa. 44:24). Again, if anyone knows the significance of the Hebrew word *elohim* — he does. Yet he sharply affirms that it is he alone who is the true *Elohim* (Isa. 46:9). If anyone would know that God is two or three persons sharing the same Deity, it would be him. But he gives absolute assurance that it is he alone who is the Holy One (Isa. 40:25; 43:15).

And who is it who says that God cannot be understood; that he is unknowable? He does not say that. He says the opposite (Jer. 9:24). If we err by believing that only one individual is God — who is it who has misled us? It would be God himself.

His words are in the Bible. His claim of being the only one in the universe who is truly God is found again and again. Likewise, in a flood of affirmations, people in the Bible give their absolute assurance to that claim. He has the world's most impressive list of character witnesses. Again and again, his prophets and people of old step forward and testify on his behalf. They affirm his word as being the very essence of truth. If we are to really believe the Bible, we must believe his testimony: He alone is God! Let us join with his prophets and people of old and testify that our Father is indeed the only true God.

> The most complex being in the universe
> is simple to understand in this regard:
> There is only one of him!

Why Do We Call Him "Father"?

Why do we call him "Father" if some other person(s) created us? Why do we call him "God" if we do not believe him? As for me, I do believe him! I am fully persuaded. It is *his* testimony, and as sovereign of the universe, his word cannot really be contested. Look how decisively he defends himself; how eloquently he explains these matters. The testimony of God will not allow me to claim allegiance to him while at the same time rejecting the first of his priorities: He is the only one who is truly God. This is a matter upon which he has never and will never compromise. He anticipates the same from those who will be his people.

I would rather place my confidence in his words than in the words of armies of theologians bent on defending centuries of post-biblical religious tradition. It is the Father who sits on the throne of the universe. The spirit of God is not another person of Deity. Rather, it is the Father himself in operational presence. The Messiah is his anointed one; his only begotten human son; his chosen king. Yet Messiah is not "the holy God." Rather, he is "the holy one **of** God" (Ps. 16:10; Acts 2:27). I now affirm with his prophets and people of old: The Father alone is the only true God!

Chapter Ten

Notes

1. To that count could be added verse 22 which effectively says "God blessed them, saying."

2. The idea that God is speaking to a preexisting Messiah in Genesis 1:26 is extra-biblical. The first instances of that unfortunate exegesis that I am aware of are found in the *Epistle of Barnabas* and in Justin Martyr. While God's people of old foresaw the day of Messiah, they never thought of him as literally existing before the time of his conception.

3. *NIV Study Bible* (Grand Rapids: Zondervan, 2002), 6. There are only four verses in the Bible in which God speaks using plural personal pronouns. Three are found in early Genesis (1:26; 3:22 and 11:7) with the fourth being in Isaiah (6:8). In none of those four verses is anyone identified as being God other than the individual who is speaking. *The NIV Study Bible* relates that in those passages God is speaking to the assembly of angelic beings in his heavenly court (1 Kings 22:19–23; Job 15:8 and Jer. 23:18). In contrast to the four verses with plural pronouns, there are many thousands of singular nouns, pronouns and verbs which are used by/for God in the Old and New Testaments. Note: Trinitarian commentators typically do not even bother to mention the plural in Ecclesiastes 12:1 which is rightly and routinely translated "Creator." It is described by Gesenius as a plural of majesty. H. W. F. Gesenius, *Gesenius' Hebrew-Chaldee Lexicon to the Old Testament* (Grand Rapids: Baker House, 1984), 139.

4. In the commentary, Wenham indicates, "The use of the singular verb 'create' in Genesis 1:27 does, in fact, suggest that God worked alone in the creation of mankind." Gordon J. Wenham, *Word Biblical Commentary*: Genesis 1–15 (Nashville: Word Books, 1987), 27–28.

5. The Messiah is in fact the first of the new creation and is God's unique agent through whom he is bringing forth the rest of that creation. The new creation is the subject of Isaiah 51:16 and Psalm 102. It is also the subject in Hebrews 2:5 where the writer specifies, "We

are speaking of the inhabited world to come." (The writer there has been quoting Ps. 102.).

6. The word *elohim* is used in the Bible to refer to gods of the nations (Ps. 96:5, etc.) and on occasions as a title of honor for notable persons (e.g. Ps. 82:6). *Elohim* takes on a unique significance when referring to YHWH. In that sense, it can be said that "he" is the only ("real") *elohim*.

7. *NIV Study Bible* (Grand Rapids: Zondervan, 2002), 5.

8. William Smith, *A Dictionary of the Bible* (Nashville: Thomas Nelson, 1986), 220. The venerable *Encyclopedia of Religion and Ethics* cleverly says that it is "exegesis of a mischievous sort" to suggest that the doctrine of the Trinity may be seen in the word "*Elohim*." *Encyclopedia of Religion and Ethics*, James Hastings, ed. (London: T. T. Clark, 1908), 24:249.

9. There are various examples of inaccurate reporting regarding the meaning of the Hebrew word *echad*. E.g., Robert Morey, *The Trinity: Evidence and Issues* (Iowa Falls, IA: World Bible Publishers, 1996), 89.

10. The misuse of the word *echad* is an example of how far afield some will go in search of a basis for a multi-person God. It must be axiomatic that arguments in favor of a multi-person God are to be as strange as the doctrine itself. Trinitarian theologians themselves have, over time, corrected the popular myths that "Let us make man" and that the Hebrew word *Elohim* referred to a Trinity. It is certain that this clamor over *echad* will be set right as well. Much confusion on the part of the public could be avoided if only people would test such ideas by whether or not anyone in the Bible actually made the point in question.

11. He goes on to write that the word "one" standing before a compound noun is "not in any way changed by its proximity to the compound noun." He indicates that, "The unwary have been taken in by the most amazing assertions that *echad* tells us that God *is more than one*!" Anthony Buzzard, *Jesus was not a Trinitarian* (Morrow, GA: Restoration Fellowship, 2007), 308–310 (emphasis original).

12. The proper definition of *echad* can readily be understood by referencing either of these two standard works on the biblical Hebrew language: Ernst Jenni and Claus Westermann, *Theological Lexicon of the Old Testament*, Translation by Mark E. Biddle (Peabody, MA: Hendrickson Publishers, 1997) or *Brown-Driver-Briggs Hebrew and English Lexicon of the Old Testament* (Peabody, MA: Hendrickson Publishers, 2000).

13. The strange idea of God as one substance in three persons is spoken of or alluded to in various post-biblical statements from the 4th century on but never in the Bible itself.

14. There seems to be no end to the promotion of self-devised non-scriptural "proofs" for a multi-person God. Currently making the rounds is the proposal that if God is not multiple persons then he would not be "perfect." E.g. Michael Reeves, *Delighting in the Trinity: An Introduction to the Christian Faith* (Downers Grove, IL: Intervarsity Press, 2012). As is typical for these "homegrown" ideas, this notion fails from its inception due to the lack of Scriptures that say such a thing! Simply put, if there was a Scripture in the Bible that had said God would be imperfect if he were not a Trinity of persons, Dr. Reeves would have had no need to write a book in which he tries to make that point. Dr. Tuggy writes that those making that argument "not only have failed to support their case, but the very sort of reasoning they use supports the opposite conclusion." See Dale Tuggy, "On the Possibility of a Single Perfect Person" in Colin Ruloff, ed. *Christian Philosophy of Religion* (Notre Dame: University of Notre Dame Press), 2014, 128-48. *Trinities.org*, November 23, 2010, http://trinities.org/dale/SinglePerfect.pdf.

15. Mystification is a rather desperate effort to defend the indefensible. Proponents of a multi-person God propose various ingenious "proofs" that God is multiple individuals. As those "proofs" fail, however, people often retreat to, "It's a mystery that cannot be understood but must be believed."

16. For Jesus and his early disciples, only one individual is God. That one is the Father (John 17:3; Eph. 4:6). Hence, there is no "mystery" spoken of in the New Testament about multiple persons being one God. This supposed mystery exists only for Christians in post-biblical times after the development of that incomprehensible notion. Designating the multi-person God idea as a "mystery" helps to obfuscate the fact that a theory which has been assigned paramount importance by post-biblical Christians is in reality both illogical and unscriptural.

The post-biblical abuse of the concept of "mystery" can be contrasted with Paul's use of the word (*musterion*) in his letters. Paul does not use the term to distract from logical or scriptural difficulties, but rather uses it to describe truths that were formerly hidden but now are known! He never identifies a multiple-person God as being one of those mysteries. Rather, Paul's mysteries are truths about the Messiah and God's blessing of salvation to people in all of the nations through this man (Rom. 5:15; 16:25–27, etc.).

Chapter Eleven

Messiah

My wife and I had never visited a Jewish synagogue. Peering from the vestibule into the main auditorium, my attention fastened on a large wooden cabinet. It was at the back of the stage and faced the audience. Its doors were particularly ornate and I noticed that there were words across the top of the cabinet in the Hebrew language.

As I was gazing at the cabinet, a friend approached. He was an instructor of biblical Hebrew at Vanderbilt Divinity School. Julie, a member of the congregation, had invited the professor and his students to visit the synagogue. Looking toward the cabinet, he asked me, "Can you read those words?" Happily, I was able to translate them. Known as "The Shema," they were the words of Deuteronomy 6:4.

As the meeting began, I was immediately impressed by the sincerity and devotion of the people. They read Scriptures and sang psalms. Children gave recitations: some in English and some in Hebrew. Still I puzzled over the extraordinary cabinet. What was its purpose? I was soon to learn. The rabbi approached it and opened the doors revealing a large scroll. It contained Scriptures written in Hebrew: books of the Bible. The cabinet that was the centerpiece of their meeting hall housed a centerpiece of their faith: Hebrew Scriptures.

I recall my interest upon hearing them reading words from "my" Bible. Perhaps for the first time, it settled in with me that when I am reading the Old Testament, I am reading words from *their* Bible. As a people, it was theirs before it was mine. As I listened, I thought about what separates me as a Christian from these dedicated worshippers.

Sharon and I were glad we had visited. While we have not been to the synagogue since, my thoughts have often wandered to those devoted people, the large wooden cabinet and the amazing words across the top:

> Hear, O Israel!
> The LORD is our God,
> the LORD is one.
> — Deuteronomy 6:4[1]

The Jewish Connection

How extraordinary: walking into a place of worship and viewing the words of Deuteronomy 6:4! What a stunning affirmation that there is only one who is God! Sharon and I tried to recall if we had ever seen those words displayed in any of our Christian churches. Unfortunately, we could not think of any. While we have often seen the 10 Commandments displayed, Moses' great declaration about God is strangely absent.

It is certain that the people at the synagogue are worshipping the God of their ancestors: the God of the Bible. They are the descendants of the prophets and God's people of old. A thousand years older than Buddhism, the religion of the Jews is ancient. Never willing to embrace a Trinitarian, multi-person view of God, orthodox Judaism represents a pure monotheism spanning thousands of years. As a Christian who is Monotarian in my faith, I celebrate that same absolute monotheism.

But if I and these Jews have the same God, why is there a gulf between us? At the synagogue, as I reflected on what separates us, I knew that it is a person: a person whom they may judge to be at best a spiritual teacher or prophet, but the one whom I judge to be the Messiah.[2] As a Christian or a Jew, what can we learn about the Messiah from the Hebrew Bible?

God's Greatest Plan — His Greatest Savior

We see that in Old Testament times, God had unfinished business. He made our world with the intent that it would be filled with righteousness. But this had not yet been accomplished. His people longed for the day in which the righteousness of God will prevail upon the earth.

They see that because of his love, YHWH will raise up a king. God's ultimate plan for deliverance will require his greatest deliverer. This king will be the servant of the LORD and will lead in the ways of righteousness. Greater than Saul, David or Solomon, he will bring justice to all the earth. He will be the LORD's anointed.

Like scenes in a grand play, God's prophets of old see visions of people and events that are beyond their lifetimes. By his power, they see things that are still future to them as though they were happening before their eyes. They watch the unfolding of the story of God's ultimate plans for humanity and foresee the king through whom those plans will be accomplished. Let us look with them at seven amazing scenes.

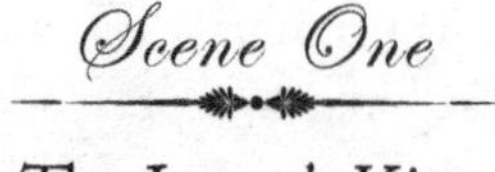

The LORD's King

The 2nd Psalm

Looking far into the future from his own day, a prophet tells us of a king…

> Why are the nations in tumult and the peoples conceiving a futile thing? The kings of the earth set themselves, and the rulers counsel together, against the LORD and against his anointed one saying, "Let us break their chains and cast away their bonds" (Ps. 2:1–3).

The prophet foresees a day in which God will anoint a special king. This will be wonderful! Pivotal for all of humanity! Rulers of the earth, however, will view the leadership of God as bondage. They will reject and oppose the LORD and his anointed one.[3]

Then we see God's response:

> But he who sits in heaven laughs. The Lord scoffs at them. He will speak to them in his anger, and terrify them in his fury, saying, "I have set my king on Zion, my holy mountain" (Ps. 2:4–6).

The decision of the LORD God is certain, immutable. He has chosen this one. He will make him king over all the earth and as God's anointed he will rule the world in righteousness.

Then the LORD's king himself speaks:

> "I will proclaim the LORD's decree: He said to me, 'You are my son; today I have begotten you. Ask of me and I will give you the nations for your inheritance, the whole earth for your possession. You will break them with an iron scepter, you will dash them in pieces like pottery'" (Ps. 2:7–9).

The king declares the LORD's decree. The LORD has said to him, "you are my son; today I have begotten you."[4] As God's human son, God will give Jesus "the nations as his inheritance — the whole earth as his possession." The scene concludes with the admonition that the rulers of the earth must serve the LORD and "kiss the son" (v. 10–12). Its last words are a wonderful promise, "Happy are those who take refuge in him."

The people will greatly honor and worship the LORD's Messiah. Kings are to do homage to him. God will truly make him king of kings. As people have bowed before David and others of old, all will bow before this one. They will not honor him as though he himself is the LORD God. However, they will worship him as the LORD's anointed king. This will glorify the God whose plans these are: the one who makes him king.[5]

When will these things be? The writer of this psalm knew as he wrote that no king in Israel had done these things. If we believe these Scriptures and this God, then we must also believe that these are events that were future for the prophet. This one will be begotten of God. He will be the son of the highest. The LORD's greatest deliverer was not yet born. When he would be, the world would be changed forever.

Scene Two

He Will Be a New Covenant

Isaiah 42

The LORD will put his spirit on him…

Look at my servant, whom I uphold; my chosen one in whom I delight. I have put my spirit upon him and he will bring justice to the nations. He will not lose heart nor be

> discouraged till he has established justice in the earth. The coastlands wait for his law (Isa. 42:1, 4).

The LORD's anointed king in Psalm 2 is his servant in Isaiah 42. He is the one by whom God will bring "justice to the nations." God loves his people Israel, but his love extends to people in all nations.

It is the LORD God himself, the one who alone made all things, who is speaking to Isaiah in this scene:

> This is what God, the LORD says, he who created the heavens and stretched them out, who spread out the earth and everything in it. He gives breath to the people on it and life to those who walk in it (Isa. 42:5).

The LORD then speaks directly to his servant:

> I the LORD have called you in righteousness. I will take hold of your hand. I will keep you and will make you to be a covenant to the people, a light to the nations, to open the eyes that are blind, to free captives from prison and release those who sit in darkness from the dungeon. I am the LORD; that is my name. I will not give my glory to any other, neither my praise to idols (Isa. 42:6–8).

God will make this man "to be" a covenant for the people and a light to the nations. There will now be a new covenant: a new arrangement between God and human beings. It will not only be with Israel — but with all peoples. And again, this servant will not just bring a covenant like Moses did. The servant himself is to be this covenant. He will be the living, breathing, walking covenant that God will make with humanity. Now, God's laws will not be ones written in stone. His laws will be those spoken by the mouth of the Messiah himself. This will not be the covenant that God made with the children of Israel when he brought them out of Egypt by Moses.[6] The coastlands do not wait for Moses' law. Rather, they wait for the law of this servant of God: The Torah of the Messiah (v. 4).[7]

This new covenant through Messiah will be God's final arrangement between himself and humanity. By Moses, Israel began learning of the ways of God. By Messiah, all peoples will learn the true ways of the LORD (Isa. 42:6).

YHWH will hold his hand and keep him. He will open blind eyes and deliver the people out of the darkness of the dungeon. God will give him amazing power and authority to act on his behalf. He will be able to do all of these things because the LORD will put his spirit upon him (Isa. 42:1).

And YHWH will cause him to receive great honor from his fellow human beings. God will never give to anyone the honor and glory he himself is due for being our Creator and the only true God (Isa. 42:8). Nevertheless, in God's plans, from the very beginning there was a unique glory that the LORD had in store for the Messiah. It was a glory unparalleled by that which he gave to other kings: This man would literally sit at the right hand of God in heaven.

We end this scene with God clarifying — this is a vision of things that were to come:

> Look, the former things that I told you have come to pass. Now I declare new things. Before they spring forth I tell you of them (Isa. 42:9).

He is telling his people of old about this servant before he is even born. Before these things "spring forth," he gives them visions and allows them to see.

If people were to ask the God of the universe what he is most proud of, he might tell them that it is this servant. Although he is not yet born, the LORD foresees him and knows that he will be wonderfully pleased with him. This man will be begotten by God: God's heir. He will be the greatest human being who will ever live. Yet he will be humble and divest himself of his royal privilege. Born to be a king, he will take the role of a servant.

Scene Three

A Prophet Like Moses

Deuteronomy18

God will put his words in his mouth...

In this scene, Moses makes an extraordinary declaration to the people:

> The LORD your God will raise up for you a prophet like me from among your brothers. You must listen to him! (Deut. 18:15).

Extraordinary! The LORD will give them a prophet like Moses. By God's power, Moses parted the sea and led the people out. He gave the terms of a great covenant; brought the Ten Commandments and even the Shema. There were to be many amazing prophets in Israel. Yet this one who will be like Moses is spoken of from days of old. Jesus is the prophet the prophets spoke about.

Then Moses quotes what God had told him about the prophet. The LORD had said:

> I will raise up a prophet from among their brothers, and I will put my words in his mouth. He will speak to them everything that I command him. It will come to pass that anyone who does not listen to my words which he will

> speak in my name, I will hold that person accountable (Deut. 18:18, 19).

God will put his words in his mouth. This prophet will tell the people everything God commands him to say. When he comes, the people are to hear him. This man will be greater than even Moses. To reject him and his words is to reject God's greatest plan, his greatest work for humanity.[8] He will be God's Messiah (Luke 2:26).

But this too was in the future for God's prophets of old. We find no prophet in all of the Scriptures who is identified as the one of whom Moses spoke — until we come to the New Testament. There we find the prophet who is like Moses, the one who is empowered to be the mediator of a new covenant, the one in whose mouth God places his words forever.

Scene Four

He Will be God's Shepherd
Micah 5

Another king will come from Bethlehem…

> And he will stand to shepherd his flock in the strength of the Lord, in the majesty of the name of the Lord his God. And they will endure, for he will be great to the ends of the earth (Micah 5:4).

The 23rd Psalm announced that YHWH himself is the shepherd of his people. Yet, he gave them leaders to shepherd and care for them on his behalf. Moses was such a shepherd (Isa. 63:11, 12). The Lord even says of King Cyrus of Persia that he is "my shepherd who will perform all of my pleasure" (Isa. 44:28). However, some shepherds of God's people did evil and the word of God was against them (Jer. 23:1, 2).

Here, Micah foresees the coming of a great shepherd of God who will not fail. He will succeed because he will depend on God as he cares for the people. This shepherd will not himself be God. Rather, the LORD will be "his" God. He will "stand to shepherd his flock in the strength of the LORD — in the majesty of the name of the LORD his God" (v. 4).

Micah foresees his origins, even his place of birth:

> But you, Bethlehem Ephrathah, though little among the clans of Judah, yet out of you will come forth for me one who will be ruler in Israel, whose origin is from of old, from ancient days (Micah 5:2).[9]

God has this shepherd in mind from the beginning. Through prophets long before Micah, God has been telling the people about his origin — the day in which he would come to be. Many commentators see the first preview of the coming of the Messiah as early as Genesis 3:15.[10] The people of the Bible know about his lineage — he will be a descendant of David, Solomon and other great kings of Israel.[11] Here, the prophet even sees the place of his origination. Micah has the honor of announcing that he will come from Bethlehem in Judah, the city of King David.

God also tells the prophet Jeremiah about this one who will come from the house of David to rule and govern his people. God says:

> "And I will raise up shepherds over the people who will care for them and they will no longer be afraid nor will any be missing. I the LORD have spoken it!" He goes on to say, "The days are coming when I will raise up a righteous branch to David. He will be a king who rules with wisdom and will do what is just and right in the land" (Jer. 23:4, 5).

Of all of God's rulers, none walk with more fidelity toward him; none care for his people as much. Of all of those who shepherd God's people, none ever loves them as much as this one.[12]

Scene Five

He Will Bear the Sins of Many
Isaiah 53

A man acquainted with suffering...

> Who has believed our message? To whom has the arm of the LORD been revealed? For he grew up before him like a tender shoot: like a root out of dry ground. He has no stateliness or majesty that we should look at him, nothing in his appearance that we should be attracted to him. He was despised and rejected; a man of sorrows and acquainted with suffering. And, like one from whom people hide their faces, he was despised and we held him to be of no account (Isa. 53:1–3).

He will be God's anointed king (Ps. 2:6); his begotten son (Ps. 2:7). Kings are to give him homage (Ps. 2:10–12). As the son of David, he is born to be king, even the king of kings. Yet in his life he divests himself of glory and privilege. From his birth, this man is exceedingly rich. God has determined that the nations are his inheritance and the entire earth his possession (Ps. 2:8). Yet he will live a life of humility and impoverishment.[13] He chooses to suffer with his people and for their sakes.

> Surely he has borne our griefs and sorrows. Yet we accounted him stricken, smitten by God and afflicted. But, he was wounded for our transgressions; he was crushed for our iniquities. Upon him was the chastening that made us

> whole and by his stripes we are healed. All of us like sheep have gone astray. Each of us has turned to his own way; and the LORD has laid on him the iniquity of us all (Isa. 53:4–6).

He will be blameless:

> He was oppressed and afflicted. Yet he did not open his mouth. Like a lamb that is led to the slaughter; a sheep that is silent before its shearers, he did not open his mouth. By oppression and judgment he was taken away. And he will die without descendants. He was cut off from the land of the living, stricken for the transgression of my people.[14] And he was given a grave with wicked men and with the rich in his death. Though he had done no violence, nor was there any deceit in his mouth (Isa. 53:7–9).

In v. 10, we learn that all of this is according to the wisdom and will of God. Then God speaks in v. 11: This one is his servant. And it is God himself who tells us that this man bears the sin of many:

> This one will find satisfaction when he sees what is accomplished by his anguish; by his knowledge my righteous servant will make many righteous; he will bear their inequities. Therefore, I will give him a portion with the great, and he will divide the spoils with the strong, because he poured out himself to death and was numbered with the transgressors. He bore the sin of many, and made intercession for them (Isa. 53:11, 12).

All are quieted upon viewing this scene. In it, people are made aware of themselves: their weaknesses, their failings. Anyone who thinks humanity does not need a savior has not taken a good look at humanity. He will truly be one of us: "a man of sorrows and acquainted with suffering" (v. 3). By him, many will be made righteous (v. 11). It is for the people that he will suffer. Like Moses, he will make intercession to God for transgressors (v. 12).[15] And, as giver and mediator of the New Covenant, his help will extend beyond Israel to all the nations.

This one will not be an angel or an "angel-man." He will not be God or a "God-man." He cannot be Deity or any kind of super-being. To do what must be done, he can be nothing other than a true human being — genuinely one of us. He must be one who suffers, fears, is tried, tested, and struggles in every sense as we do.

We also see here a picture of the death and resurrection of the Messiah. This servant will suffer and die for the sake of the people. He will be given a grave with wicked men and with the rich in his death (v. 9). Yet, God will not allow him to remain dead. It is *because* he pours out himself to death, that God will "give him a portion with the great" (v. 12).

Like our earlier scenes, this is also in the future to God's ancient prophets. Though set primarily in "past tense" language, it is another example of prophetic prolepsis. These events actually occur in Isaiah's future. There is no instance in the Hebrew Bible in which it is said that anyone had fulfilled this prophecy of the "suffering servant" who makes many righteous. That remains the case until we reach the New Testament (Acts 8:30–35).[16]

Scene Six

In Stunned Silence, They Watch as He Dies

The 22nd Psalm

In anguish, the LORD's servant speaks…

My God, my God, why have you forsaken me?[17] Why are you so far from delivering me, so far from the words of my groaning? O my God, I cry in the daytime, but you do not answer; also at night — but I find no rest. But you are holy, you who are enthroned on the praises of Israel. Our fathers put their trust in you; they trusted and you delivered them. They cried out to you and were delivered. They trusted you and were never disappointed. But I am a worm and not a man. I am scorned by men and despised by all. All those who see me mock me: they sneer and shake their heads (Ps. 22:1–7).

People mocking him say with sarcasm:

He trusts in the LORD; let the LORD deliver him! Let him deliver him, seeing he delights in him! (Ps. 22:8).[18]

Still, his faith is in his God. Listen as he cries out again:

But you are he who brought me out from the womb; you caused me to trust in you even at my mother's breast. From my birth I was cast upon you; you have been my God from my mother's womb. Do not be far from me, for trouble is near; there is no one to help (Ps. 22:9–11).

His suffering is beyond measure:

Many bulls have encircled me; strong bulls of Bashan have surrounded me. They open their mouths wide at me, like a ravening and roaring lion. I am poured out like water, and all of my bones are out of joint. My heart is like wax, it is melted within me. My strength is dried up like a potsherd, and my tongue sticks to the roof of my mouth. And you lay me in the dust of death. Dogs have encircled me. A band of evil men has surrounded me; they have pierced my hands and my feet.[19] I can count all of my bones. People stare at me and gloat. They divide my garments among them, and they cast lots for my clothing[20] (Ps. 22:12–18).

Though he will be begotten by God, this man will humble himself even to a terrible death at the hands of evil men. Yet, YHWH is his strength (v. 19). Four times he speaks of his God (vv. 1, 2 & 10). He says: "you have been my God from my mother's womb." He will be a man of amazing faith. He declares, "You caused me to trust in you even at my mother's breast." He will trust in the Lord even to death. And he will be a wonderful worshipper of God. He will cause others to worship also. The Messiah speaks to the Lord saying:

> I will declare your name to my brothers. In the midst of the congregation I will praise you (Ps. 22:22).[21]

Scene Seven

Second Only to God
Psalm 110

He will be King David's Lord — For Eternity...

Anointed by God! Yet he will die at the hands of evil men. What then will his end be? David, progenitor of kings of Israel, introduces our final scene. Looking far ahead from his own time, he sees the Lord God speaking to someone David refers to as "my lord":

> The Lord said to my lord, "Sit at my right hand until I make your enemies a footstool for your feet" (Ps. 110:1).

The One who alone is God is on the throne of the universe. He always has been and always will be. However, David sees a stunning new development: God seats his anointed king at his own right hand.[22] What great honor and glory are bestowed on this one! For a man to sit at the right hand of God is beyond amazing! This man will be second only to God. God will make him lord over all.[23] This is the LORD's doing, and it will be wonderful.

It is not a god or a "God-man" who David sees being told to sit at God's right hand. Neither will any angel nor other heavenly being have that honor. It is one of the greatest of all mysteries that from the beginning, God has reserved this glory for a man, a man who perfectly models God's love and character to all creation. Even the angels of God are in admiration of him. Angels who saw Adam fail God now rejoice when they see how this man chooses to obey him.

In this scene, we see yet another declaration by God regarding the Messiah:

> The LORD has sworn an oath and will not change his mind: "You are a priest forever according to the order of Melchizedek" (Ps. 110:4).

It is good news! The one whom God seats at his right hand will be both king *and* priest for the people. In perfect harmony with God, he will act on behalf of the rest of us.

Resurrection!

While we saw him die in Scene Six, it is not possible that he will remain dead. As was the case in Isaiah 53, our present scene demonstrates the certainty, power and glory of resurrection. Though he will die, the Messiah must live again to fulfill this prophecy: to sit at God's right hand in heaven and be a priest "forever." Indeed, God will raise him from the dead to eternal glory, a glory that he has had in store for him from the beginning of time.

Here too, if we are to believe King David and these Scriptures, we must believe that this is a scene of things that were in David's future. When he spoke these words, there was no king in Israel who was David's lord.

In eternity past, there was no one seated on a throne at the right of God. In the spectacular vision of Isaiah 6, the prophet sees the LORD in all of his majesty with his heavenly court. There are many beings there including mighty seraphs. Yet there is no throne at God's right hand. It is not until the Messiah is born, walks with his fellow men, brings the terms of the New Covenant, seals that covenant with his own blood, dies, is raised again to life and is taken up into heaven, that the directive is given, "sit at my right hand."

We also know that this scene is future to the prophet because of the declaration that this one will be a priest. In all of the Hebrew Bible, the prophets never speak of anyone having fulfilled this role of being a priest after the order of Melchizedek. It is not until the New Testament that we find this one who is made to be a priest "forever" according to God's great plan.[24]

One Lord — Forever!

Through all eternity, the Messiah will be God's ultimate lord. Throughout history, kings in Israel died and were replaced by others. But the Messiah will never die again. He will live forever and never be replaced (Luke 1:32, 33).[25]

Likewise, kings in Israel ruled over "Israel." At the same time, different kings were ruling in other nations. The Messiah, however, will rule over all the nations. God gives him "the nations as his inheritance, all of the ends of the earth as his possession."[26] He will be the one lord over both Jews and Gentiles. YHWH causes his human son to be the one king — one ruler — one lord over all.

Moses gave a wonderful covenant to Israel. The Messiah, however, will "be" God's final covenant — with all of humanity. And unlike Moses who died and left his covenant in writing to be read by people, the Messiah lives forever. He will eternally speak his law and administer his covenant.

This lord will not even be born for centuries after David has died. As a prophet of God, David is seeing far ahead. In the resurrection, David himself will forever serve this one whom God will seat at his own right hand.[27]

From the beginning, God determined that through eternity, the Messiah would have preeminence over his own fathers. God has chosen to give him the throne of his father David. In the resurrection, David does not reassume that throne as the superior of the Messiah. In that day, David will call the Messiah *adoni*, "my lord." In the resurrection, if we were to ask David what he is most proud of, I suspect it would be that God chose one of his offspring to be lord of all — forever.[28]

What will the end of this suffering servant be? His end will be wonderful! Glorious! YHWH will make him lord of all! In the resurrection, David and every other lord and king will bow their knees to the Messiah. Moses will bow his knees to him. Messiah is the one who brings God's ultimate Torah — God's ultimate covenant with humanity. There will be a day of resurrection, and in that day, David's son will be his lord! As God's vice-regent, the Messiah will reign as lord of lords and king of kings — forever.

Why I Am a Christian

The LORD of hosts has sworn saying, "It will come to pass as I have planned; it will be as I have purposed" (Isa. 14:24).

Imagine a God who can foresee the marvelous things in the scenes above. Imagine a God who designs such things for humanity. Consider this one who cares that much for us! How could I not serve a God of such love and power? He is truly our Father — my Father.

The gods of the religions of men have no scenes to show us. The gods of the "cosmic unknown" have no plans. Apparently they do not care for our plight! In reality, they can foresee nothing because they themselves are blind. They plan nothing for us, because it is humanity in its foolish moments that gives them their existence!

I am forever dedicated to the one who alone is God. I am in awe of his astounding abilities and wonderfully drawn to his love. But if I am to embrace this God, I must embrace his plans for bringing righteousness to the earth. I must embrace his Messiah, the man by whom those plans will ultimately be accomplished. I must also embrace God's New Covenant which he is making with all of the nations. Through the Messiah, God will bring forth a new creation upon the earth.

Yet there is another important reason why I am a Christian: it is my admiration and love for God's anointed one. From his birth, he is the heir of God. His inheritance will be the nations. As the son of David, he is born king of the Jews. Yet this man divests himself of privilege and takes the role of a servant. He is forever my role model! How shall I not esteem this one who would so concern himself with the desperate needs of his fellow human beings?

Perhaps I will visit the synagogue again someday. I would enjoy learning more about the Jewish people and their faith. Perhaps they would be interested in hearing about my Christian faith as well. They might find it interesting that as a Christian Monotarian I like them, faithfully embrace only one — rather than two or three persons — as God. I might tell them about my faith in the LORD's anointed one — his Messiah. It was one of their prophets who said he would be "a light to the nations." He has indeed become light to me. It is by him that I have come to know God. That is the reason I am a Christian.

Chapter Eleven

Notes

1. My translation of Deuteronomy 6:4 takes the second part of the declaration to be quantitative. That is the approach of many versions. (i.e., "There is only one individual who is the true YHWH"). Hence, the word for "one" (*echad*) serves to indicate a single individual (i.e. Abraham is "one" man — Ezek. 33:24). Both phrases in the Shema could be taken as covenantal — qualitative. (The LORD is our God, the LORD alone.) That is the view of the New Revised Standard Version and the New Living Translation. It also agrees with the Jewish Publication Society's 1985 version of the Tanakh. In that approach, the word *echad* is used in its sense of exclusivity — "only" or "alone." (Cf. 1 Chron. 29:1: "Solomon alone" was chosen by God to be king.) The end result is the same. The covenant God of Israel is the only true/real God (e. g. 2 Kings 5:15). The *Jewish Study Bible* sees either approach (quantitative or qualitative) as "possible" though it favors the qualitative. See *The Jewish Study Bible* (Oxford: Oxford University Press, 2004), 380.

2. The word Messiah is from *mashiach* or "anointed." *Mashiach* is used in the Hebrew Bible to refer to various kings. In this chapter and otherwise, the author uses the word without qualification to refer to "the" anointed one — "the" Messiah.

3. See Acts 4:25–28.

4. "Begotten" here is from *yalad* which is the usual word for begetting of children. There is a basis here for the fathering of the Messiah by a miracle of God. This would agree with the New Testament birth narratives of Messiah as given in Matthew 1:18–20 and Luke 1:26–35. This view would also have support of the Septuagint in Psalm 110:3 in which God says to the Messiah, "I have begotten you from the womb before the morning." In any event, this passage stands in stark opposition to the post-biblical tradition of a supposed "eternal begetting" of the son. Psalm 2:7 establishes that there is *a point in time* ("today") in which the son is begotten. The Bible in Basic English captures the sense of it with, this day have I "given you being."

5. See Philippians 2:9–11; Luke 1:30–35; Acts 2:36.

6. See Hebrews 8:8–13.

7. See Galatians 6:2.

8. See John 12:48–50.

9. This shepherd has an origin (*motsaah*). *Brown-Driver-Briggs* clarifies that *motsaah* in this verse is a reference to "his origin." *Brown-Driver-Briggs Hebrew and English Lexicon* (Peabody, MA: Hendrickson Publishers, 2000), 426. It should be noted, however, that he did not literally originate before the days of his birth. Rather, his origin was revealed — seen by God's prophets from days of old. The Bible in Basic English picks up on this with, "whose going out has been *purposed* from time past, from the eternal days."

10. Dr. Joe Martin gives this same understanding of Micah's prophecy. Martin references Genesis 12:3; 49:10; Numbers 24:17; 2 Samuel 7:16 and Psalm 2:2 as additional Scriptures which from early times foreshadow Messiah's coming into existence. Martin, Joe, "O Bethlehem, Bethlehem..." *The Restitution Herald and Progress Journal*, Jan., 2014.

11. See Jeremiah 33:14–16.

12. This of course brings us to the parable in John 10 in which the Messiah is the "good shepherd." Here too, the Messiah shepherds on behalf of his God. It is the sheep God "gives him" of which he is the shepherd (John 10:27–29; 17:9).

13. See 2 Corinthians 8:9. We see in Romans 8:17 that Messiah's people are "joint-heirs" with him.

14. The language here does not allow for the interpretation that this is a personification of Israel suffering for the sake of the nations. Rather, it is clearly a man who suffers for Israel.

15. Regarding the Messiah as intercessor, note 1 Timothy 2:5, Hebrews 4:14–16; 9:24. We see the example of Moses in the role of intercessor in Psalm 106:21–23.

16. Also see Luke 24:26, 46 and 47.

17. See Matthew 27:46; Mark 15:34.

18. See Matthew 27:43.

19. See Luke 24:39, 40.

20. See Matthew 27:35; Luke 23:34.

21. See Hebrews 2:12.

22. It should be noted that Psalm 110:1 is not a picture of an earlier status quo in heaven with one sitting at the right hand of God from eternity past. The psalm begins with one being instructed "to sit" at God's right hand. That corresponds well to the various earlier

declarations of the Lord in which he declares that there is no one beside(s) him (Isa. 45:5, 6 etc.).

23. "Lord said to my lord." Again, the Hebrew word for "Lord" is "YHWH" which refers to the Lord God. On the other hand, the word "lord" in the second part of the statement is not "YHWH." Rather, it is from the Hebrew *adoni* which never refers to the Lord God but is used for human superiors or occasionally angelic beings: "lords" who are not God. Hence, the phrase in Psalm 110:1 is: "YHWH said to *adoni*." That means that the Messiah is identified as being a "lord" who is not Deity. It is not unusual for the word *adoni* here to be misreported by commentators as being *adonai*. For a full consideration of the Messiah as being *adoni* and not YHWH or *adonai*, see Anthony Buzzard, *Jesus Was Not a Trinitarian* (Morrow, GA: Restoration Fellowship, 2007), 85–87.

24. The author of Hebrews expounds on this "priest according to the order of Melchizedek" (Ps. 110:4). It should be noted that in the Scriptures (Old and New Testaments) Jesus is never said to actually be Melchizedek. Rather, he is a priest "after the order of Melchizedek" (Heb. 5:6, 10; 6:20; 7:1, 10–17, 21).

25. See Romans 6:10.

26. Psalm 2:8.

27. In the N.T., Jesus picks up on the seeming conundrum of King David referring to his own descendant as "lord" (Matt. 22:41–45). It was of course a puzzle as to why and how David — progenitor of kings — would someday call one of his own descendants his superior. Jesus' raising of the matter was an unanswerable strike at the views of the Sadducees who had shortly before been arguing against resurrection. Without resurrection, how will David who was by then long dead, ever call one of his distant descendants "lord"?

28. Psalm 110:1 is the most favored verse from the Hebrew Bible found in the N.T. According to one count, it is quoted or referenced there some 25 times. YHWH seating his human Messiah at his right hand represents the essential framework for the entire N.T. Psalm 110:1 together with v. 4 assures that Messiah will be a true man — not YHWH nor an angel, and that there will be a resurrection of the Messiah and by extension other human beings. Those verses also assure that a man will be stationed at God's right hand in preparation for the establishing of God's ultimate rule on the earth: "Sit ... until I make your enemies a footstool."

Chapter Twelve

Jews, Gentiles and the Battle over God

Blessed is the nation whose God is the Lord*; the people whom he has chosen for his inheritance.*

— Psalm 33:12

A Nation Speaks

From the man harvesting wheat in his field, to the mother baking bread; from the most humble of servants, to the greatest king: These are people bound together by relationship with their God. The nation is ancient Israel. Their God is YHWH — the Lord.

He is The One! It is he who has made them. These people are in his care. They will speak of their God so that all may know him. They rejoice! They sing of him!

> Make a joyful noise to the LORD, all the earth! Serve the LORD with gladness! Come into his presence with singing! Know that the LORD, he is God! It is he who made us, and we are his; we are his people, and the sheep of his pasture. Enter his gates with thanksgiving, and his courts with praise! Give thanks to him; bless his name! For the LORD is good; his steadfast love endures forever, and his faithfulness to all generations (Ps. 100, ESV).

They were his people: Abraham, Sarah, Moses, David and a myriad of others bowed only to the LORD as God. By their words and the lives they lived, they speak to us even to this day. They tell the world that the gods of the nations are created by men, but this God has created us.

Six Amazing Words

שמע ישראל יהוה אלהינו יהוה אחד

Shema 'Yisrael, YHWH Eloheinu, YHWH echad

Six words in the Hebrew language — yet they are likely the most celebrated words in that language. Spoken in the era in which the nation was born, these six words came to characterize both the nation and its people. Translated, they are:

> Hear, O Israel! The LORD is our God, the LORD is one.
> — Deuteronomy 6:4

Moses cries out — "Hear, O Israel!" And about what is he so passionate? It is that the LORD is their God. Wonderfully heralded, this supremely important declaration has come to be called the Shema. Named for the first Hebrew word in the proclamation, *shema* literally means, "Hear!" — "Listen!"[1] Those six words resound in ancient Israel. Their laws and precepts are predicated upon relationship to their God. In the Shema, "The One" is affirmed again. His first priority stands: "He alone is God." His prime directive is understood: This nation will "serve only him as God."

How Many Shall They Love?

As Moses declares the Shema, he proclaims:

> And you shall love the Lord your God with all your heart, and with all your soul, and with all your strength (Deut. 6:5).

How shall a person love *him* with *all* his heart, *all* his soul and *all* his strength if he is serving any other as God? If he forsakes the Lord to serve others, the commandment is broken. If others are promoted as being the eternal God along with him, that too breaks the commandment. To love anyone other than YHWH as a supposed person of Deity divides one's heart and diminishes the love that is due to him as the only true God.[2] The declaration in the Shema regarding who God is and the words about a person loving him with all his heart, soul and strength, are inextricably bound together. Without that love, the words of the Shema are rendered ineffective in one's life. But, likewise, without knowing who God is, the love a person should have toward the Lord alone will be misdirected. Those who understand that we are to love YHWH with all of our hearts should feel the need to be accurately informed regarding him and about how many "he" is.

His people will honor his prophets. They will bow before his kings and rulers. They will bow their knees to his Messiah when he is born. When it comes to who their God is, however, they will love only the Lord.

The Children Know Him

On the occasion when Moses gives the Shema to the nation, he instructs the people to recite to their children the things he is telling them:

> Keep these words in your heart that I am commanding you today. Diligently recite them to your children and talk about them when you are at home and when you walk along the way, when you lie down and when you get up (Deut. 6:6, 7).

Let us walk in ancient Israel. Let us talk to the youths tending the sheep. Let us ask the children playing along the way. What will they tell us about their God? They will tell us that he is the LORD: that he alone is God. Around the evening meal, at their going to bed, when rising in the morning, when they go out for the day — a nation of people and generations of their children will speak these words: "The LORD is our God, the LORD is one."

Jesus and Original Christianity

Jesus was a descendant of David and of Abraham (Matt. 1:1). Born in Israel, he was raised by Jewish parents in a Jewish community. He grew up attending the synagogue, learning the Scriptures and the words of the prophets. His earliest followers were people who from their youth were wholly dedicated to YHWH alone as God.

It is Jesus the Jew and his Jewish disciples who were the original teachers of Christianity. They were the true fathers of the Christian church. There was a wonderful continuity between the Jewish founders of Christianity and God's prophets of old. They all believed that only one individual is God: The Father of Jesus Christ. The first Christians were solidly grounded in YHWH alone as the God of Israel and in Jesus as his Messiah, his greatest anointed king. Jesus himself summarized these very things at the beginning of his great intercessory prayer which is recorded in the Gospel of John:

> Father ... this is eternal life: that they may know you, the only true God, and Jesus Christ whom you have sent (John 17:3).

Jesus did not come to bring the world a different definition of God. He came to affirm the same one that God's prophets and people of old had been proclaiming from the beginning. Confirming that the Father is the only true God, Jesus then speaks of himself not as God, but as God's Messiah, the Christ. The God of Israel is the God of Jesus. Original Christianity is the realization of true biblical faith from Abraham to John the Baptist.

A Different Christianity

In the centuries after the Bible was written, non-Jewish people from the Hellenistic world entered the church. They were from backgrounds with very different ideas from those of the Bible. For thousands of years they had worshipped many individuals as divinity. In their pantheons, there had even been families of deity.[3]

A New "Expanded" God

The overarching message of the Bible is not merely that there is one God. Rather, it is the more definitive declaration that there is only *one individual* who is God. That individual is YHWH — the Father of us all. Without the heritage of centuries of devotion to only one as God, the new Gentile converts often found themselves confused. Lacking a good understanding of the Hebrew Scriptures regarding the Messiah, they were often befuddled by such things as the disciples of Jesus bowing before him and calling him "Lord." Would that not mean that Christ was also God in addition to YHWH? They even proposed that God's own spirit is another person of Deity from the Father. Yet contrary to all of this, it was the Father himself who said:

> I am the LORD, and there is no one else; other than me there is no God. I strengthen you, though you do not know me, so that all may know; from the east and from the west, that there is no one other than me; I am the LORD, and there is no one else (Isa. 45:5, 6).

What these new converts were doing eventually resulted in a reconfiguring of the biblical understanding of God's spirit and his Messiah. By the end of the 4th century CE, they were recasting them as divine persons who together with the Father were inexplicably supposed to be one God. But as we saw earlier in this book, when the prophets of old spoke of God's spirit working and moving in the earth, they never said that it was another person from the Father. Rather it was the spirit of the Father himself.[4] And to the prophets, God's Messiah was his ultimate anointed king: the "Lord Messiah," but not the "LORD God."

From the 4th century till now, Gentile Christians have wrestled with the contradictions of the notion that God is multiple persons. How can two or three persons who are fully God not be two or three Gods? Did not the Bible say there is only one? And does it not repeatedly say that the Messiah is a human being? Christians have strained to see their idea of a multi-person God in the Bible. They have struggled against its insistence that there is only one individual who is

God. Ultimately they concluded that there are two or three persons who are fully God, but that they are mysteriously just one God.[5]

The new theory about God was such a mystery, however, that no one in the Bible ever heard of it. There is no instance in the entire Bible where anyone argues for a two or three person God. Of the Scriptures that say there is "one God," not one of them says two or three persons are the one God. On the other hand, as we have seen, a great corpus of Scriptures actually tells us that only one individual is God. Moses said:

> So know this today, and take to heart, that the Lord, he is God in heaven above and on the earth below; there is no one else (Deut. 4:39).

Later, King Solomon also affirms that God is one individual:

> So that all the peoples of the earth may know that the Lord is God, and that there is no one else (1 Kings 8:60).

The people of the Bible speak often of God, his spirit, and his Messiah. However, they never meant multiple persons who are one God. That was a mistake that God's prophets of old and the original Christians never made.

Touted as a mystery, the idea of multiple persons as one God is actually the clashing together of two hopelessly inharmonious ideas: that three persons are each fully God, but there is only one God. The complexity, contradiction and confusion which accompany this theory are not worthy of the true God of heaven and earth. Regrettably, the clarity, simplicity and beauty of faith in only one individual as God have been replaced by an ongoing theological fog which envelops Christians to this day. Good people have struggled to believe in God and Christ not because of this confounding idea, but in spite of it.

"Trinity" — A New Name for God

In time there came to be a new Gentile name for the new Gentile idea of God. In the third century CE a Christian by the name of Tertullian proposed a Latin word to describe God, his spirit and his Messiah. The term was *trinitas* (Trinity).[6] The word originally referenced any triad or grouping of three things. Hence, it did not in itself have reference to God. Tertullian was not a Trinitarian and for him the one God (*ho theos*) is still the Father.[7]

With no name in the Bible which identified a three person God,[8] "Trinity" eventually caught on and in time came to be treated as a name for the new "three in one" version of God. The word "Trinity" became integrated with Gentile Christian worship. It found its way into poems, songs and liturgy. Christians today are often surprised to learn that it is not a Hebrew or Bible name for God. We have seen it used so much in matters which are associated with the Bible that we make the assumption that it is in the Bible. It is peculiar to see well-intended Christians sometimes incorporating the word "Trinity" into the names of their churches, not realizing that they have adopted a very non-biblical, Gentile name for a post-biblical configuration of God.

New Church Fathers / A New Orthodoxy

The Harper Collins Encyclopedia of Catholicism states:

> Today, however, scholars generally agree that there is no doctrine of the Trinity as such in either the OT or the NT. ... Trinitarian doctrine as such emerged in the fourth century, due largely to the efforts of Athanasius and the Cappadocians.[9]

The architects of the multi-person version of God became a cadre of new church fathers. Now often revered as "the early church fathers," they were not early enough. Blending the Bible with Greek philosophy and ideas from their own religious pasts, they were actually among the early free thinkers of Christianity. These were people who were intent on making their new Christian faith correspond with their pre-Christian backgrounds.[10] The resulting symbiotic relationship between Gentile Christianity and Greek philosophy becomes apparent.[11] Many of the best of Trinitarian scholars today acknowledge that the Trinity was a post-biblical development with roots in the philosophy of that day. For example, Trinitarian scholar and noted church historian Cyril C. Richardson of Union Theological Seminary recognizes that the Trinity is "not a doctrine specifically to be found in the New Testament. It is a creation of the fourth-century church."[12]

Likewise, Professor Shirley C. Guthrie, Jr. of Columbia Theological Seminary writes:

> The Bible does not teach the doctrine of the Trinity. ... The language of the doctrine is the language of the ancient [post-biblical] church taken from classical Greek philosophy.[13]

Without the deep roots in understanding of the one God that Jesus and his early disciples had, these Gentile Christians were re-interpreting God, Christ and the Bible. In many ways they were reinventing Christianity, even reinventing God. Today, their views are supposed to be conservative and mainstream. When compared to the Christianity of Jesus, however, they were liberal — radical — offbeat. Nevertheless, what began as a peculiar reinvention of God went on to become self-proclaimed orthodoxy.[14]

Without direct statements in the Bible that multiple persons are the One God, the new converts came to rely on proof-texting. Isolating verses from their Jewish context, they proposed new meanings to various Scriptures and gave creative new definitions to some Hebrew words and phrases. When even that proved inadequate, new language was found to express their ideas about God. Such phrases as "three persons," "coequal persons," "coessential (consubstantial) persons," "copowerful persons," "coeternal persons" and a variety of others are all expressions fitted to multi-person God theories, but are absent from the Bible. And such language is contrary to the Bible's grand theme that only YHWH is God. He himself said:

> For I am God, and there is no one else; I am God, and there is no one like me (Isa. 46:9).

A coalescing of philosophical ideas and Gentile Christianity is found at the pivotal Council of Nicaea.[15] Convened by Emperor Constantine in the spring of 325 CE, bishops debated issues regarding the nature of Christ. However, by now *all* of the parties had largely lost touch with the Jewish roots of Christian faith. Ultimately they concluded that Christ is to be understood as a God-person and equal to the Father. That was an astounding departure from the Bible. It was the Father himself who rhetorically had said:

> "To whom then will you compare me? Who is my equal?" says the Holy One (Isa. 40:25).

There is no one with whom to compare him: no one who is his equal! He could have said, "Who indeed is my coequal?" Hence, the coequality provisions of the new version of God — provisions which insist that the Messiah is "coequal" with the Father — are particularly disturbing. Not only are they absent from the Bible, they are directly contradicted by a variety of specific scriptural statements. Not the least of these is Jesus' own words:

> "My Father is greater than all" (John 10:29).
> "The Father is greater than I am" (John 14:28).[16]

Many centuries after Moses, the new "church fathers" proposed to tell people what to believe about the Hebrew Bible and the Hebrew God. They were of course destitute of Scriptures which actually stated their view that multiple persons are the one God. In light of that deficiency, subsequent generations of Christians concluded that those post-biblical church fathers were more advanced than original Christians. We now find the pejorative term "primitive Christianity" applied to the ministries of Jesus and his early Jewish followers.[17]

The new orthodoxy evolved over time. Gentile Christians literally spent centuries wrestling over their understanding of God and Christ. At the First Council of Constantinople in 381 CE, it was declared that the holy spirit is also a God-person and equal to the Father.[18] It will not be until 451 CE at the Council of Chalcedon that they will formalize the utterly incomprehensible idea that Jesus had two natures in one person and one subsistence.[19] It is in the wake of such philosophical thinking that we find terms like "God-man" and "dual nature" added to the Gentile Christian vocabulary. Such phrases were of course unknown to Jesus — the Lord and founder of the Christian Faith — the original Christians, and God's true prophets of old.[20]

New Church Creeds

With councils, and the advent of the new orthodoxy, came the issuing of dogmas. Over time the post-biblical church fathers locked in their confusion by means of church creeds. They hammered out creedal statements that would be recited by Christians. The orthodoxy of the new church fathers rested on their own devised creeds and not on the Bible itself. Dr. Richardson states:

> My conclusion, then, about the doctrine of the Trinity is that it is an artificial construct. It tries to relate different problems and to fit them into an arbitrary and traditional threeness. It produces confusion rather than clarification; and while the problems with which it deals are real ones the solutions it offers are not illuminating. ... There is no necessary threeness in the Godhead.[21]

The problem for the new orthodoxy was even more acute than the lack of Scriptures stating it. Again, the idea of multiple persons as one God is in direct opposition to the great body of Scriptures insisting that only one individual is God. Key in this is the Shema itself. The Shema is "the" biblical creed with regard to God. It remains the creed of devout Jews to this day. It rules out the idea of multiple persons being the one God. Because of this, there has been a tendency for Gentile Christians to diminish the Shema or simply disregard it.[22]

In that light, it is notable that Christians often celebrate the first of the 10 Commandments. That commandment is summarized in the negative directive: "You shall not have any other gods before me" (Ex. 20:3). By comparison, the positive statements in the Shema are more illuminating. In the Shema is found not only the declaration of who God is — YHWH alone — but also the essential affirmation that a person is to love the LORD with all of his heart, soul and strength!

Some frail attempts have been made by multi-person pundits to reinterpret the Shema in keeping with the new version of God. Some have suggested that the words in the declaration: "Hear, O Israel! The LORD is our God, the

Lord is one" must refer to multiple persons of Deity who are together a "compound one."[23] The word "God" is then taken as referring to the "essence" or "substance" in which the supposed persons exist. Confusing to even think about, this reinvention of the Shema is very awkward and comes late. Nothing is said in Deuteronomy 6:4 about "substance," "essence," or "multiple persons" as being a "compound one." No one in the entire Bible proposes such meanings for Moses' words.[24]

In their scriptural context, it is unmistakable that the words of the Shema uncompromisingly affirm what all of God's prophets and people of old confessed about him: There is only one individual who is God — he is YHWH. Some twelve times in the sixth chapter of Deuteronomy "the Lord" is referred to by "he," "him," and "his." Singular personal pronouns define a single person. Moses says:

> Verse 1 — Now this is the commandment, the statutes and the decrees that the Lord your God directed me to teach you to observe in the land that you are about to enter into and possess...
>
> v. 2 keep all **his** decrees and **his** commands
>
> v. 4 Hear, O Israel! The Lord is our God, the Lord is one.
>
> v. 10 into the land that **he** swore to your fathers
>
> v. 13 **him** shall you serve... by **his** name
>
> v. 15 **he** will destroy
>
> v. 17 diligently keep... **his** decrees, and **his** statutes as **he** has commanded you.
>
> v. 23 **he** brought us out from there to give us the land that **he** had promised
>
> v. 25 If we observe... as **he** has commanded

How many people will hear Moses speaking the words above and walk away thinking that the LORD, God of Israel, is two or three persons existing as a compound one? Again, how many people will be thinking that the word "God" actually means the "essence" or "substance" in which multiple persons exist?[25] The answer is clear on both counts — none! On the other hand, how many will walk away knowing that there is only one individual who is God? The answer is certain — all of them! They will know no other God and no other persons with Deity. They will know only him! The Shema is a proclamation about one amazing individual, YHWH himself.[26] He is their Father.

The Creed of Jesus

Christians today often recite creeds which were devised by post-biblical Gentile Christians centuries after Christ. They do that, while at the same time having never learned the biblical creed which God himself gave to Moses. It is that creed which Jesus affirms. When he is approached by a Jewish man who asks him which is the most important of all of the commandments, Jesus responds that it is:

> *Hear, O Israel! The Lord is our God, the Lord is one.*
>
> — JESUS (Mark 12:29)

Christians today seldom reflect on those amazing words which were spoken by the founder of our faith. That is unacceptable. It is tragic that a great many Christians are unaware that Jesus even spoke those words, words which he himself pronounced to be of paramount importance. Has not our attention been drawn away from the essential teaching of Jesus about God and diverted to creeds developed centuries after the Bible?[27]

Why has the creed of Jesus been so tragically neglected by post-biblical Christians? Isn't it because his creed does not teach the later dogma that God is multiple persons? Isn't it because his creed does not assert that he himself is also God in addition to his Father? Furthermore, isn't the creed of Jesus neglected — perhaps avoided — because it declares that only one individual is God, thus completely *disallowing* that two or three persons are the one God? When will we as Christians stand up boldly for Jesus and his teaching about God? When will we join with the man who asked the question, "which is most important of all?" and respond as he did to the words of Jesus? —

> Well said, teacher! You have truly said that he is one and there is no other but him (Mark 12:32).

When will we as Christians come to love and celebrate Jesus' creed and affirm that only one individual is God? When will our children learn the words of Jesus about God? When will our clergy finally abandon a stubborn affirmation of post-biblical ideas that they themselves admit have never made sense? When will a clergyman run to Jesus, and against all others, unceasingly speak his words about God? Again, it is Jesus who said that his Father is "the only true God" (John 17:1–3).

And notice again, as was the case in Deuteronomy 6, that the pronouns in Mark 12 allow for no other possibility than that the one who alone is God is a "him," not a "them." Jesus' declaration in v. 29 ("the Lord is one") has a singular verb of being. Even a first year student of New Testament Greek can affirm that more literally the phrase is, "the Lord *'he is'* one."[28] In that light, the man speaking with Jesus goes on to say:

> And to love him with all the heart, with all the understanding and with all the strength, and to love one's neighbor

> as oneself is more important than all burnt offerings and sacrifices (Mark 12:33).

And how does Jesus respond to the man's affirmation?

> When Jesus saw that he had answered wisely, he said to him, "You are not far from the kingdom of God" (Mark 12:34).

Jesus recognized that the man had "answered wisely." On the other hand, what would Jesus say to us today who come ignoring the words he spoke, while at the same time we sternly affirm and defend the words of Gentile Christian orthodoxy that multiple persons are the one God? Might not Jesus say to us that we are not speaking wisely, but foolishly? Will we incur the wrath of Jesus by loving and clinging to the creeds of the Gentile church fathers, while minimizing or disregarding his own words? Can we not at least honor and respect him in this matter as much as the good man did in Mark's account above? Might not that man who inquired about "which commandment is most important" and then rightly affirmed to Jesus that there is no other God but YHWH stand against us in the day of judgment?

Church creeds and statements of faith which propose multiple persons as one God simply must give way to the creed of Jesus: only one individual is God — the Father. Likewise, our various post-biblical statements of faith must give way to YHWH's own words: "I am God, and there is no one like me" (Isa. 46:9). Why not let go of our post-biblical Gentile Christian traditions about a multiple person God? Why not revise our statements of faith? Let us boldly rewrite them so that they rest upon and quote the actual words of Jesus in Mark 12:29 and John 17:3. Let our statements of faith quote the words of YHWH himself in Isaiah 46:9.

As a Christian, deciding about this matter is not difficult for me. It is the creed of God given by Jesus which is to be relied on unconditionally. Words found in the Bible itself are of necessity always preferable to those of later theologians and church councils. In the case of those later decisions and writings, inspiration may be doubted. Utmost confidence should be placed in the Bible, and Christians should all agree that in Scripture true inspiration is certain. We must put an end to interpreting the Bible through the lens of later theologians and councils. Rather, we must reverse that approach and test later doctrinal developments by the Bible itself. When we do, those later innovations all collapse.

Forced Orthodoxy Prevails

Multi-person orthodoxy ultimately triumphed not because it was a good idea or because it was biblical — it was neither. Rather, it prevailed because of persecution. With the coming of Emperor Constantine the Great and his embracing of Christianity, Christians were allowed to exist freely in the Roman world. However, that freedom applied only to people who adhered to the version of Christianity approved by Constantine and his successors. This important fact can be seen following the Council of Nicaea. Bishops who refused to vote in agreement with the conclusions reached at the council did so under threat of banishment by the emperor. In fact, the leader of the minority party was deposed and exiled to Illyricum. Later, Constantine would have a change of mind; banish the leader of the first party and bring back the leader of the minority party. Still later, he would again bring back the leader of the original party. The price of peace for Christians was the loss of control over what they would believe and practice. Ultimately, authority in matters of faith now rested with the emperors.[29]

When people today sometimes laud Constantine and his successors for ending the persecution of Christians, they forget that it was at the expense of other Christians who disagreed with the new mandated theology. Constantine's successors continued inflicting suffering on men and women who dared to differ. Some 55 years after Nicaea, emperors Gratian, Valentinian II and Theodosius I decreed to the citizens of Constantinople that all who embraced the doctrine of the Trinity would enjoy their favor. Then the edict continues:

> The rest, however, whom we adjudge demented and insane, shall sustain the infamy of heretical dogmas, their meeting places shall not be called churches, and they shall be smitten primarily by Divine Vengeance and secondly by the punishment of Our Power, which we have received by Divine favor.[30]

To resist multi-person orthodoxy now meant being declared demented, insane and subject to punishment by the government of the land. A short time later, the emperors go on to command the proconsul of Asia that "all churches shall presently be surrendered to those Bishops who ... affirm the concept of the Trinity."[31]

No one in the Bible was ever persecuted for denying or affirming a multi-person God. No one in the Bible had ever proposed such an idea. It was more than three centuries after Christ that Constantine's successors were turning reality on its head by making a concerted effort to suppress people who held to the true, biblical understanding of God as one individual. Christians of all stripes had been persecuted in times prior to Constantine's conversion in 312 CE. Now persecutions were reserved for those Christians who would not walk in lockstep with the dictates of the emperors, including adherence to the new multi-person orthodoxy.

Orthodox Christians observed Constantine's brutality and yet went on to honor him as a saint.[32] While they themselves had earlier endured great persecutions, strangely they now became friends of the persecutors. In fact, Trinitarian Christians came to persecute minority Christians in the centuries subsequent to Constantine. Hence, the persecuted became the persecutors. In that regard, those Gentile Christians were really more the children of the emperors than of Jesus who was non-violent (John 18:36) and insisted that his disciples are to "love their enemies" and to pray even for "those who persecute them" (Matt. 5:44). Thus, with the advent of state-approved and state-enforced Christianity came centuries of Christian on Christian hate.

Christians were now deprived of the freedom to choose what they would believe in regard to the very God they worshipped. Free inquiry was dead, as was freedom of speech. Even to question these particular matters became a taboo which is part of Gentile Christian DNA to this day. Sadly, many Christians even now verbally abuse and "dutifully" oppose anyone who trusts in Christ but does not embrace the doctrine of the Trinity. They do so without realizing that their proclivity to harm dissenters can be traced not to Jesus, but to the dark days of Constantine and his successors.

Multi-person orthodoxy was born in confusion, nurtured at the bosoms of post-biblical bishops, guarded with violence by emperors and sustained by an ongoing intimidation against dissenters that continues even to this day.[33]

The Jews Are Right About God

You [Samaritans] worship what you do not know; we worship what we know, for salvation is from the Jews.

—Jesus (John 4:22)

The knowledge of God was committed to the Jews. They were given the honor and responsibility of holding forth the one true God to the rest of humanity. From Abraham to Jesus, faithful Jews continued to do that. To this day, many orthodox Jews resist every hint of a multi-person God. There have been honorable Jews over the centuries who embraced death rather than accept that anyone other than the LORD himself is God. Those Jews knew the importance of these words:

> It is the LORD your God you must follow, him you shall fear. You will keep his commandments, his voice you shall obey, him only you shall serve, and you shall hold to him (Deut. 13:4).

Ancient Israel was never known as being the nation which believed that its God was multiple persons. Rather, Israel was renowned as the nation that believed in one God and that YHWH alone was that God! Faithful Jews have never had a problem with regard to how many persons are the one true God. From Abraham till now — that simple fact they have right.[34]

The Jews Have a Problem

Nevertheless, the Jews do have a problem. The revelation about God's Messiah was also given to the Jews. It was their prophets who foresaw him. The Messiah would in fact be that son of Abraham by whom God determines to bring his ultimate covenant to mankind. It is he whom God commissions to rule the nations in peace. The Jews were given the responsibility for proclaiming the one true God. But to maintain fidelity to him, they must also receive and proclaim his Messiah.

But now we see this peculiar circumstance: While many Jews look for the Messiah to come, a significant part of humanity has embraced Jesus as being that Messiah. Have Jews too quickly dismissed the possibility that Jesus is the one for whom they have waited?

Jews are not wrong to oppose the post-biblical Christology of Gentile Christians which transformed Jesus from Jewish Messiah to being a "God-person." That notion about him would have been just as unacceptable to Jesus as it has been to devout Jews over time. Jesus and faithful Jews have this in common: an unswerving dedication to only one individual as God. That one is the Father of the nation of Israel *and* the Father of Jesus. Following his resurrection, Jesus told Mary Magdalene:

> But go to my brothers and tell them, I am ascending to my Father and your Father, to my God and your God (John 20:17).

Have Jews allowed post-biblical Gentile Christians to color, if not dictate, their views about Jesus? Have such unfortunate ideas as him being a "God-man" or an "angel-man" prevented Jews today from giving him a fair hearing on his own merits? Jesus never claimed to be an angel or a "God-man." His claim was to be the Jewish Messiah (John 4:25, 26). The scriptural basis for his claim was the Jewish Bible (John 5:39).

If indeed Jesus is God's Messiah, then it is tragic that Jews would misjudge him. For Jews to cling to Moses' law while Jesus is even now establishing the new eternal Torah of Messiah is to miss the point of God's own words to Moses regarding him:

> I will raise up a prophet from among their brothers, and I will put my words in his mouth. He will speak to them everything that I command him. It will come to pass that anyone who does not listen to my words which he will

> speak in my name, I will hold that person accountable (Deut. 18:18, 19).

Ideally, it is Jews who should lead in the matter of humanity coming to accept God's true Messiah. Again, according to Jesus himself, "Salvation is from the Jews." But how can they lead if they themselves fail to understand that Jesus is the Messiah? Do not Jews today owe it to themselves and all of humanity, to take a fresh look at the all-important question of Jesus the Jew? Perhaps if they do, it will inspire Christians to seek to know God again as one individual rather than two or three. The day could come when Christians and Jews alike will begin to pray as Jesus did. Together we might in unison say that it is "eternal life" to know the Father as "the only true God" and Jesus as "the Messiah," his anointed king (John 17:3).

Christians Can Do Better

Christians do not need to embrace the eastern religions, "New Age," or other philosophies. We do not need to discover Judaism, the Law of Moses, or Islam. Christians today need to rediscover original Christianity. Let us reclaim the spirit and heart of the first Christians. Let us recover their devotion to Jesus as the true Messiah and to the Father alone as the only true God. Let us again embrace YHWH's own first priority: He is the only one who is truly God. Let us choose to obey from our hearts his prime directive: We shall serve him as the only true God and no one else.

I am a Christian — a Gentile Christian — but above all a Christian. As such, I have determined that my allegiance must be to Christ himself: not to (C)catholic or "orthodox" Christianity, post-biblical church fathers or extra-biblical church creeds. It is interesting to see many Protestant Christians today who on one hand disavow allegiance to the bishops of the "high" churches, while "in" the other hand clutching the non-biblical doctrines which came from just such bishops in earlier centuries.

My refrain is that of the wonderful hymn:

> On Christ, the solid Rock, I stand;
> All other ground is sinking sand,
> All other ground is sinking sand.[35]

We as Christians can do better — in Christ! I believe that we can and must do better in terms of our understanding about the one true God and his Messiah. And we owe it to Christ, to ourselves, and to all of humanity to do better in our conduct: better in our relationships with the people of this world and better in our conduct with one another as Christians. That is particularly the case with ill-treatment of minority (non-orthodox) Christians. Is it not Jesus himself who said that his followers are to be the salt of the earth — the light of the world? We as Christians can do better![36]

If Christians today are saved, it is not because they believe in a complicated configuration of God called the Trinity. Unfortunately, too many Christians have bought into the strange contradiction that God wants people to be saved, but in order for them to be saved they must confess faith in the complex, incomprehensible, theologically loaded idea of multiple persons being one God. Does that not cast a roadblock in the path of many people? Why would God condition salvation on such a confusing and contradictory concept?[37]

The doctrine of the Trinity is a theory forever in search of proof. If it were actually biblical, the Jews who knew God before Christianity would have been declaring it all along. If it was really true, people would just read it in their Bibles and no one would even have to ask questions. The confusing post-biblical idea about multiple persons being one God never deserved to be believed by Christians — much less elevated to become the central doctrine of the church, a belief which is supposed to identify a person as a Christian.

We can understand how post-biblical Gentile Christians were derailed in this matter. They had their own religious and philosophical pasts against them. For example, in their pantheons, had they not long believed in such ideas as various "persons" who were deity and of the same substance? Did not that create a mindset which could more readily slip into the notion of multiple persons being one (God) substance in Christianity?[38] Such ideas may have been acceptable to those Gentile Christians, but should we as Christians today still rest our faith on such reasoning?

We can understand that Christians adopted a view that God is multiple persons under the weight of persecutions by emperors who suppressed any other understanding of God. But we as Christians today are no longer under the decrees of "Christian" emperors. Now, we have only self-imposed requirements to conform to our own Gentile church tradition. But why should we? The truth is better!

Will we really believe that bishops and philosophers, centuries after Christ, somehow became the fathers of the Christian church? And will we today still discount the fact that Christians over the centuries acted with cruelty against their fellow human beings in the name of Christ? Will we excuse them on the utterly lame pretext that "things were different then"? When will we become enough like Jesus that we no longer avert our attention from evil deeds or diminish their significance because it was "Christians" who were doing them?[39]

And perhaps it is the case that ordinary Christians of early centuries were often unable to read the Scriptures for themselves. But what is our excuse now? We have the Scriptures massively available to us. Great numbers of us as Christians can read them. Will we then always rely on our clergy to tell us what we "must" believe in regard to the very God whom we worship? Our clergy are often wonderful people with admirable qualities. However, we must remember that typically they themselves grew up being told what to believe in the matter of defining God. They are people who likely had to confess faith in multiple persons as God or be denied entrance into a Christian seminary. The result has been a clergy that is often more wedded to Gentile church heritage than to Jesus and the Scriptures themselves.

And how long will we entertain people who come to us asserting that they can "prove" the doctrine of the Trinity? Will we forever allow ourselves to be mesmerized by proof-texting, faulty syllogisms and non-scriptural examples? Will we always permit long lists of convoluted arguments for a multiple person God to stand, instead of what should be clear and direct scriptural statements about God? Will we continue to allow the allure of a supposed "mystery" to steal from us the power of the simplicity of the one true God and his Messiah?

And will we cling to the notion that we are invincible? We need to quit believing our own Christian propaganda that Christianity could never be wrong in the matter of defining God. We can read in our New Testament that God declared the Jews — his own chosen people — to be in error in refusing the Messiah. The Apostle Paul tells us as Gentile Christians that we must not think too highly of ourselves lest we should also fall short (Rom. 11:20, 21). If God's people, the Jews, could err *en masse*, do we imagine that we as Gentiles cannot?[40]

Let us embrace again the simplicity of the one true God and stop insisting that people must accept a complex notion about multiple persons as God — a notion that we ourselves agree we have never understood. When will we stand up for the sufficiency of faith in YHWH who alone really is God (John 17:3)? When will we defend Jesus as being what he said he was: the Christ of God — God's son? When will we stand up for those who are seeking to come to Christ and defend them from the burden of confessing the one God as being multiple persons? That is a confession that no one in the Bible was ever instructed to make.

We must no longer be content to live in the haze that lingers over these critical issues. We who have been heirs of confusion must now become the people who celebrate the glory of the Father as the only true God and Jesus as God's true human Messiah. We as a generation of Christians today can do better. And if we can — then we must.

I Stand with the Children!

As for me, while others decide what they will do, I stand with the children of ancient Israel. They know their God. There is so much humanity could learn from them. In ancient Israel, the truth about how many persons are the one God can be understood by a child of five! The children in Israel can count how many Gods there are on one finger. They can count how many persons are that one God on the same finger. YHWH himself is the only true God!

Yet to this day, people of great learning often cannot grasp what every child in Israel knew. Intelligent men and women are often found worshipping gods of their own making. Great efforts are expended in the quest of all that *is not* God. From idol worship to deism; from God as nature to the gods of the cosmic unknown: all of these only fail us.

Again, good people are often stumped by the futile reasoning and contradictions of the concept of a multi-person God.

One could fill a large library with the writings of those who are forever asserting they can "prove" this peculiar post-biblical notion. If the idea were true, they could save all their paper and ink, because God's prophets and his people of old would simply have said it — over and over again. The children in Israel would have been reciting it. But they did not!

My creed is in the Bible itself. I can say, "The Lord is my God, the Lord is one." My allegiance to God is not in any sense divided. I can truthfully say that I love the Lord with all of my heart, all of my soul and all of my strength. I am wholly devoted to the one who alone sits on the throne of the universe. He is the Father of his people, the Father of Jesus Christ, and my Father. He alone is God.

Of whom shall *we* sing? Let us sing of the Lord. Of whom shall *we* speak? When we are at home and when we are away, when we lie down and when we rise up — let us speak of him. And what shall we recite to *our* children? Let our children and their children know: "The Lord is our God, the Lord is one!"

Shema! But will *we* listen? Let us say with ancient Israel: "We too will serve the Lord, because he is *our* God." If there are only ten people on the face of the earth who will hold to this One, let us take our stand with them. It is better to serve YHWH in a tent than to serve others as God in the greatest halls of mankind. He is "THE ONE"!

Chapter Twelve

Notes

1. The Shema or "Shema 'Yisrael" as a prayer and in liturgy is often extended and recited as Deuteronomy 6:4–9; 11:13–21 and Numbers 15:37–41.

2. Of course, this relates to whom we love as being God. It does not prevent a person from loving the Messiah, fellow believers, spouses, children, parents, etc. in the various ways that are appropriate for them.

3. The most famous is the family of Zeus who was supposed to be the father of Aphrodite, Athena, Apollo and others. The Greeks pictured these deities as being various individuals who were the same substance. That is essentially the concept employed by Gentile Christians in their idea of three "persons" who are one substance, what Trinitarian professor William Placher calls "stuff" (i.e. God-stuff). See William Placher, *A History of Christian Theology — An Introduction* (Philadelphia: The Westminster Press, 1983), 75.

4. Jesus has this same understanding of the spirit in mind in Matthew 10:20.

5. Dale Tuggy tells us that the formula of "three persons as one God" was not a part of post-biblical Christian vocabulary until the 4th century CE. Dr. Tuggy indicates that "there is simply no mention of a tripersonal God before the latter half of the 300s." He believes that the "trinity" of earlier times is "just a triad, the founding member of which is the one God" (personal correspondence, February 12, 2015). Also see Dale Tuggy's "10 Steps Towards Getting Less Confused About the Trinity — #8 — trinity vs. Trinity." http://trinities.org/blog/10-steps-towards-getting-less-confused-about-the-trinity-8-trinity-vs-trinity/.

6. *Trinitas* is a Latinization of *he trias* which is Greek for "the triad." It is thought that Tertullian was the first to use this term in Latin with reference to God, God's spirit and Christ. The Greek term had been used earlier in similar fashion by Theophilus of Antioch (*Ad Autolycum* 2.15).

7. Tertullian was not a Trinitarian. He identified the one God as the Father, not the Trinity and did not accept the required coequality provisions of the Trinity. He believed that the son was not equal to the Father. He also believed that the son had a beginning at a point in time. See Dale Tuggy, "Tertullian the Unitarian" (2013) http://trinities.org/blog/podcast-episode-11-tertullian-the-unitarian. Also see William C. Placher, *A History of Christian Theology — An Introduction* (Philadelphia: The Westminster Press, 1983), 73.

8. The word "God" itself is never used in the Bible to reference the Trinity. Anthony Buzzard states: "If one takes the evidence of Scripture as a whole, there is not a single occasion on which the word 'God' means the triune God!" Anthony Buzzard, *Jesus Was Not a Trinitarian* (Morrow, GA: Restoration Fellowship, 2007), 31.

9. "God" and "Trinity," Richard P. McBrien, ed., *Harper Collins Encyclopedia of Catholicism* (San Francisco: Harper Collins, 1995), 564 and 1271.

10. William Placher writes that Christians of the era "sought an alliance with classical philosophy against popular religion." He goes on to indicate, "Two schools of Greek philosophy, Platonism and Stoicism, deeply influenced early [post-biblical] Christian thought." William C. Placher, *A History of Christian Theology — An Introduction* (Philadelphia: The Westminster Press, 1983), 56.

11. To that should be added that Gentile Christians were influenced by Philo of Alexandria and other Hellenistic Jews who from around 200 BCE to 100 CE went to great extremes in efforts to reconcile Jewish religion with Hellenistic philosophy.

12. Cyril C. Richardson, *The Doctrine of the Trinity* (Nashville: Abingdon Press, 1958), 17.

13. Shirley C. Guthrie, Jr., *Christian Doctrine*, Rev. ed. (Louisville, KY: Westminster Press, 1994), 76 and 77.

14. The word orthodoxy means essentially "right opinion." The word in its meaning is not related to the Greek Orthodox Church as such, though the church adopted the word as part of its name in proposing that it is the church of "right opinion."

15. Much has been written regarding the council of Nicaea. Those favoring orthodoxy tend to write of the council in undeservedly positive terms. Others have used the council to propose unwarranted speculations. One of the more recent such cases is the fictional absurdities in the best-selling book *The Da Vinci Code*. Dan Brown, *The Da Vinci Code* (New York: Anchor Books, 2009). In any event, a balanced view of the council must recognize that it was a step toward

the revision of "God" from the biblical Jewish and early Christian perspective (he is a "single individual") to the Gentile orthodox view ("multiple persons" as one God).

16. Jesus is subordinate to his Father both functionally and ontologically. No Scripture says that Jesus was only functionally subordinate to God. Jesus places his Father as ontologically being "the only true God," and himself not as God but as the Christ (John 17:3).

17. Jesus had promised his earliest followers that the spirit would guide them into all truth (John 16:13). It is beyond reason, however, to apply those words to Gentile Christians who, in centuries after Christ, were proposing a reinvention of God as multiple persons.

18. For an overview of the First Council of Constantinople, see Charles Freeman, *A.D. 381: Heretics, Pagans, and the Dawn of the Monotheistic State* (New York: Overlook Press, 2009).

19. For a review of events leading up to the Council of Chalcedon see Phillip Jenkins, *Jesus Wars: How Four Patriarchs, Three Queens and Two Emperors Decided What Christians Would Believe for the Next 1,500 Years* (New York: Harper Collins Publishers, 2011).

20. One particularly offensive aspect of the Trinity is the doctrine of *anhypostasia* which requires people to believe that Messiah has a "human nature," but is not really "a human being" as such ("man," but not "a man"). For a critical consideration of the two natures theory see Alvan Lamson, "On the Doctrine of Two Natures in Christ," *Four American Unitarian Tracts*, Published by Dale Tuggy, 2007, available at www.lulu.com.

21. Cyril C. Richardson, *The Doctrine of the Trinity* (Nashville: Abingdon Press, 1957), 148 and 149.

22. The Shema expresses a timeless truth — that only one individual is God and that individual is YHWH. As Pastor Jack L. Stone has said, "Whatever God was in eternity he is now. His nature and being doesn't change" (personal correspondence, 4-28-14).

A recent example of the diminishing of the Shema by post-biblical Gentile Christians is that of Craig Evans who asserts that: "Jesus' affirmation of the Shema is neither remarkable nor specifically Christian." Craig Evans, *Word Biblical Commentary on Mark*, 34b (Nashville: Thomas Nelson, 2001), 261. I would respond that Jesus' affirmation of the Shema is very remarkable (he declared it to be the greatest of all the commandments) and solidly Christian (Jesus himself taught the same timeless truth regarding God being only one individual — John 17:3). It would also seem that Dr. Evans here makes a tacit admission that the Shema does not speak of a multi-person

God. It is hard to imagine Evans writing from his Trinitarian perspective that the Shema is not remarkable nor specifically Christian if it were actually speaking of the Trinity.

23. This relates to the abuse of the Hebrew word *echad* (one, alone, single) which is erroneously proposed by some to refer to a "compound one." Again there is a review of the word *echad* in chapter 10 of this book.

24. It can be noted by even the casual Bible reader that the word "LORD" (YHWH) is accompanied by singular verbs and pronouns continuously (thousands of times) throughout the Hebrew Bible. That further confirms the obvious: a single self (one individual) is being referenced when we read about YHWH.

25. For the benefit of "Social-Trinitarians," we might also ask how many people will walk away thinking the word "God" here refers to an eternal group of three divine friends?

26. It is the Father who is YHWH (Isa. 63:16). He is the only one who is the LORD and it is he who created all things (Neh. 9:6).

27. Among the creeds, the Nicene (325 CE), Nicene-Constantinopolitan (381 CE) and Chalcedonian (451 CE) are particularly problematic. They represent the fruits of endless confusion and terrible infighting among post-biblical Gentile Christians as they sought to establish the non-scriptural notion of a multi-person God. In that, they struggled to make Jesus a "God-person." They also determined to see God's own spirit as a separate individual — another God-person in addition to the Father. On the other hand, the Apostles' Creed which is likely based on some early rules of faith is truer to the Scriptures. That creed knows nothing about any one being God other than the Father. It rightly affirms Jesus to be the "Christ," "God's son" and "Lord" but does not propose him to be God, God the son or a God-man. Likewise, the spirit of God is mentioned in the creed but not as a God-person. While the Apostles' Creed is truer to the Scriptures than the others, it is nonetheless widely agreed to have not been authored by the apostles of Jesus and dates later in its present form.

28. Properly parsed, the verb *esti* is 3rd person singular, present, indicative.

29. Arius, leader of the minority party, and Athanasius of the majority party each paid the price of banishment for being unrelenting in their views. Athanasius was exiled a total of five times by four different emperors. Both men died without ever retracting their positions. Their banishments testify to the extent of the emperors' invasiveness and exercise of power in matters regarding Christian doctrine and faith.

30. Clyde Pharr, ed., *The Corpus of Roman Law (Corpus Juris Romani), Theodosian Code* (Nashville: Department of Classics, Vanderbilt University, 1946), 16:1, 2.

31. Ibid. 2, 3. The proconsul was Ausonius. We may be reminded of how far the reach of legislated orthodoxy has extended by considering the infamous "Blasphemy Act" which became law in England in 1697. The act made it a crime for "any person educated in or having made profession of the Christian religion ... to deny the Holy Trinity." The Trinitarian aspect of the act was repealed (to the benefit of unitarians) by the "Doctrine of the Trinity Act" which was passed in 1813.

32. Constantine came to be widely revered as a saint in the Eastern Church. This was in spite of the fact that after his conversion to Christianity he persecuted Jews and minority Christians, and put to death his wife, a son, nephew, nephew's wife, and other family members.

33. It is to our shame as Christians that it took the coming of the Enlightenment, the influence of non-mainstream Christians (such as the Anabaptists, and unitarians) and the development of the western democracies to bring an end to church/state sponsored violence against minority (non-orthodox) Christians in the West.

34. It must be remembered that over the centuries, Jews have been very diverse in their beliefs. My references in this chapter of the book are to the many Jews who have diligently held to the LORD (Adonai) as being the only true God, and who have looked for the coming Messiah according to the Hebrew Scriptures.

35. Edward Mote, "The Solid Rock," c. 1834.

36. Have we not reached a point where we as Christians can dialogue on issues without condemning one another "to hell" on the basis of post-biblical doctrines and creeds? Can we not abandon intimidation, name calling and coercion in favor of persuasion with mutual Christian respect?

37. See my article, J. Dan Gill, "Yet Another Music City Miracle! Must One Believe in the Doctrine of the Trinity to be Saved?" http://www.21stcr.org/multimedia/articles/music_city_miracle.html.

38. For a summary of the debate over *homoousios* see William Placher, *A History of Christian Theology—An Introduction* (Philadelphia: The Westminster Press, 1983), 75–79.

39. The rationalizing of such persecutions by Christians can still be seen today. A notable example of this is the zealous defense of

John Calvin by some modern Calvinists regarding the awful "Servetus Affair." For a balanced consideration of that matter, read the analysis of attorney and former Calvinist, Stanford Rives, *Did Calvin Murder Servetus?* (Charleston, SC: Booksurge Publishers, 2008).

40. In all of this, it should never be thought that Christ intends that there be a separation between Gentiles and Jews within Christianity (Gal. 3:28; Col. 3:11). There is to be one Lord over all (Rom. 10:12). Jewish Christians have at times brought separation by promoting the Law of Moses and failing to grasp the sufficiency of the eternal Torah of the Messiah (Gal. 2:16; 3:26–29; Heb. 13:20). On the other hand, it was post-biblical Gentile converts who developed and promoted critical differences regarding who God is. When Gentile Christians evolved the notion of God as multiple persons, they were separating themselves from the roots of Christian faith in that matter. Those roots run deep in YHWH alone as the only true God and Jesus as the Christ of God (John 17:3).

Selected Bibliography

Allen, Leslie C. *Word Biblical Commentary: Psalms 101-150*. Word Books, 1983.

American Unitarian Association. *Sixteen American Unitarian Tracts*. Boston, Bowles and Dearborn, 1827. Rep. Dale Tuggy, 2008.

Anderson, Hugh. *The Gospel of Mark (The New Century Bible* Commentary). Eerdmans, 1981.

Armstrong, Karen. *The Battle for God*. Ballantine Books, 2001.

———. *The Great Transformation. Alfred A. Knopf, 2006.*

———. *A History of God. Gramercy Books, 2004.*

Armstrong, Richard A. *The Trinity and the Incarnation*. 1904, rep. Kessinger, 2005.

Barclay, William. *The Gospel of Mark*, Westminster John Knox, 1975.

———. *A Spiritual Autobiography. Eerdmans, 1975.*

Barrett, C.K. *Essays on John*. SPCK, 1982.

———. *The Gospel According to St. John. Westminster, 1978.*

Bateman, Herbert. "Psalm 110:1 and the New Testament." *Bibliotheca Sacra* 149, Oct-Dec., 1992.

Bauckham, Richard. *God Crucified: Monotheism and Christology in the New Testament*. Eerdmans, 1999.

BeDuhn, Jason David. *Truth in Translation: Accuracy and Bias in English Translations of the New Testament*. University Press of America, 2003.

Beisner, E. Calvin. *God in Three Persons*. Tyndale House, 1984.

Blanchard, John. *Does God Believe in Atheists?* Evangelical Press, 2000.

Boice, J. M. *The Sovereign God*. Intervarsity Press, 1978.

Borg, Marcus and N. T. Wright. *The Meaning of Jesus: Two Visions*. HarperCollins, 2000.

Bowker, John. *God: A Brief History*. DK Publishers, 2003.

Brown, Colin. "Trinity and Incarnation: In Search of a Contemporary Orthodoxy." *Ex Auditu* 7, 1991. 83-100.

Brown, Dan. *The Da Vinci Code.* Doubleday, 2003.

Brown, Harold O. J. *Heresies: Heresy and Orthodoxy in the History of the Church.* Hendrickson, 1998.

Brown, Michael L. *Answering Jewish Objections to Jesus,* Baker Books, 2000.

Brown, Raymond. *The Birth of the Messiah.* Geoffrey Chapman, 1977.

———. *The Gospel According to John. Doubleday, 1970.*

———. *An Introduction to New Testament Christology. Paulist* Press, 1994.

———. *Jesus: God and Man. MacMillan, 1967.*

Bruce, F. F. *Canon of Scripture.* Intervarsity Press, 1988.

———. *Commentary on the Greek Text of the Acts of the Apostles.* Eerdmans, 1975.

———. *The Epistle to the Hebrews (New International Commentary on the New Testament).* Eerdmans, 1990.

———. *The Gospel and Epistles of John. Eerdmans, 1994.*

———. *Jesus: Lord and Savior. Intervarsity Press, 1986.*

Bruce, F. F. et al. *The Origin of the Bible.* Tyndale House, 2003.

Brunner, Emil. *The Christian Doctrine of God.* Lutterworth Press, 1962.

Bultmann, Rudolf. "The Christological Confession of the World Council of Churches." In *Essays Philosophical and Theological.* SCM Press, 1955.

Buswell, J. O. *A Systematic Theology of the Christian Religion.* Zondervan, 1962.

Buzzard, Anthony. *The Coming Kingdom of the Messiah: A Solution to the Riddle of the New Testament.* Restoration Fellowship, 2002.

———. *Jesus was Not a Trinitarian: A Call to Return to the Creed of Jesus.* Restoration Fellowship, 2007.

———. *The Law, The Sabbath and New Covenant Christianity.* Restoration Fellowship, 2005.

Buzzard, Anthony and Charles Hunting. *The Doctrine of the Trinity: Christianity's Self-Inflicted Wound.* International Scholars Publications, 1998.

Caird, C. B. "The Development of Christ in the New Testament." In *Christ for Us Today*. SCM Press, 1968.

Carden, Robert. *One God: The Unfinished Reformation*. Grace Christian Press, 2002.

Carson, D. A. *The Gospel According to John*. Apollos, 1991.

———. "The Purpose of the Fourth Gospel: John 20:31 Reconsidered," *Journal of Biblical Literature* 106/4, 1987: 639-651.

Casey, Maurice. *From Jewish Prophet to Gentile God*. Westminster/ John Knox Press, 1991.

Cave, Sydney. *The Doctrine of the Person of Christ*. Duckworth, 1962.

Chang, Eric H. H. *The Only True God*. Xlibris Corporation, 2009.

Chang, Eric H. H. and Bently C. F. Chan. *The Only Perfect Man*, 2nd. Ed. EHHC, 2016.

Chan, Francis. *Forgotten God Reversing our Tragic Neglect of the Holy Spirit*. David C. Cook, 2009.

Chandler, Russell. *Understanding the New Age*. Word Publishing, 1988.

Chapman, Colin. *The Case for Christianity*. Eerdmans, 1981.

Cole, R. Alan. *Mark (Tyndale New Testament Commentaries)*. Eerdmans, 1983.

Cooper, David. *The Messiah: His Redemptive Career*. Biblical Research Society, 1938.

Creed, J. M. *The Divinity of Jesus Christ*. Fontana, 1964.

Cullmann, Oscar. *The Christology of the New Testament*. SCM Press, 1963.

Cupitt, Don. *The Debate About Christ*. SCM Press, 1979.

Demmitt, Greg. "The Christologies of Barton Stone and Alexander Campbell, and their Disagreement Concerning the Preexistence of Christ." *A Journal from the Radical Reformation* 12:2 (2005).

Dever, William G. *What Did the Biblical Writers Know and When Did they Know It?* Eerdmans, 2001.

———. *Who Were the Early Israelites and Where Did They Come From?* Eerdmans, 2003.

Dorner, J. A. *History of the Development of the Doctrine of the Person of Christ*. T & T Clark, 1889.

Dunn, James D. G. *Christology in the Making*. SCM-Canterbury Press, 2003.

———. *The Theology of Paul the Apostle*. Eerdmans, 1998.

———. *Unity and Diversity in the New Testament*. SCM Press, 1977.

Ehrman, Bart D. *Jesus: Apocalyptic Prophet of the New Millennium*. Oxford University Press, 1999.

———. *The Orthodox Corruption of Scripture*. Oxford University Press, 1993.

———. *Truth and Fiction in The Da Vinci Code*. Oxford University Press, 2004.

———. *How Jesus Became God. HarperOne, 2014.*

Erickson, Millard J. *God in Three Persons*. Baker Books, 1995.

———. *Making Sense of the Trinity*. Baker Books, 2000.

Eyre, Alan. *The Protesters*. The Christadelphian, 1975.

Farrar, F.W. *The Bible: Its Meaning and Supremacy*. Longmans, Green and Co., 1897.

———. *The Gospel According to St. Luke. The Cambridge Bible for* Schools and Colleges. Cambridge University Press, 1902.

Fitzmyer, Joseph. *A Christological Catechism*. Paulist Press, 1991.

———. *The Gospel According to Luke I-IX (Anchor Bible)*. Doubleday, 1981.

Fortman, Edmund J. *The Triune God*. Baker, 1972.

Franklin, Eric. *Christ the Lord*. Westminster Press, 1975.

Freeman, Charles. *A.D. 381 Heretics, Pagans, and the Dawn of the Monotheistic State*. The Overlook Press, 2008.

———. *The Closing of the Western Mind*. Vintage Books, 2002.

Goguel, Maurice. *Jesus and the Origins of Christianity*. Harper, 1960.

Goppelt, Leonhard. *Theology of the New Testament*. Eerdmans, 1982.

Goudge, H. L. "The Calling of the Jews." In *Judaism and Christianity*, ed. Lev Gillet, J.B. Shears & Sons, 1939. 45-56.

Grensted, L. W. *The Person of Christ*. Nisbet & Co., 1933.

Grillmeier, Aloys. *Christ in Christian Tradition*. Westminster John Knox Press, 1975.

Groothuis, Douglas R. *Unmasking the New Age*. Inter Varsity Press, 1986.

Guthrie, Shirley C. *Christian Doctrine,* Rev. Ed. Westminster/John Knox Press, 1994.

Hamilton, H. F. *The People of God: An Inquiry into Christian Origins.* Oxford University Press, 1912.

Hanson, A. T. *Grace and Truth: A Study in the Doctrine of the Incarnation.* SPCK, 1975.

———. *The Image of the Invisible God.* SCM Press, 1982.

Hanson, R. P. C. "The Doctrine of the Trinity Achieved in 381." *Scottish Journal of Theology* 36 (1983): 41-57.

Harnack, Adolf. *History of Dogma.* Dover Publications, 1961.

———.*Lehrbuch der Dogmengeschichte. Wissenschaftliche Buchge* sellschaft, 1983.

———. *What Is Christianity?* Williams and Norgate, 1901.

Harpur, Tom. *For Christ's Sake.* Beacon Press, 1987.

Harris, Murray J. *Jesus as God: The New Testament Use of Theos in Reference to Jesus.* Baker, 1992.

Harvey, Anthony. *Jesus and the Constraints of History.* Duckworth, 1982.

Hemphill, Joel W. *To God the The Glory.* Trumpet Call Books, 2006.

———. *Glory to God In the Highest.* Trumpet Call Books, 2010.

Hervey, Arthur. *The Genealogies of Our Lord and Savior Jesus Christ.* Macmillan, 1853. Rep. Kessinger, 2007.

Hick, John, ed. *The Myth of God Incarnate.* SCM Press, 1977.

Hillar, Marian. *The Case of Michael Servetus (1511-1553): The Turning Point in the Struggle for Freedom of Conscience.* Edwin Mellen Press, 1997.

———, trans. *The Restoration of Christianity: An English Translation* of Christianismi Restitutio by Michael Servetus. Edwin Mellen Press, 2007.

Hinchliff, Peter. "Christology and Tradition." In *God Incarnate, Story and Belief,* ed. A. E. Harvey. SPCK, 1981.

Hodgson, Leonard. *Christian Faith and Practice.* Blackwell, 1952.

———. *The Doctrine of the Trinity. Charles Scribner's Sons, 1944.*

Holt, Brian. Jesus: God or the Son of God? TellWay, 2002.

Hurtado, Larry. Lord Jesus Christ: Devotion to Jesus in Earliest Christ*ianity*. Eerdmans, 2003.

———. *How on Earth Did Jesus Becoma a God?* Eerdmans, 2005.

Jenkins, Philip. Jesus Wars. Harper One 2010

Jervell, Jacob. *Jesus in the Gospel of John*. Augsburg, 1984.

Jocz, Jacob. *The Jewish People and Jesus Christ*. SPCK, 1962.

Johnson, Luke Timothy. *The Creed: What Christians Believe and Why It Matters*. Doubleday, 2003.

Kaiser, Christopher B. *The Doctrine of God: A Historical Survey*. Crossways, 1982.

Kirkpatrick, A. F. *The Book of Psalms (XC-CL). The Cambridge Bible for Schools and Colleges*. Cambridge University Press, 1901.

Knox, John. *The Humanity and Divinity of Christ*. Cambridge University Press, 1967.

Kopecek, Thomas. *A History of Neo-Arianism*. Philadelphia Patristic Foundation, 1979.

Küng, Hans. *On Being a Christian*. Doubleday, 1976.

Kuschel, Karl-Josef. *Born Before All Time? The Dispute over Christ's Origin*. Crossroad, 1992.

Lackey, P. R. *The Tyranny of the Trinity*, 2nd. Ed. AuthorHouse, 2008.

La Due, William J. *The Trinity Guide to the Trinity*. Trinity Press International, 2003.

Lampe, Geoffrey. *Explorations in Theology 8*. SCM Press, 1981.

———. *God as Spirit*. SCM Press, 1983.

Lamson, Alvan. *The Church of the First Three Centuries*. Walker, Fuller, and Company, 1865.

Lawson, John. *Introduction to Christian Doctrine*. Francis Asbury, 1980.

Lebreton, Jules. *History of the Dogma of the Trinity*. Benziger Brothers, 1939.

Levine, Amy-Jill, *The Misunderstood Jew*. HarperCollins Publishers. 2006

Lewis, C.S. *Christian Reflections*. Eerdmans, 1995.

———. *Mere Christianity*. HarperCollins, 2001.

Little, Spence. *The Deity of Christ.* Covenant Publishing, 1956.

Loofs, Friedrich. *Leitfaden zum Studium des Dogmengeschichte (Manual for the Study of the History of Dogma),* 1890. Niemeyer Verlag, 1951.

———. *What Is the Truth About Jesus Christ?* Charles Scribner's Sons, 1913.

Macleod, Donald. *The Person of Christ.* Intervarsity Press, 1998.

Marshall, Howard. *Acts, Tyndale Commentaries.* Eerdmans, 1980.

———. "Jesus as Lord: The Development of the Concept." In Eschatology and the New Testament. Hendrickson, 1988.

Matthews, W. R. *God in Christian Experience,* 1930, rep. Kessinger, 2003.

———. *The Problem of Christ in the Twentieth Century. Oxford* University Press, 1950.

McBrien, Richard P. *Encyclopedia of Catholicism.* HarperCollins, 1995.

McGiffert, Arthur. *A History of Christian Thought.* Charles Scribner's Sons, 1954.

McGrath, Alister. *Christian Theology: An Introduction.* Blackwell, 2007.

Meier, John P. A. *Marginal Jew: Rethinking the Historical Jesus.* Doubleday, 1994.

Metzger, Bruce. *A Textual Commentary on the Greek New Testament.* United Bible Societies, 1971.

Meyer, H.A.W. *Commentary on the Gospel of John.* Funk and Wagnall, 1884.

Milton, John. "*On the Son of God and the Holy Spirit.*" Rep. in A Journal from the Radical Reformation 5:2 (1996): 44-64.

Moltmann, Jürgen. *The Spirit of Life.* Fortress Press, 1992.

Morey, Robert. *The Trinity: Evidence and Issues.* World Publishing, 1996.

Morgridge, Charles. *The True Believer's Defence Against Charges Preferred for not Believing in the Deity of Christ,* 1837. Rep. Christian Educational Services, 1994.

Morris, Leon. *The Gospel According to John (New International Commentary on the New Testament).* Eerdmans, 1995.

Morris, Robert. *The God I Never Knew.* Waterbrook Press, 2014.

Mounce, William D. *Word Biblical Commentary: Pastoral Epistles.* Thomas Nelson, 2000.

Murray, Michael. *Reason for the Hope Within.* Eerdmans, 1999.

Navas, Patrick. *Divine Truth or Human Tradition.* Authorhouse, 2011.

Netland, Harold. *Encountering Religious Pluralism.* Inter Varsity Press, 2001.

Newman, John Henry. *Select Treatises of St. Athanasius.* James Parker and Co., 1877.

Nicoll, W. Robertson. *Expositor's Greek Commentary.* Eerdmans, 1967.

Nolan, Albert. *Jesus Before Christianity.* Orbis Books, 1992.

Norton, Andrews. *A Statement of Reasons for Not Believing the Doctrines of Trinitarians,* 1833. Rep. University of Michigan, 2005.

O'Carroll, Michael. *Trinitas: A Theological Encyclopedia of the Holy Trinity.* Liturgical Press, 1987.

Oehler, Gustav. *The Theology of the Old Testament.* Funk & Wagnalls, 1893.

Ohlig, Karl-Heinz. *One or Three? From the Father of Jesus to the Trinity.* Peter Lang, 2003.

Olson, Roger and Christopher Hall. *The Trinity.* Eerdmans, 2002.

Olyott, Stuart. *The Three Are One.* Evangelical Press, 1979.

Orr, James. *The Virgin Birth of Christ.* Charles Scribner's Sons, 1912.

Packer, J. I. *Knowing God.* Intervarsity Press, 1998.

Paine, L. L. *A Critical History of the Evolution of Trinitarianism.* Houghton Mifflin and Co., 1900.

Pannenberg, Wolfhart. *Jesus—God and Man.* Westminster Press, 1968.

Partner, Peter. *Christianity: The First Two Thousand Years.* Seven Oaks, 2002.

Peake, Arthur S., ed. *Peake's Commentary on the Bible.* Thomas Nelson and Sons, 1919.

Pettingill, William and R. A. Torrey. *1001 Bible Questions Answered.* Inspirational Press, 1997.

Pfeiffer, Charles F. and Everett F. Harrison, eds. *The Wycliffe Bible Commentary.* Moody Bible Institute, 1990.

Placher, William C. *A History of Christian Theology*. The Westminister Press, 1983.

Purves, George T. "The Influence of Paganism on Post-Apostolic Christianity." Rep. in *A Journal from the Radical Reformation* 8:2, 1999, 25-50.

Quick, Oliver. *Doctrines of the Creed*. Nisbet, 1938.

Rahner, Karl. *Theological Investigations*. Helicon, 1963.

Rees, Thomas, trans. *The Racovian Catechism*, rep. Christian Educational Services, 1994.

______. *A Sketch of the History of Unitarianism*. Christian Educational Services, 1994.

Reim, Günther. "Jesus as God in the Fourth Gospel: The Old Testament Background." *New Testament Studies* 30, 1984: 58-60.

Réville, Albert. *History of the Dogma of the Deity of Jesus Christ*. Philip Green, 1905.

Rhodes, Ron. *The Heart of Christianity*. Harvest House, 1996.

———. *Reasoning from the Scriptures with the Jehovah's Witnesses*. Harvest House, 1993.

Richardson, Cyril C. *The Doctrine of the Trinity*. Adingdon Press, 1958.

Robinson, John A.T. "The Fourth Gospel and the Church's Doctrine of the Trinity." In *Twelve More New Testament Studies*. SCM Press, 1984.

———. *The Human Face of God. Westminster Press, 1973.*

———. *The Priority of John. SCM Press, 1985.*

Rubenstein, Richard. *When Jesus Became God: The Struggle to Define Christianity During the Last Days of Rome*. Harvest Books, 2000.

Sanders, E. P. and Margaret Davies. *Studying the Synoptic Gospels*. SCM Press, 1991.

Schaeffer, Edith. Christianity Is Jewish. Tyndale House, 1975.

Schrodt, Paul. *The Problem of the Beginning of Dogma in Recent Theology*. Peter Lang, 1978.

Schweizer, Eduard. *The Good News According to Mark*. John Knox Press, 1970.

Segal, M. H. *A Grammar of Mishnaic Hebrew*. Oxford, 1927.

———. "Mishnaic Hebrew and Its Relation to Biblical Hebrew and to Aramaic." Jewish Quarterly Review, Old Series 20 (1908-1909): 647-737.

Showers, Renald and George Zeller. *The Eternal Sonship of Christ: A Timely Defense of This Vital Biblical Doctrine*. Loizeaux Brothers, 1993.

Snaith, Norman. *Distinctive Ideas of the Old Testament*. Epworth Press, 1944.

Snobelen, Stephen. "'God of gods and Lord of lords': The Theology of Isaac Newton's *General Scholium* to the *Principia*." Osiris 16, 2001.

Southern, Randy. T*he World's Easiest Guide to Understanding God*. Northfield, 2003.

Spurgeon, Charles. *The Treasury of David*. Baker Book House, 1983.

Stott, John. *The Authentic Jesus*. Marshalls, 1985.

Strobel, Lee. *The Case for Christ*. Zondervan, 1998.

Swindoll, Charles. *Jesus: When God Became a Man*. W Publishing Group, 1993.

Swindoll, Charles and Roy Zuck, eds. *Understanding Christian Theology*. Thomas Nelson, 2003.

Terry, Milton. *Biblical Hermeneutics*. Zondervan, 1975.

Toon, Peter. *Our Triune God*. Victor Books, 1996.

Trakatellis, Demetrios. *The Pre-Existence of Christ in Justin* Martyr: An Exegetical Study with Reference to the Humiliation *and Exaltation Christology*, Harvard Dissertation Series 8, Missoula, Montana: Scholars Press, 1976.

Treffry, Richard. *An Inquiry into the Doctrine of the Eternal Sonship of Our Lord Jesus Christ*. John Mason, 1837.

Turner, Nigel. Grammatical Insights into the New Testament. T & T Clark, 1965.

Van Buren, Paul. *A Theology of the Jewish-Christian Reality*. Harper & Row, 1983.

Wachtel, Bill. "Christian Monotheism: Reality or Illusion." *The Restitution Herald*, April, 1985.

Wainwright, Arthur. *The Trinity in the New Testament.* SPCK, 1980.

Walvoord, John and Roy Zuck, eds. *The Bible Knowledge Commentary.* Victor, 1983.

Watts, John D. W. *Word Biblical Commentary: Isaiah 34-66.* Word Books, 1987.

Wenham, Gordon J. *Word Biblical Commentary: Genesis 1–15.* Word Books, 1987.

Werner, Martin. *The Formation of Christian Dogma.* Harper, 1957.

Whale, J. S. *Christian Doctrine.* Cambridge University Press, 1952.

Whidden, Woodrow, Jerry Moon and John Reeve. *The Trinity.* Review and Herald, 2002.

White, James. *The Forgotten Trinity.* Bethany House, 1998.

Whiteley, D. E. H. *The Theology of St. Paul* Blackwell, 1980.

Wilbur, Earl Morse. *Our Unitarian Heritage: An Introduction to the History of the Unitarian Movement,* Beacon Press, 1943.

Wiles, Maurice. *The Remaking of Christian Doctrine.* SCM Press, 1974.

Williams, George Huntston. *The Radical Reformation.* 3rd edition. Truman State University Press, 2000.

Wilson, Ian. *Jesus: The Evidence.* Harper & Row, 1984.

Wilson, John. *Unitarian Principles Confirmed by Trinitarian Testimonies.* Rep. University of Michigan, 2005.

Wilson, Marvin. *Our Father Abraham: Jewish Roots of the Christian Faith.* Eerdmans, 1989.

Wright, N. T. *"The Historical Jesus and Christian Thought."* Sewanee Theological Review 39, 1996.

———. *Jesus and the Victory of God. Augsburg Fortress, 1997.*

Yancey, Philip D. *The Bible Jesus Read.* Zondervan Publishing House, 1999.

Zahrnt, Heinz. *The Historical Jesus.* Harper & Row, 1963.

Zarley, Kermit. *The Restitution of Jesus Christ.* Triangle Books, 2008.

Index of

Scripture and Other Ancient Writings

Old Testament

Genesis

Exodus

Jeremiah

Lamentations

Ezekiel

New Testament

Acts

Other Ancient Writings

Index of

Subjects and Names

D

E

N

O

P